Jane's

Battleships

OF THE 20th CENTURY

Jane's
Battleships
OF THE 20th CENTURY

TEXT BY BERNARD IRELAND

ILLUSTRATIONS BY TONY GIBBONS

HarperCollins*Publishers*

In the U.S. for information address:
HarperCollins*Publishers* Inc.
10 East 53rd Street,
New York,
NY 10022.

In the U.K. for information address:
HarperCollins*Publishers*
77-85 Fulham Palace Road,
Hammersmith,
London W6 8JB.

First Published in Great Britain by
HarperCollins*Publishers* 1996

3 5 7 9 10 8 6 4 2

© HarperCollins*Publishers* 1996

All paintings © Tony Gibbons

ISBN 0 00 470997 7

Editor: Ian Drury
Design: Amzie Viladot
Production Manager: Bridget Scanlon

Colour reproduction by Colourscan, Singapore
Printed in Italy by Rotolito Lombarda SpA, Milan, Italy

Royal Sovereign, Resolution and Revenge were part of the 1st Battle Squadron of the Grand Fleet in 1917. These 15-in gun dreadnoughts were the ultimate guarantors of the blockade that was strangling the German economy and eroding popular support for the war.

Contents

HMS Agamemnon belonged to the last class of
predreadnought battleships built for the Royal Navy.
During World War I she became the flagship of the
Mediterranean fleet and the surrender of the
Ottoman Empire was signed aboard her in 1918.
Note the stern gallery.

continued overleaf...

Contents continued

Jutland *veteran*
HMS Malaya *seen
with American
battleships* Alabama
and South Dakota
*during their feint off
Norway in 1943.*

Introduction

The big gun held sway at sea for centuries. Fleets were built around it and battles, even wars, decided by it. For long, the antidote was a bigger gun or more protection. Or the speed with which to escape.

The capital ship, which had evolved slowly over centuries, developed rapidly with the increasing pace of industrialisation and technology. Within half a century, it had achieved its ultimate expression. However, perceptions change. What seemed then to be the way to do things, now appears archaic. Lines of battle pounding each other to scrap metal is directly equivalent to two armoured warriors hacking at each other with broadswords. There had to be a better way to do it.

The true battleship killer was the torpedo. To destroy a large ship in combat, one ultimately has to sink it. To do so, the hull must be opened to the sea. By striking beneath a ship's armour, the torpedo could achieve exactly that, but even after it had achieved a measure of reliability, torpedoes suffered for want of what (today) would be called a delivery system. Torpedo boats could be swatted by battleships' gunfire before they could get in range. Submarines, with their slow submerged speed, required the target to steam obligingly by.

Aircraft provided the ultimate solution. At risk of over-extending the analogy above, our armoured, sword-wielding warrior had no protection against a swarm of hornets. And these hornets had killer stings.

This book traces the development of the capital ship through that final exhilarating phase of its long existence. Technology gave the ship designer better guns, better armour plate and better machinery. After World War I, international agreement then imposed limitations on their application. Designers then had to make choices, driven by the

The monstrous anger of the guns: HMS Royal Oak *unleashes a broadside from her 15-in main armament. Battleship armour kept pace with battleship firepower during the 20th century, and it remained difficult to sink a capital ship with gunfire alone.*

perceptions and attitudes of the fleets for which they worked. The British Royal Navy, confident in its long supremacy, adopted the Fisher approach: the biggest guns and the highest speed providing protection by enabling the ships to dictate the parameters of battle. With more limited resources and more focused objectives, the Germans thought defensively, arming their battleships with smaller calibre main armament and accepting more moderate speeds as the price of thorough protection.

The USA, washed by two vast oceans inevitably thought big: survivability and endurance were complemented by big guns. For a long period, speed was of lower importance. When it was demanded, US battleships rapidly grew in size.

A further aspect covered here is the paper exercise. Every ship designer, like every architect, has the dream of creating his ideal, unfettered by restrictions in size or cost. As will be demonstrated in the following pages, limitations of one sort or another inevitably manifest themselves as any design. progresses.

Except in the USA, where a surprising number of states have acquired their eponymous ships as museum items, the battleship has effectively passed from the scene. Or has it? In the post-Cold War era of littoral combat, a new type of ship is being postulated. The 'Arsenal Ship' would be a floating magazine of vertically launched missiles. She would have minimal crew numbers and would rely greatly on the evolving concept of Collective Engagement Capability to saturate a given target precisely and with impunity. If this sounds familiar to the reader, it apparently did so to those who proclaimed the concept. The first units are numbered (provisionally) from the point where the last battleship hulls left off...

Bernard Ireland
Fareham 1996

Austria-Hungary

Right: Erzherzog Franz Ferdinand *in the Austro-Hungarian naval base at Pola, seen here during a Royal Navy visit just before World War I.*

The last major fleet action before the battle of Tsushima in 1905 took place in 1866. In a confused, close-range melee in the Adriatic, the Austro-Hungarian navy defeated that of the new Kingdom of Italy. The battle of Lissa was the first and only time two fleets of ocean-going armoured warships faced each other during the nineteenth century, and its influence on warship design lasted long afterwards.

The Austro-Hungarian navy suffered even more than the army in the steady reduction in military expenditure that lasted into the first decade of the 20th century. By 1914, the navy consisted of four modern dreadnoughts, three 12-inch gunned pre-dreadnoughts and a dozen elderly battleships and armoured cruisers. The new battleships and cruisers completed on the eve of World War I were the work of a few dedicated officers who managed to overcome the institutional lethargy for which the Imperial regime was notorious. However, even these few modern units could play little role in a World War, ranged against Great Britain and France. With Italy eventually joining the Allies, the Mediterranean was no place for Austrian surface ships.

The war was to be prosecuted more successfully by German-supplied submarines and torpedo boats, rather than the great ships acquired at such cost.

In 1918 the Austro-Hungarian Empire was dismembered by Allied powers convinced that national self-determination would solve the long-running problems of the Balkans. The fleet was divided among the victorious nations, most units being scrapped in the 1920s.

Radetzky class

Austria-Hungary was one of several powers to continue building predreadnoughts even after the all-big gun revolution had begun. Although dreadnought designs were considered by the Austro-Hungarian navy in 1905, a compromise design emerged similar to the British Lord Nelsons or the French Dantons. Four 12-inch guns were the main armament, but the secondary battery was extremely powerful: eight 9.4-inch 45 cal weapons. A tertiary battery of 20 3.9-inch weapons guaranteed that fire control would be impossible in a close-range action. Although the Austrian 12-inch gun was as good as those of any other navy, the 9.4-inch was not capable of penetrating the armour of most foreign dreadnoughts beyond a few thousand yards.

On a displacement of 14,500 tons, the Radetskys carried a formidable armament. It was achieved by reducing protection to a 9-inch belt, tapering to 4-inch at the bows

and stern. The main belt reached almost to the stern, and its thickest section, covering the area from forward of the front turret to aft of the rear turret was closed off by 6-inch bulkheads. It extended 5 feet below the waterline. Internal fore and aft bulkheads of high tensile steel were intended to provide a good measure of protection against underwater attack.

Two sets of 4-cylinder vertical triple expansion engines delivered 20,000 hp for a designed maximum speed of 20 knots. All three exceeded 20 knots on trials.

Radetsky came to Britain for the coronation review in 1911. All three Radetskys cruised in the Mediterranean on the eve of World War I, but their war service was limited to a few bombardments of the Italian and Montenegrin coasts. In 1919 *Erzherzog Franz Ferdinand* was interned at Venice, her sisters at Spaleto; all three were scrapped in Italy in the 1920s.

Radetzky class data

Displacement, standard	14,722 tons
Displacement, full load	15,851 tons
Length overall	456 feet (139 m)
Beam	80 feet 4 in (24.5 m)
Design draught	26 feet 7 in (8.1 m) mean
Complement	876

Class: *Erzherzog Franz Ferdinand, Radetzky, Zrinyi*

Armament:
4 × 12-in (2 × 2)
8 × 9.4-in (4 × 2)
20 × 3.9-in guns
6 × 11-pdr guns
5 × 47-mm guns
3 × 17.7-in torpedo tubes

Machinery:
4-cylinder Vertical Expansion engines,
  20,600 ihp
2 shafts
20.5 knots

Armour:
Belt ....9 in
Barbettes and main turrets 9.8 in
Secondary turrets ......8 in
Deck ....2 in
Conning tower...........9.8 in

Viribus Unitis class

Vice-Admiral count von Montecuccoli authorised the construction of the Empire's first dreadnoughts without parliamentary approval. With Italy pressing ahead with the *Dante Alighieri*, there was not enough time to pander to Hungarian nationalists and other interest groups who persistently blocked the budgets for their own political ends. To win Hungarian approval, the fourth unit, *Szent István*

was ordered from the Danubius shipyard at Fiume. The yard had never attempted such a large vessel and *Szent István* was three years building, while *Viribus Unitis* was completed in 26 months.

The class were based on the pre-dreadnought Radetzkys but with a single-calibre main armament of 12 × 12-inch guns in four triple turrets on the centre line: the first battleship to be so equipped. Although the Italians were the first to design and lay down a battleship with triple turrets, the Austrians managed to complete theirs first. Arcs of fire for both main and secondary armament were very wide, but the ships were not very steady firing platforms.

The main and upper armoured belts were 15–16 feet deep. Lateral bulkheads were supposed to protect the machinery

spaces and magazines from torpedo hits, but the class proved vulnerable to underwater damage. During World War I the number of 66-mm (11-pdr) singly mounted on the main turrets was reduced from 18 to twelve.

On 10 June 1918 *Szent István* was sunk off Premuda island, 30 miles south of Pola by two torpedoes from the Italian MTBs *MAS 15* and *MAS 21*. On 1 November 1918, only hours after being taken over by the newly-created Yugoslav navy, *Viribus Unitis* was sunk in Pola harbour by Italian frogmen operating from the CMB *Locusta*. The 375-lb warhead did tremendous damage and the internal subdivision did not save her. *Prinz Eugen*, ceded to France, was expended as a target in June 1922; *Tegetthoff*, ceded to Italy, was scrapped in 1924–25.

Viribus Unitis class data:

Displacement, standard ....19,698 tons
Displacement, full load ....21,255 tons
Length overall ....499 feet 3 in (152.18 m)
Beam ....89 feet 8 in (27.34 m)
Design draught...............27 feet (8.23 m) mean
Complement 1,050

Class: *Viribus Unitis, Tegetthoff, Szent István, Prinz Eugen*

Armament:
12 × 12-in guns (4 × 3)
12 × 5.9-in guns
18 × 11-pdr guns
4 × 21-in torpedo tubes

Machinery:
4 Parsons turbines, 25,000 shp
4 shafts
20 knots

Armour:
Belt ....up to 11 in
Turrets ....11 in
Barbettes ....11 in
Decks ....1.9 in
Conning tower...........11 in

France

French battleships 1900–1960

In the first editions of *Jane's Fighting Ships*, the navies were listed in order of size. The Royal Navy predominated, and each book began with page after page of British battleships. After the British came the French. Yet in 1898, the very year the first Jane's title was launched, Germany announced an unprecedented naval expansion programme. Once directed to the construction of a High Seas Fleet, the enormous industrial power of Wilhelmine Germany catapulted the German navy up the 'league table' until on the eve of World War I, Germany was second only to Great Britain. The rapidly expanding navies of America and Japan jockeyed for position too, the latter aided after 1905 by their demolition of the Russian navy at Port Arthur and Tsushima. By 1906 the French navy, for decades the second strongest fleet in the world, had fallen behind its traditional rivals both in terms of quantity and quality. Nowhere was this more obvious than in battleships. French cruisers, while easily distinguished by their multiplicity of low funnels, were not significantly inferior to their potential opponents.

Left: Suffren, seen here during the Dardanelles operations, was typical of the French battleships built at the beginning of the century. Badly damaged by Turkish batteries in March 1915, she was lost with all hands off Portugal in 1916 after being torpedoed by a U-Boat.

Below: In 1942 the French fleet scuttled itself at Toulon to prevent the Germans seizing control. This is the Strasbourg.

Yet French capital ships had been built slowly, to bizarre designs and not until 1895 was there a serious attempt to build a homogenous class. By the turn of the century, the bulk of the French battlefleet was made up of individually-designed battleships, with different specifications and their own handling characteristics. France was slow to adopt the almost universal layout of a main armament in two turrets, one before and one aft of the superstructure. Many French battleships persisted with a lozenge arrangement: one big gun forward, one aft and one on either side. Theoretically, this provided excellent arcs of fire, but they could only fire three guns on the broadside.

Trained and prepared for much of the nineteenth century for another naval war with Britain, the French navy was famous for the '*Jeune Ecole*': a school of thought which stressed the use of cruisers to raid enemy commerce and light craft to attack capital ships. In other words, how a navy outnumbered in battleships, as the French would be in any conflict with Britain, could still prosecute a successful campaign. Perhaps the emphasis on commerce-raiding and torpedo boats attracted the most fertile minds in the service. There was certainly no attempt to undermine British numerical advantage in battleships with qualitative superiority. The Navy

Minister, Pelletan even held up the construction of the two République class battleships, determined to concentrate on cruisers and torpedo craft.

French battleships remained easy to identify, even when they finally adopted a two turret layout for their main armament. Pronounced tumblehome, with secondary armament on overhanging sponsons as well as aft turrets sometimes a deck lower than the fore turret set them apart from other nations' battleships. French yards had enough excess capacity to export: selling battleships to Russia and influencing Russian battleship design until the disaster in the Far East. However, the

pace of construction was noticeably slower than France's main competitors.

France was as unprepared for the revolutionary *Dreadnought* as any other nation. But whereas Germany was able to develop the Helgoland class dreadnoughts within two years, the French navy persisted with the Danton class. These were heavily-armed battleships by predreadnought standards: the standard main armament of four 12-inch guns was backed by a secondary armament of 9.4-inch weapons, all in turrets. Equivalents to the British Lord Nelsons, they were the most powerful predreadnought battleships, but just as obsolete as their predecessors when compared to all big gun designs. The 9.4-inch gun could not penetrate battleship scales of protection at anything but point blank range. Although alternative armament was discussed: another two or even four 12-inch guns should have been possible on their displacement, the Dantons retained their mixed battery. Whereas the Lord Nelson class was abruptly terminated in favour of more dreadnoughts, France persisted with building Dantons. Six were completed before attention was turned to a dreadnought design.

The first French dreadnought was not launched until September 1911. The turret layout was as wasteful of firepower as early British and German designs. However, at least the French managed to dispense with the ram bow which was still a feature of many dreadnought designs, even on the eve of World War I. The battle of Lissa cast a long shadow over battleship design. The Courbet class dreadnoughts were obviously French, sporting three low funnels with the same profile of those found on the earlier capital ships.

Alliance with Britain enabled France to concentrate her fleet in the Mediterranean by 1914, leaving the northern coast to be protected by the

Left: St. Louis, Charlemagne *and* Suffren *seen at the Dardanelles in February 1915. Note the false bow waves painted on all three battleships. Obsolete by World War I, these predreadnoughts were still useful for shore bombardment.*

Royal Navy. The primary concern of the French navy at the beginning of the war was to transport units from the army in North Africa to mainland France. The presence of the German battlecruiser *Goeben* was cause for concern, but she soon bolted for Constantinople. French battleships ventured into the Adriatic to prevent the Austro-Hungarian fleet blockading Montenegro, but these confined waters were soon dominated by minefields and submarines.

In 1915 France commissioned the first of three Provence class 'super dreadnoughts', armed with ten 13.4-inch (34 cm) guns. By 1918 *Paris* and *Bretagne* were equipped with flying-off platforms on 'B' turret.

While the French dreadnoughts were all refitted during the 1920s, the economic and political climate prevented any new construction. When France did develop her first-war capital ships, they were radical in the extreme: 'all or nothing' armour, and the main armament concentrated forward in two quadruple turrets. Interestingly, the Dunkerque class battlecruisers were the first capital ships to be designed to carry aircraft from the outset, with Loire Nieuport 130 flying boats in a hanger aft and launched from a 72-feet catapult that could be rotated through 360 degrees.

Graceful and elegant warships, the Dunkerques and Richelieus found

themselves fighting both the Axis and Allied powers during World War II. In splendid defiance of the experience of World War II, *Jean Bart* was even completed 1945–49 and joined the French squadron sent to Egypt in the 1956 Anglo-French debacle at Suez. Carrying no less than 52 large calibre anti-aircraft guns (57– and 100-mm), *Jean Bart* had one of the most powerful AA fits ever mounted on a battleship. When she was scrapped in 1969 she was the last battleship extant in Europe.

Below: *The powerful battleship* Richelieu *fired her first broadsides in anger against British forces attacking the French Mediterranean fleet in 1940. She later joined the Free French forces and served in the Arctic and Pacific 1944-5.*

Danton class

In 1906 the French announced plans to increase naval construction in response to the massive building programme underway in Germany. Over the next 14 years it was proposed to expand the fleet from 20 predreadnoughts (half so elderly as to be unfit for war) to a total of 38 capital ships.

The first class of battleship constructed to fulfill this grandiose (and never to be realized) plan was the Danton class, of which the nameship was laid down in February 1906. Like the British Lord Nelsons laid down nine months previously, the Dantons represented an interim class between dreadnoughts proper and the bulk of the world's predreadnought battleships. Instead of the usual main armament of four 12-inch guns, a secondary battery of 6-inch guns and a range of lighter weapons, the Dantons had a much more powerful secondary battery of 9.4-inch guns, all sited in turrets. Beamier and longer than the Nelsons, the Dantons had three secondary turrets per side for a total of twelve 9.4s.

The British terminated the Lord Nelsons after just two units. With Dreadnought such a success, it was obvious that all subsequent capital ships would be in her guise. The value of an intermediate calibre battery, be it 9.2-inch in the case of the Nelsons, 9.4-inch with the Dantons, or even 10-inch with the Japanese *Aki* proved quesionable. Fire control was complicated: it was difficult to distinguish between the shell splashes of the main and secondary armament. The intermediate calibre weapons were not able to penetrate the main armour of any contemporary battleship but lacked the rate of fire of 6-inch guns which made the lighter weapons arguably more useful against cruisers or torpedo boats.

Notwithstanding these considerations, the construction of the Dantons continued. Three were laid down in 1907 and, incredibly, another pair in 1908 by which time Britain, Germany and the USA were well into dreadnought-building programmes. Various schemes were suggested to improve these anachronistic battleships: substituting two or four more 12-inch guns for the 9.4-inch secondary battery was one. Equally practically, it was proposed to arm them with 9.4-inch guns alone.

The Dantons were the first French class to be turbine-driven, with a 30 per cent increase in power over the preceeding Vérité class. The 26 boilers exhausted by a distinctive five funnels. Armour protection was to usual French standards, with a

10-inch belt protecting the vitals, and a great deal of internal subdivision. Struck by two torpedoes from the German submarine *U-64* on 19 March 1917, south of Sardinia, *Danton* remained afloat for about 40 minutes, enabling most of her people to escape. Several contemporary battleships sank like stones after similar damage. *Voltaire* survived two lightweight torpedoes from the Austrian *UB-48* in 1918.

All served in the Mediterranean during World War I. *Mirabeau* and *Vergniaud* served in the Black Sea against the Bolsheviks in 1919, the former grounding badly during a blizzard off the Crimea. Refloated after lightening, including the removal of 'A' turret, she never returned to service and was condemned in 1921. *Condorcet* became a barrack ship in 1931 and was used briefly (and eventually scuttled) by the Germans at Toulon in 1944.

Danton class data:

Displacement, standard	18,360 tons
Displacement, full load	19,600 tons
Length overall	480 feet 11 in (146.58 m)
Beam	84 feet 8 in (25.8 m)
Design draught	28 feet 8 in (8.74 m)
Complement	921

Left: Danton was one of the most powerful predreadnought battleships, but she was rendered obsolete by the all big-gun ship. Nevertheless, France continued to build a class of six, all out of date before they were completed.

Class: *Danton, Condorcet, Diderot, Mirabeau, Vergniaud, Voltaire*

Armament:
4 × 12-in guns (2 × 2)
12 × 9.4-in guns (6 × 2)
16 × 2.9-in guns
10 × 47-mm guns
2 × 18-in torpedo tubes

Machinery:
4 Parsons steam turbines, 22,500 shp
4 shafts
19 knots

Armour:
Belt ....up to 10 in

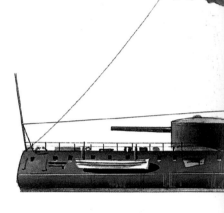

Main turrets	12.6 in
Barbettes	11 in
Secondary turrets	8.7 in
Deck	2.75 in
Conning tower	11.8 in

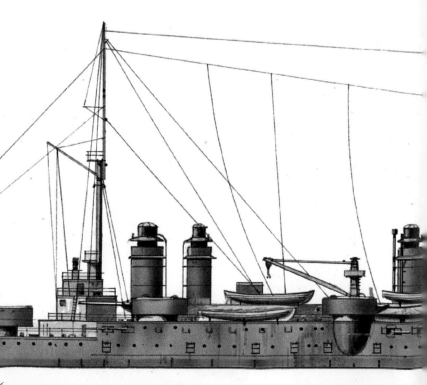

Below: République *in the unusual scheme worn by many French battleships serving in the eastern Mediterranean during 1915. The provision of turrets for most of her secondary armament was innovative at a time when many navies persisted with casemates too low to be serviceable in heavy seas.*

République class

After a long succession of 'one-off' designs, leading to the contemporary criticism that the French navy was a fleet of prototypes, the French laid down a class of three battleships between 1894 and 1896. The Charlemagnes were distinctively Gallic, with a pronounced tumblehome and secondary armament mounted in overhanging sponsons. While respectably armed with the usual four 12-inch guns, their armour was Harvey nickel-steel, not the more modern and stronger Krupp cemented steel. Like the individual designs they followed, they displaced little more than 11,000 tons and were not really a match for the latest British or American designs.

The design was modified in 1898 to produce the *Jéna*, and again in 1899 for the similar *Suffren*, but with the two Républiques, the French finally started work on a large enough displacement to create a powerful unit that did not skimp on either firepower or protection. *République* was laid down at the end of 1901. The forward and after 12-inch turrets were located on the forecastle and upper decks respectively, and twelve of the 6.4-inch secondary guns were housed in six twin turrets, three on each beam on the forecastle deck; the other six secondary guns were to be found in two upper deck casemates forward, and in four main deck casemates.

Having finally perfected the predreadnought battleship, it was unfortunate that the *République* took so long to complete. By the time she fitted out, five years after she was laid down, she had been rendered obsolete by the British *Dreadnought*. Even the Russian shipyards, rapidly expanding to meet the demands of modern warship design managed to build battleships faster than this. Both Républiques served in the Mediterranean during World War I; *République* was stricken in 1921, and *Patrie* in 1928.

République class data:

Displacement, standard	14,605 tons
Length overall	439 feet (133.81 m)
Beam	79 feet 7 in (24.26 m)
Design draught	27 feet 7 in (8.41 m)
Complement	766

Class: *Patrie, République*

Armament:
4 × 12-in guns (2 × 2)
18 × 6.4-in guns (18 × 1)
25 × 3-pdr guns
2 × 18-in torpedo tubes

Machinery:
Triple expansion steam engines
Three shafts
19 knots

Armour:
Belt	up to 11 in
Decks	up to 2.75 in
Secondary guns	up to 5.9 in
Conning tower	12 in

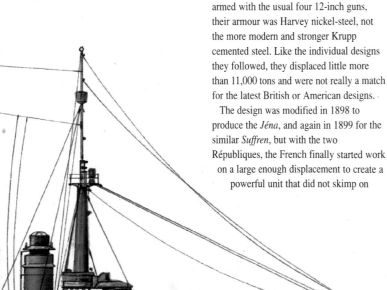

Left: By the time she was completed, in 1911, Dantons' mixed armament of four 12-in guns and twelve 9.4-in guns was outmatched by the twelve 12-in guns carried by typical dreadnoughts.

Battleships of the 20th Century

Courbet class

France did not begin her first dreadnoughts until 1910. So slow was the pace of French naval construction that all suitable slips were occupied until that autumn by the six units of the Danton class predreadnoughts. The lessons of the dreadnought era were absorbed by French designers between 1906 and 1910, but it was not until the advent of M. Délcasse as navy minister and Admiral de Lapéyrère as commander-in-chief that modern battleships were designed for the fleet.

The Courbets were ahead of contemporary thinking in that they abandoned the last vestiges of the ram bow, which had lingered on among European and American battleships although the day of ramming was clearly long gone. Superfiring centre-line turrets kept length to a minimum, important because of the limitations of French dry docks. The provision of director fire control was ahead of both British and US practice

However, these modern features were counter-balanced by several backward-looking aspects of the design. The Courbets stuck to 12-in calibre for the main armament at a time when the Britain and American were moving into the era of the 'super-dreadnought' with 13.5- or even 14-in guns. The poorly located wing turrets wasted firepower as did the poor distribution of the otherwise powerful secondary armament. Armour protection was adequate and was based on a belt running from the bows to within a few feet of the stern. The upper belt formed a substantial redoubt for the secondary armament. The heavy weight of armour at the ends tended to make the ships pitch most uncomfortably in any sort of sea.

Right: Courbet's profile bears more than a passing similarity to the Dantons'. Entering service just in time for World War I, the Courbets were based at Malta in 1914, ready to engage the Austro-Hungarian fleet if it sortied from the Adriatic.

In 1914 and 1915 *Courbet* was flagship of the French Mediterranean Fleet, and on 16 August 1914 sank the Austro-Hungarian cruiser *Zenta* during a foray into the Adriatic. *Courbet* was modernized between 1921 and 1924, the fore funnel being altered and the pole foremast being replaced by a tripod mast. Another refit in 1928 and 1929 saw the two foremost funnels trunked into a single uptake, the boilers replaced and the torpedo tubes deleted. Four 2.95-in anti-aircraft guns were added. A training ship by the time France was overrun in 1940 *Courbet* escaped from Cherbourg to the UK, where she because an AA ship. She was expended as a breakwater for the 'Mulberry' artificial harbour on the Normandy coast on 10 June 1944, and was broken up after the war.

Jean Bart was also built at Brest but completed some five months earlier than *Courbet*, on 5 June 1913. The Austrian *UB-14* torpedoed *Jean Bart* on 21 December 1914, but she survived albeit at the cost of her wine stores. Demilitarised in 1936 and renamed *Océan* she served as a harbour-training ship. She was scuttled in Toulon on 27 November 1942, and was thereafter used by the Germans as a target. In 1944 she was raised, and in 1945 was scrapped.

Paris was built by Forges et Chantiers de la Mediterranée at La Seyne, and completed in August 1914. Like *Courbet*, she was modernized in 1923–4, but emerged with two funnels forward instead of one. In 1939 she was a harbour training ship, but escaped to the UK in June 1940 and was used an accommodation ship for Polish seamen. She was handed back to France in 1945 and scrapped in 1956.

France was built at St Nazaire, and also completed in August 1914. She was flagship of the Mediterranean Fleet in 1916, serving at Corfu and Mudros. She was lost on 26 August 1922 when she struck an uncharted rock in Quiberon Bay during a storm. Salvage proved impossible and the wreck was left to its fate after some parts were removed.

Courbet class data:

Displacement, standard	23,100 tons
Displacement, full load	26,000 tons
Length overall	551 feet 2 in (168 m)
Beam	91 feet 6 in (27.9 m)
Design draught	29 feet 6 in (9 m)
Complement	1,108

Class: *Courbet, France, Jean Bart, Paris*

Armament:
12 × 12-in guns (6 × 2)

22 × 5.5-in guns
4 × 47-mm guns
4 × 18-in torpedo tubes

Machinery:
2 Parsons steam turbines, 28,000 shp
4 shafts
20.5 knots

Armour:

Belt	up to 10.6 in
Belt ends	7.1 in
Decks	2.76 in
Barbettes	11 in
Turrets	up to 11.4 in
Casemates	7.1 in
Conning tower	11.8 in

Below: Courbet as completed. The turret layout enabled them to fire with six 12-in guns on targets all but directly ahead or directly astern, although the broadside was obviously limited to ten guns. A rangefinder was fitted above the bridge during World War I and in her 1928 refit the forward pair of funnels were trunked together.

Right and below: While the last French predreadnoughts had taken the sensible step of mounting at least some of the secondary armament in turrets, the Courbets reverted to casemates for their 5.5-in guns. Sited below the main turrets, they must have been sporting to serve when the main armament was firing.

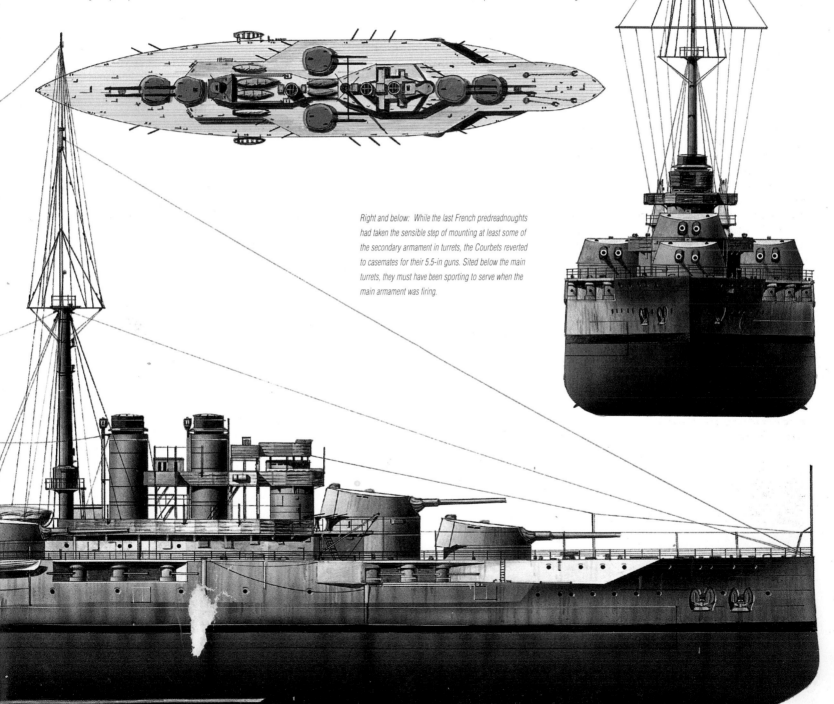

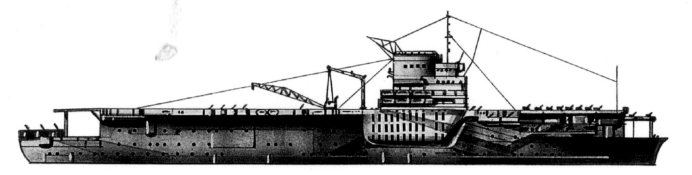

Normandie class

While the Royal Navy was increasing its main armament calibre again, from 13.5-inch to 15-inch with the Queen Elizabeths, the French decided to stay with their 13.4-inch guns, but mount two more of them in their next class of battleships. It was decided to fit these in three quadruple turrets: the first to be fitted in any navy. This saved enough weight for the extra two guns to be shipped on the same displacement as the Bretagne class. Each turret contained what was in effect two twin mounts on a single barbette. To provide cruising economy, and as a safeguard against the poor performance of French-built turbines, reciprocating machinery was coupled to the outer shafts. The turbines powered the inner shafts and were designed for steaming ahead only.

The outbreak of war slowed construction severely as the workforce vanished. French conscription was so thorough that the French army fielded as many men as the Germans from a population half that of the German Empire – and thousands of men volunteered before their call-up date in the heady days of August 1914. *Flandre*, *Gascogne* and *Normandie* were launched in the autumn of 1914, with *Languedoc* following in May 1915. However, work was suspended soon after. Although the workforce was restored to full strength, France had little need for extra battleships while her armies were engaged in a life-or-death struggle against Germany.

The French navy considered completing them after World War I. To take account of lessons learnt during the war, a 1919 study concluded that the Normandies would require a speed of 21.5 knots (and thus new turbines), lengthening the hull and fitting anti-torpedo bulges, and elevating the main armament to achieve a maximum range of 25,000 metres. Thought was apparently given to developing them as battlecruisers, with six 17-inch guns and a speed of 32 knots; but all these ambitious schemes were abandoned as economic reality sank in. All were broken up in the 1920s, except for the *Béarn* which was not launched until 1920 and was converted into an aircraft carrier. Completed in 1927, she was equipped to carry 40 aircraft. However, her speed of 21.5 knots was clearly inadequate. In 1940 she escaped to Fort de France, Martinique where she was decommissioned. Re-commissioned into the Free French fleet, she was overhauled and rearmed at New Orleans in 1944. Used to carry troops and supplies to the French army fighting in Indochina during the 1950s, she survived as an accomodation ship until sold to Italian shipbreakers in 1967.

Normandie class data:

Displacement, standard	24,833 tons
Length overall	577 feet 8.5in (176.4 m)
Beam	88 feet 5in (27 m)
Design draught	28 feet 6in (8.7 m)
Complement	1,124

Class: *Flandre, Gascogne, Languedoc, Normandie, Béarn.*

Armament:
12 × 13.4-in guns (3 × 4)
24 × 5.5-in guns
4 × 47-mm guns
6 × 17.7-in torpedo tubes

Machinery:
2 Parsons turbines
2 triple expansion steam engines
40,000 shp
4 shafts
21 knots

Above: Béarn, the fifth unit of the Normandie class, was begun in December 1913. Work was stopped in 1915 and only resumed in 1920 to clear the slipway. While her sisterships were all scrapped, she was converted to an aircraft carrier and is shown here as she appeared in 1945 after refitting in the USA.

Armour:
Belt	up to 11.8 in
Decks	up to 2.75 in
Barbettes	11.2 in
Turrets	up to 13.4 in

Lyon class

Design work for the Lyon class battleships, based on an enlargement of the Normandie class, was begun in mid-1913. Projected designs included a 27,500-ton ship mounting 14 × 13.4-inch guns or 8 × 15-inch guns, a 28,500–29,000-ton ship mounting 16 × 13.4-inch or 10 × 15-inch guns, and even a ship mounting 20 × 12-inch guns. Based on the data below construction was scheduled to have begun in 1915, but the outbreak of World War I halted the project at the design stage.

As in the Nomandies, the main armament was to be carried in quadruple turrets, one forward, one amidships and a superfiring pair aft, all on the centre-line. The 5.5-inch secondary armament was to be in casemates fore and aft. Armour details were never finalised.

Plans for the post-war French navy were rendered irrelevant by the financial consequences of the Great War. France received two former enemy battleships, the German dreadnought *Thuringen* and the Austro-Hungarian *Prinz Eugen*, but both used as targets and promptly scrapped. No new battleship construction was possible until the 1930s.

Lyon class data:

Displacement, standard ....27,500 tons
Displacement, full load ....29,600 tons
Length overall ....638 feet 2 in (194.5 m)
Beam ....95 feet 2 in (29 m)
Design draught ....30 feet 2 in (9.2 m)
Complement ....Not known

Class: *Duquesne, Lille, Lyon, Tourville.*

Armament:
16 × 13.4-in
24 × 5.5-in QF
6 × 17.7-in torpedo tubes

Machinery:
2 turbines
2 sets Triple Expansion engines
4 shafts
23 knots

Armour:
not known

Above: The Normandie class as they would have appeared on completion. By the time Languedoc left her slip in May 1915 it was obvious that they would have to be left unfinished until the ground war against Germany had been won. The first battleships designed to carry quadruple turrets, the Normandies were not completed after World War I and their hulls were scrapped.

Below: The Lyon class was to have followed the Normandies, with construction beginning in 1915. With sixteen 13.4-in guns in four quadruple turrets, they would have carried more heavy guns than any other battleship afloat. They were never laid down, French shipyards concentrating on only warships which could be completed in time to see service during the war.

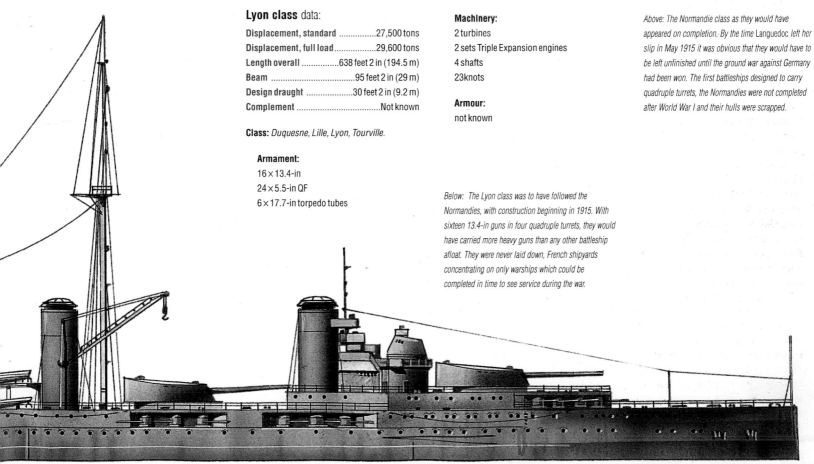

Dunkerque class

France was allowed by the 1921–22 Washington agreements to build 70,000 tons of battleship tonnage (i.e. two units of the maximum 35,000 tons displacement), but the right was not exercised until 1932–34. Although the ships were of only 26,500 tons apiece, their 30 knot speed and eight 13-inch guns completely outclassed the German pocket battleships, laid down between 1929 and 1932. Thus it was that France, building to well within limits, stimulated the dictatorships to build the two Scharnhorsts (laid down in 1935) and the first two Vittorio Venetos (laid down 1934 and greatly over-size).

The 13-inch (33 cm) calibre was new to the French but the unusual grouping of it in two, superfiring quadruple turrets was not entirely original. Quadruples had been planned for the Normandie class, abandoned after World War I. The close grouping was based on the 'all or nothing' principle, by which most armour was devoted to covering the smallest area that would protect the vitals. The two British Nelsons (laid down in 1922) had concentrated their main battery in the shortest length of hull, inspiring the French to do likewise. Two quadruple turrets were also some 1700 tons lighter than four doubles. Armour protection was still relatively light, designed to protect the ship against the 11-inch guns of the German pocket battleships.

French capital ships and cruisers were known until World War I for their idiosyncratic appearance. Suddenly, during the thirties this changed, their warships having a grace and flair that became distinctive, although 'all or nothing' left ships with 'soft' ends, and massive flooding, particularly forward, was a real hazard. *Strasbourg* was slightly different to *Dunkerque*, with a rangefinder mounted much higher in the tower bridge and the conning tower integrated with the superstructure, despite some concerns about the amount of topweight.

On the outbreak of war, *Strasbourg* joined the hunt for the elusive raider *Graf Spee*: she was one of the few Allied ships that might have been able to bring the 'pocket battleship' to action. Both were sent into the Atlantic when *Scharnhorst* and *Gneisnau* made their first convoy raid but were transferred to the Mediterranean in April 1940. Both ships were at Mers-el-Kebir (Oran) in July 1940 when the British attacked, following the refusal of a surrender ultimatum. *Strasbourg* escaped but *Dunkerque* was heavily damaged. Both were again together at Toulon in November 1942 when the French destroyed their fleet rather than allow the Germans to seize it. Although eventually salvaged, neither again went to sea and they were scrapped in the 1950s.

Dunkerque class data:

Displacement, standard ....26,500 tons
Displacement, full load ....35,500 tons
Length overall ....703 feet 9 in (214.5 m)
Beam ....102 feet 3 in (31.16 m)
Design draught ....28 feet 6 in (8.69 m)
Complement 1,431

Class: *Dunkerque, Strasbourg*

Armament:
8 × 13-in
16 × 5.1-in DP
8 × 37-mm AA
32 × 13.2-mm AA

Machinery:
4 Parsons geared turbines
4 shafts

112,500 shp
29.5 knots

Armour:
Belt ....up to 9.5 in
Bulkheads ....up to 9 in
Main deck ....up to 5.1 in
Lower deck ....up to 2 in
Torpedo bulkheads ....up to 1.6 in
Turrets ....up to 13 in
Barbettes ....13.6 in
Secondary turrets up ..to 3.5 in
Conning tower............10.6 in

Below: Having pioneered quadruple turrets with the Normandie class left incomplete during World War I, France persisted with the idea and built two classes of capital ship during the 1930s with their armament concentrated forward in two quadruple turrets. Concentrating the guns and magazines together saved a great weight of armour.

Above: Both Dunkerque class were scuttled at Toulon in November 1942. This photograph was taken during an RAF reconnaissance sortie over the port and shows the Strasbourg on the far right. She had escaped the 1940 British attack on the French fleet at Mers-el-Kebir.

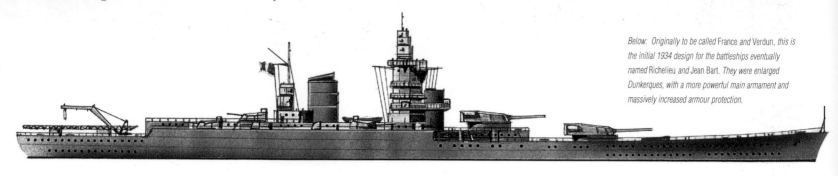

Below: Originally to be called France *and* Verdun, *this is the initial 1934 design for the battleships eventually named* Richelieu *and* Jean Bart. *They were enlarged* Dunkerques, *with a more powerful main armament and massively increased armour protection.*

Richelieu class

The comparatively modest armament and displacement of the two Dunkerques may have set a good example, but neither Italy nor Germany seemed over-awed. France therefore looked at a more powerful version, armed with 15-inch guns. There was a very close class resemblance, with the obvious major difference in the quirky funnel structure. By combining funnel casing and after superstructure, topweight was saved and boiler gases exhausted abaft the optical systems. As in the Dunkerques, the designers separated the big turrets to make it less likely that a single hit could put both out of action. A protective deck was also provided forward and aft in the otherwise 'soft' end.

The two completed units had an interesting war in that they both started by fighting the Allies, the *Richelieu* finishing by joining them. *Richelieu* was laying at Dakar in Senegal in July 1940 when the British adopted a similar line to that taken at Mers-el-Kebir. The attack was a failure (the *Richelieu* hitting HMS *Barham* with a 15-inch shell) but an aircraft from the carrier *Hermes* put a torpedo into the battleship's after end. The damage was beyond the capacity of Dakar to deal with and the ship remained inactive until being repaired (as a Free French unit) in the United States. With her damaged guns replaced by weapons taken from *Jean Bart*,

she emerged from the New York Navy Yard with new radar but without her aircraft. After taking part in operations off Norway in early 1944, she joined the British Pacific fleet as a fast escort for the aircraft carriers.

On 19 June 1940 *Jean Bart*, escaped from the St. Nazaire fitting out basin minutes before German aircraft arrived overhead. She reached Casablanca on 22 June where she remained for the rest of the war. By the time of the Allied landings in North Africa, the guns in the forward turret had been made operational (none had been fitted in the after turret before she left France). *Jean Bart* opened fire on the US landing forces and was rewarded with eight 16-inch hits from USS *Massachusetts* and aircraft bombs. She returned to Brest in 1945 and, despite the obvious obsolesence of the battleship, she was completed in time to take part in the Anglo-French attack on Egypt in 1956. She was decommissioned in 1961 and scrapped in 1970.

A third unit (*Clemenceau*) had not reached the launch stage when France was overrun in 1940. The Germans captured the citadel in the Salou dock at Brest and towed it to an isolated anchorage where it was sunk in 1944 by US aircraft. A fourth 'half-sister' (*Gascogne*) was never commenced.

Richelieu class data:

Displacement, standard ....38,500 tons
Displacement, full load.................47,500 tons

Length overall ....813 feet 3 in (247.85 m)
Beam ....108 feet 9 in (33 m)
Design draught ....31 feet 9 in (9.63 m)
Complement 1,670

Class: *Jean Bart, Richelieu, Clemenceau.*

Armament:
8 × 15-in guns (2 × 4)
9 × 6-in guns (3 × 3)
12 × 3.9-in guns (6 × 2)
16 × 37-mm guns
8 × 13.2-mm machine guns

Machinery:
4 Parsons geared turbines, 155,000 shp
4 shafts
32 knots

Armour:
Belt ....up to 13.6 in
Main deck ....up to 6.7 in
Lower deck ....1.6 in
Turrets ....up to 16.9 in
Secondary turrets ......up to 5.1 in
Conning tower............13.4 in

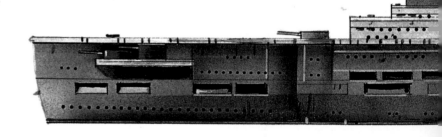

Above: Before she was completed, the French navy examined plans to convert Jean Bart into a hybrid battleship/aircraft carrier. There was also discussion about increasing the main armament to 16-in calibre, but all these plans were overtaken by the German attack in 1940.

Left: Richelieu *after her refit, with 40 mm AA mountings covering the quarterdeck in place of the catapult and flying boat.*

Above: *The after control position was located on the funnel which was canted aft to keep it clear of gases. Note the 3.9-in 40 mm AA guns.*

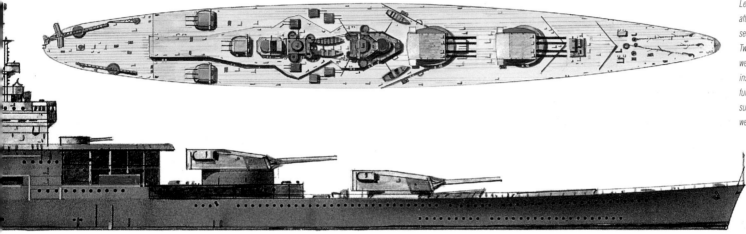

Left: *Three 6-in turrets aft provided Richelieu's secondary armament. Two more triple turrets were to have been installed between the funnel and the forward superstructure, but they were never fitted.*

Above: Richelieu *as she looked before her refit in the USA, with a Loire 130 flying boat on the catapult. Richelieu helped defeat a British attack on Dakar in September 1940, hitting the battleship Barham with one 15-in shell.*

Left: *Fairey Barracudas overfly* Richelieu *in 1945 when she served as a fast carrier escort with the British Pacific fleet. Placed in reserve in 1956, Richelieu was scrapped in 1968.*

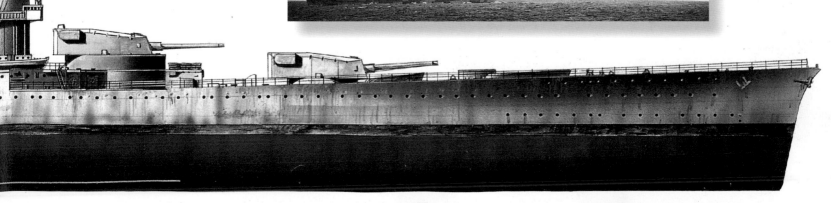

Germany

Tirpitz and the beginnings of German naval expansion

Like the nation itself, the Imperial German Navy dated only from 1871. Founded on the antiquated and ineffective Royal Prussian Navy, it grew modestly under the leadership of the Army, which was still by far the State's most potent force. Then, in 1888, Germany gained its third Kaiser in Wilhelm II.

Wilhelm was passionately interested in naval affairs and, fired particularly by the theories of Alfred Thayer Mahan, he believed that a powerful battle-fleet would be the key to Germany's "place in the sun", the acquisition of an overseas empire and the prestige and trade that would follow. The British Empire, headed by his grandmother, Queen Victoria, was a living exemplar for his beliefs.

In August 1889, Wilhelm was created an honorary Royal Navy Admiral of the Fleet, enabling him to lead a German squadron at the great Fleet Review at Spithead, and be attended with the ceremony that he loved. It served only to fire him with envy. The resulting naval race was a primary cause of the First World War.

Left: Germany's first predreadnoughts were the innovative 10,000 ton Brandenburg class, armed with six 11-in guns. By World War I, two had been sold to Turkey and the other two were relegated to coastal defence duties in 1915.

The new Kaiser was single-minded in his determination for a change of course. Bismarck, architect of the German nation, was a wily, world-class statesman who got his way by diplomacy and restraint. Too able by half, he was dismissed by Wilhelm, who wanted somebody that he felt he could control. The Chancellor had, in any case, virtually damned himself by expressing the opinion that Germany should aspire to be a seapower of the "second rank".

In 1897 an irrevocable step was taken by the appointment of two new State Secretaries – Tirpitz at the Navy Office and von Bulow at the Foreign Office. Rear Admiral Alfred Tirpitz (ennobled 'von Tirpitz' by the Kaiser in 1902) had been in command of the Far East Cruiser Squadron but proved to be an able administrator and tactical politician, totally in tune with the ideas of his master. Wilhelm's strident behaviour was matched by his belief that the new technological revolution would transform the nation into a world power but, internationally, he created more apprehension than admiration.

Tirpitz' first action was to present a lengthy memorandum. Its potentially-explosive theme identified England as "the most dangerous enemy (sic)" and argued for a carefully-structured fleet, to be concentrated "between

Below: Oldenburg: one of the second class of German dreadnoughts. Built at Gdansk (then Danzig) she survived the battle of Jutland and was surrendered in 1918. Awarded to Japan, she was broken up in Holland in 1920.

Germany

Heligoland and the Thames". The Royal Navy, although larger, had too many commitments to concentrate the necessary strength in the North Sea and, therefore would not risk a war. By default, so powerful a German fleet could defeat that of either Russia or France, while making Germany a worthwhile ally where it mattered.

The Admiral was a 'battleship man'; believers in *guerres de course*, or defeat of superior fleets by massed torpedo craft or submarines, could expect poor career prospects. His 'spiritual massage' of opponents in the Reichstag won him the necessary support for the First and Second Navy Bills of 1898 and 1900. Where the First caused the British no undue alarm, the Second was a different matter. Without cost limitation, it sought to double the size of the German fleet to 38 battleships and 58 assorted cruisers. There was discussion of further growth to 45, or even 48, capital ships. By 1905, with the demolition of the Russian fleet by the Japanese, Germany already ranked the world's third sea power, after Great Britain and France.

Above: The more conventional Kaiser Friederich III class followed the Brandenburgs. They were armed with four 9.4-in and up to 18 6-in guns.

Tirpitz was well matched after 1904 by Britain's 'Jackie' Fisher, who, as First Sea Lord, reorganised the bulk of the Royal Navy's strength on the Channel (i.e. 'Home') Fleet, the Gibraltar-based Atlantic Fleet and the Malta-based Mediterranean Fleet. This was made possible by the Anglo-Japanese alliance of 1902 and the Anglo-French *entente* of 1904, which allowed a re-distribution of assets, so that 75 per cent were immediately available for North Sea operations.

Wilhelm, the self-styled "Admiral of the Atlantic" announced that the Navy Bills' programmes would be pursued "… to the last detail. Whether the British like it or not …" The Race was on.

Above: Admiral von Tirpitz: architect of Germany's High Seas Fleet and the aggressive naval policy that helped cause World War I.

Below: Before Tirpitz, the German fleet was one of the minor navies. The four Sachsen class were designed for coast defence in the early 1870s. Displacing 7900 tons, they were armed with six 26 cm (10.2-in) guns in open barbette mountings.

German predreadnoughts

First fruits of the Wilhelmian era were the four Brandenburgs, built between 1890 and 1894. Of a size, and almost exactly contemporary with the two British Barfleurs they were far more innovative. At a time when the *de rigueur* main battery was four guns disposed in twin mountings, forward and aft, the Brandenburgs shipped an extra twin 28 cm (11-inch) abaft the machinery space. With no real secondary battery, their smaller weapons were a strange mix of 10.5 cm (4.1-inch) and 8.8 cm (3.5-inch) guns. In contrast to the British design, which concentrated protection over the vitals, leaving 'soft' ends, the German spread thinner armour over a full-length belt.

The five Kaisers that followed (1895–1902) showed a reversion to orthodox design. Although some ten per cent larger all round, their main battery was of four 24 cm (9.4-inch) guns. An enlarged superstructure, however, accommodated fourteen 15 cm (6-inch) weapons in casemates and gunhouses. Protection was concentrated over the armament, the main belt being very narrow. The five Wittelsbachs that followed (1899–1904) and, while improvements on the Kaisers, embraced the same philosophy, i.e. that the higher rate of fire of the 9.4 outclassed the extra weight of the 11-inch.

Above: Preussen: *one of the five Braunschweig class.*

The final classes of German predreadnoughts, the five Braunschweigs (1901–1906) and the five Deutschlands (1903–1980), were closely related, and products of the Second Navy Bill. In re-adopting the 11-inch gun, in an improved model, a powerful secondary battery of fourteen 17 cm (6.7-inch) and greater protection, standard displacement jumped to about 13,200 tons. This was still 2000 tons short of the contemporary British King Edward VIIs, Royal Navy battleships having increased in size at a greater rate. Their German peers were aimed particularly at short-range North Sea and Baltic operations, their dimensions being limited also by dockyard facilities.

The first and the last

Capital ships in the High Seas Fleet were organised in six squadrons of battleships and one of battlecruisers. Squadrons I to III comprised the cutting edge of the battle line and, of these, Squadron II was drawn from the ten units of the Braunschweig and Deutschland predreadnought classes. Their 18 knots maximum speed made them something of a liability. The remaining three classes of predreadnought were assigned by class to Squadrons IV to VI; brought forward from reserve in 1914, they were used primarily for training in the Baltic and for guarding the Baltic exits against incursions by the enemy.

Until Jutland the High Seas Fleet battle line went to sea routinely to cover Hipper's battlecruisers on raids against the English East Coast. The idea was to entice and destroy inferior British forces but, until 31 May 1916, the British always arrived too late. On this occasion the trap functioned, but brought about a pitched battle with the whole Grand Fleet: Jutland.

During the daylight phases of the action, the six ships of Squadron II kept mainly on the disengaged side of Scheer's fleet but tacked on to the main line after darkness fell. This part of the line became embroiled with British destroyers at very close range. One of the seventeen torpedoes launched hit the Deutschland class *Pommern*, which blew up, the only German battleship to be lost that day.

The low speed and limited fighting value of Squadron II led to Scheer disbanding it after Jutland, along with most of Squadrons IV to VI. New ships were joining the fleet but the main reason was that skilled personnel were required to man the large numbers of U-boats now being completed to conduct the all-out campaign against Allied commerce.

Six predreadnoughts were permitted the German fleet by the conditions of the armistice. Two, *Schleswig-Holstein* and *Schlesien*, survived to see service in World War II.

Deutschland class

The five Deutschlands were of the same dimensions as the preceding Braunschweigs, but marginally-improved protection increased displacement and draught. They appear to have been tender as a result, as their funnels were only half-cased and the four upper deck guns of the secondary armament were sited in casemates rather than in gunhouses. The secondary armament of fourteen 17 cm (6.7-inch) was powerful, but ten were casemated at main deck level, too low to have been of much use in any sea. A tertiary battery of twenty 8.8 cm guns completed the classes' not-inconsiderable fire-power which, under water, was complemented by no less than six torpedo tubes. These demanded considerable space on so small a ship. The compartment for two broadside tubes intruded into the centre boiler space, while two more were sited immediately abaft the forward magazine space. A fifth pointed forward from the forefoot, the sixth right aft, to port of the centreline rudder.

Laid down in 1903–5, they were powered by triple-expansion machinery driving three propellers. The centreline screw was of slightly smaller diameter than the wing propellers, probably to increase tip clearance beneath the hull, reducing vibration. The Deutschlands' protection was adequate for its day. Over the length of the machinery spaces, below the main belt and glacis, there were two longitudinal torpedo bulkheads. That the *Pommern* blew up from a single torpedo hit at Jutland thus suggests that she was hit, not amidships as reported, but in way of a main magazine.

The four surviving units went to serve the German navy postwar and, as the most modern and powerful units allowed, were much modified. Externally, the bridgework was extended aft, the forward funnel was trunked into the second, and the foremast converted to a lofty, tubular tower supporting a short baseline rangefinder. *Schleswig-Holstein* entered the record books by firing the first major shots of World War II, the target being the Polish military installations on the Westerplatte, at Danzig (Gdansk).

Above: Schleswig-Holstein as a cadet-training ship between the wars. These battleships, already obsolete in 1914, were the most powerful ships allowed to Germany after World War I.

Below: Schleswig-Holstein *was retained by the German navy between the wars and fired some of the first shots of World War II. This is how she appeared in 1941-2. In December 1944 she was bombed and sunk by the RAF in Gotenhafen.*

Deutschland class data:

Displacement, standard	13,190 tons
Displacement, full load	14,220 tons
Length, overall	418.6 feet (127.6 m)
Beam	72.8 feet (22.2 m)
Design draught	27 feet (8.23 m)
Complement	745

Class: *Deutschland, Hannover, Pommern, Schlesien, Schleswig-Holstein,*
Completed 1906–1908

Armament:
Four 11-in guns (2 × 2)
Fourteen 6.7-in (14 × 1)
Twenty 8.8-cm guns
Six 17.7-in torpedo tubes

Machinery:
Triple expansion steam machinery
  20,000 ihp
Three shafts 18 knots

Armour:
Belt	up to 9.45 in
Bulkheads	up to 6.7 in
Decks	up to 1.57 in
Turrets	up to 11 in
Barbettes	up to 9.84 in

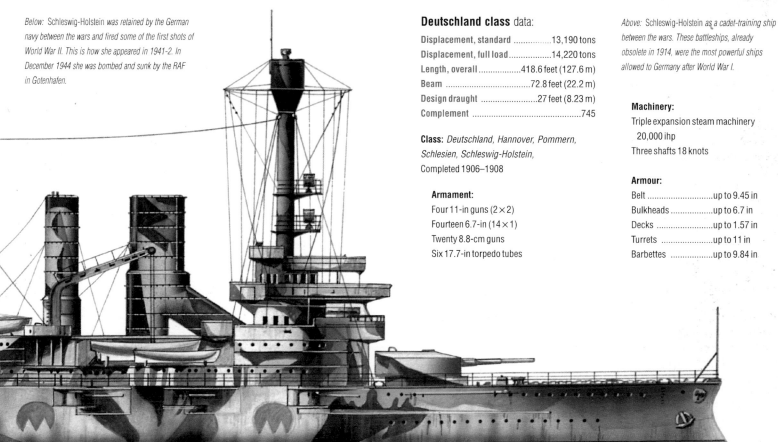

Nassau class

The 'Dreadnought' revolution was really no more than a realisation by all major fleets that capital ship armaments were a hotch-potch of out-dated ideas. It is to the credit of a navy as young as that of the Germans that they reacted as quickly as any to a period of rapid change.

Whether or not they were influenced in any way by the British Lord Nelsons, then in preparation, can only be a matter of conjecture, but the design committee first arrived at very similar 'half-way house' conclusions. Their original proposals were for twin (28 cm) 11-inch turrets fore and aft, with four wing turrets, mounting either two 9.45s or a single 11-inch apiece. They then decided to be bold, producing a preliminary draft for a ship with wing turrets mounting two 11-inch apiece. This arrangement was adopted for the four Nassaus, the so-called

'hexagonal' layout permitting a concentration of six heavy guns in axial fire either ahead or astern, while giving a full eight-gun broadside. With 12-inch guns the disposition would not have been possible on reasonable dimensions and, even with 11-inch, the beam had to be increased considerably, resulting in a comparatively stubby length-on-breadth ratio of 5.45. Even the much-criticised Dreadnought layout permitted theoretical six-forward, six-aft, eight-broadside main battery fire on only ten barrels, so the Nassau solution cannot really be judged particularly successful.

Heavy-calibre wing turrets gave designers additional problems. Turret trunks were very close to the ship's side, making them more vulnerable and complicating the provision of longitudinal torpedo bulkheads. Turrets, trunks and magazines also intruded into the boiler spaces, squeezing available volume

but producing advantage in forcibly dividing boiler and machinery spaces into three separated elements, increasing survivability.

A further drawback of the arrangement was that the six large turrets and the adoption of a heavy 6-inch secondary armament accounted for over 14 per cent of the all-up displacement. The turrets thus needed to be sited as low as possible for stability purposes, which obliged the twelve secondary mountings to be casemated at main deck level and of doubtful use in any sea. The Germans claimed that their 11-inch weapon had only marginally less hitting power than the British 12-inch, and a higher rate of fire.

Contemporary figures suggest that projectile muzzle energy of the 12-inch would be about 22 per cent greater, while the impact effect of the 850 lb (386 kg) round would be considerably more than the 595 lb

(270 kg) round of the 11-inch, 45-calibre with which the Nassaus were fitted.

Steam turbines were not yet in production in Germany, the ships taking triple-expansion machinery. Boilers were at first, coal-fired but later given partial oil-firing. A full-length belt was fitted, but its 12 inch thickness was very limited in area, tapering upward to about 8 inches and to between three and four inches at either end.

At Jutland, all four of the class were involved in the desperate, close-range nocturnal scrap with British light forces. In the course of the melee, the *Nassau* collided with the destroyer *Spitfire* (which survived) and the *Posen* with the *Elbing* (which did not). Before she met her fiery end, the British armoured cruiser *Black Prince* hit the *Rheinland* with a couple of secondary 6-inch shells. All four were scrapped by terms of the armistice.

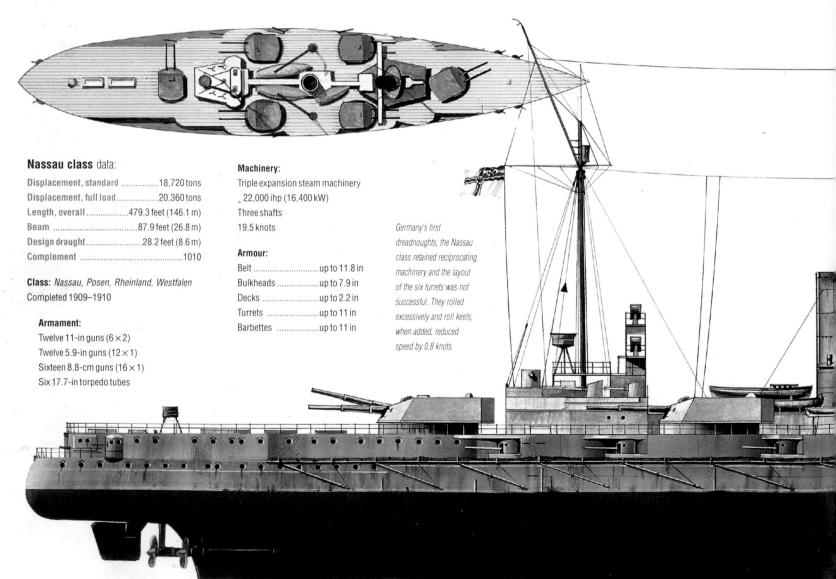

Nassau class data:

Displacement, standard	18,720 tons
Displacement, full load	20,360 tons
Length, overall	479.3 feet (146.1 m)
Beam	87.9 feet (26.8 m)
Design draught	28.2 feet (8.6 m)
Complement	1010

Class: *Nassau, Posen, Rheinland, Westfalen*
Completed 1909–1910

Armament:
Twelve 11-in guns (6 × 2)
Twelve 5.9-in guns (12 × 1)
Sixteen 8.8-cm guns (16 × 1)
Six 17.7-in torpedo tubes

Machinery:
Triple expansion steam machinery
22,000 ihp (16,400 kW)
Three shafts
19.5 knots

Armour:

Belt	up to 11.8 in
Bulkheads	up to 7.9 in
Decks	up to 2.2 in
Turrets	up to 11 in
Barbettes	up to 11 in

Germany's first dreadnoughts, the Nassau class retained reciprocating machinery and the layout of the six turrets was not successful. They rolled excessively and roll keels, when added, reduced speed by 0.8 knots.

Left: Westfalen *displays the residual ram bow typical of early dreadnoughts. She was used as a training ship from the end of 1918 until 1920 when surrendered to Britain for breaking up.*

Left: All four of the Nassau class were in the thick of the night action at Jutland. They sank the British armoured cruiser Black Prince *which blundered into them, but also rammed and sank the German light cruiser* Elbing.

Helgoland class

It was known that the four British Orions, to be laid down in 1909/1910, would be fitted with 13.5-inch main batteries. The four Helgolands, of 1908/1909, were therefore up-gunned in anticipation. The increase in size was from 28 cm (11-inch) to 30.5 cm (12-inch) but the Germans view was that the latter weapon was superior to its larger British counterpart. Its much higher muzzle velocity certainly gave it – if contemporary tables can be relied upon – a 31 per cent advantage in muzzle energy. The British preferred the reliability and lower wear of a low-velocity gun, and a projectile, weighing 1250 lb (568 kg) against 858 lb (390 kg), which had far greater destructive power.

Still harbouring misgivings about superimposed main battery turrets, the Germans repeated the 'hexagonal' layout of the Nassaus. With the larger barbette and turret dimensions of the 12-inch, however, this necessitated an increase in beam to 28.5 metres. This represented a 6 per cent increase on that of the Nassaus, but length was increased by over fourteen per cent. The improved L/B ratio of 5.84 gave them

an extra knot or so in speed for a comparatively modest increase in power. The stubby Nassaus were very quick on the helm, with a small turning circle. Like them, the Helgolands had twin rudders, in line with the wing shafts and, with a bit of effort, could also be turned quickly. The three, closely-spaced funnels were very distinctive, resulting from the boiler spaces being compressed between the structures of the large wing turrets and their magazines.

The *Helgoland* herself received a 15-inch hit at Jutland. Striking just above the waterline, forward of the forward turret, the shell broke up on the 6-inch belt but, even without exploding, it caused a 1.5-metre hole and considerable structural damage.

Helgoland class data:

Displacement, standard	22.570 tons
Displacement, full load	24,500 tons
Lengths, overall	548.6 feet (167.2 m)
Beam	93.5 feet (28.5 m)
Design draught	28.9 feet (89.8 m)
Complement	1110

Class: *Helgoland, Oldenburg, Ostfriesland, Thuringen*
Completed 1911–1912

Left: Ostriesland with the zeppelin L31 (shot down in September 1916 overs Potters Bar). Zeppelins scouted ahead of the High Seas Fleet during most major sorties.

Armament:
Twelve 12-in guns (6 × 2)
Fourteen 5.9-in guns (14 × 1)
Fourteen 8.8-cm guns (14 × 1)
Six 19.7-in torpedo tubes

Machinery:
Triple expansion machinery
  28,000 ihp (20,900 kW)
Three shafts
20 knots

Armour:

Belt	up to 11.8 in
Bulkheads	up to 11.8 in
Deck	up to 2.2 in
Turrets	up to 11.8 in
Barbettes	up to 10.6 in

Von der Tann

Germany's first battlecruiser, *Von der Tann* was ordered under the 1907–8 programme in response to the British Invincible class. Built at Blohm & Voss, Hamburg, Shipping 11-inch guns instead of the British 12-inch, she was substantially better protected than her future enemies. *Von der Tann* was also

the first German capital ship to be fitted with turbines, achieving a top speed on trials of 26.8 knots. Although coal-fired, the boilers were designed to have tar oil sprayed on the coal for maximum speed. With forced draught she could achieve 79,007 shp for 28 knots.

The two midships turrets were sited en echelon, with much wider permissable arcs than the first British battlecruisers. The mountings allowed 20 degrees elevation for a maximum range of 22,747 yds (20,800 m). The secondary armament of ten 5.9-inch guns was more powerful than the weak 4-inch batteries of the Invincibles, and the casemates were protected by 6-inches of armour. The main armour belt was 10-inches thick, tapering from 5– to 4-inches at the bow and 4– to 3-inches at the stern. Vertical protection included a 2-inch armour deck with 2-inch slopes. There was a 1-inch torpedo bulkhead. *Von der Tann* was the only German battleship to have the officers' quarters in the bows.

Von der Tann was part of Hipper's battlecruiser squadron during World War I. She took part in the notorious raid on Scarborough on 16 December 1914. On Christmas Day she became the first capital ship to be damaged (albeit due to a collision) by a carrier-based airstrike when British seaplanes buzzed the Schillig Roads.

Below: The battlecruiser Von der Tann *was built in response to the British Invincible class. Armed with 11-in guns, she was much more heavily armoured.*

Missing the Dogger bank action, she nevertheless played a key role at Jutland. She sank HMS *Indefatigable* in the opening minutes of the battlecruiser engagement and remained at her station even after hits by heavy shells and a succession of malfunctions left her with none of her main armament serviceable. *Von der Tann* joined *Derfflinger* at the back of Scheer's line when the High Seas Fleet escaped back to Germany.

Surrendered at Scapa Flow, she was scuttled there in June 1919. The wreck was raised in 1930 and broken up at Rosyth.

Left: Konig Albert sailed with her sistership Kaiser on the German navy's only major overseas deployment before World War I. They visited South America and South Africa in 1913.

Von der Tann class data

Displacement, standar	19,064 tons
Displacement, full load	21,700 tons
Length overall	563 feet (171.7 m)
Beam	87 feet (26.6 m)
Design draught	26 feet 7 in (8.1 m)
Complement	923

Class: *Von der Tann*
Completed 1911

Armament:
8 × 11-in guns (4 × 2)
10 × 5.9-in guns
16 × 3.5-in guns
Four 17.7-in torpedo tubes

Machinery:
Parsons turbines, 42,000 shp
4 shafts
27 knots

Armour:

Belt	10 in
Deck	2 in
Turrets	up to 9 in
Casemates	up to 6 in
Conning tower	up to 10 in

Kaiser class

The British and German designers adopted the principle of superimposition at the same time, so that the British Neptune and the German Moltke and Kaiser classes were all able to command a full ten-gun broadside from ten barrels. All three classes had two turrets mounted en echelon in the waist, the mounting on the disengaged side having a firing arc limited by superstructure and the opposite turret. While the Neptune and Moltkes had the waist turrets separated by the after funnel, the Kaisers increased the arcs somewhat by siting both mountings in a gap amidships. This resulted in the boiler spaces being widely separated in two groups, reflected in the distinctively-placed funnel/mast combinations, which made them instantly recognisable. The boiler arrangement increased survivability, while the new disposition allowed the waist turrets to be moved further inboard, giving greater scope for protection.

With more axial mountings, the length and displacement needed again to be increased and the existing power was also increased for the required 20-knot speed. The class adopted steam turbine propulsion, but the innovation was planned to go further. For *Prinzregent Luitpold* (only) the centreline propeller was to be driven by a 12,000 bhp two-stroke diesel. Unfortunately for the ship, the plan was somewhat in advance of contemporary technology, and she 'made do' with only two machinery sets. The intention, of course, had been to allow economic cruising, at 12 knots.

Five units were built, the extra hull being the *Friedrich der Grosse*, designed from the outset to be fleet flagship. At Jutland, despite the proximity to the flag, they went virtually unscathed, only the *Kaiser* being hit. Two 12-inch projectiles from the *Agincourt* caused little damage. The complete class was scuttled at Scapa Flow in 1919, all being subsequently salvaged and scrapped locally.

Kaiser class data:

Displacement, standard	24,530 tons
Displacement, full load	26,790 tons
Length, overall	565.6 feet (172.4 m)
Beam	95.1 feet (29.0 m)
Design draught	29.4 feet (8.95 m)
Complement	1085

Class: *Friedrich der Grosse, Kaiser, Kaiserin, Konig Albert, Prinzregent Luitpold.*
Completed 1912–1913

Armament:
Ten 12-in guns (5 × 2)
Fourteen 5.9-in guns (14 × 1)
Eight 8.8-cm guns (8 × 1)
Five 19.7-in torpedo tubes

Machinery:
Steam turbines 31,000 shp (28,100 kW)
Three shafts 21.5 knots

Armour:

Belt	up to 13.8 in
Bulkheads	up to 7.87 in
Deck	up to 2.4 in
Turrets	up to 11.8 in
Barbettes	up to 11.8 in

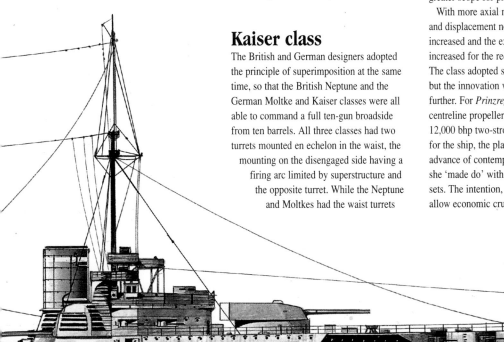

Konig class

In 1909–1910 the British commenced the four Orions, whose ten-gun 13.5-inch main battery was disposed in the rational manner of two superimposed turrets fore and aft, and a single turret on the centreline amidships. Despite all five mountings being on the centreline, little extra length was required because the barrels of the superimposed 'B' and 'X' positions could overlap the lower 'A' and 'Y' turrets. The advantage of the layout (itself a refinement of the 1907 Delawares') was greatly improved arcs of fire in broadside (although the number of barrels theoretically available for chase fire had diminished) and a smaller area of armour required for the protection of the waist mounting.

The four Konigs of 1911–1912 followed this precedent, more flexibility in space being available since the adoption of compact steam turbine machinery. With no wing turret barbettes to cause obstruction, a double torpedo bulkhead was possible along the both sides of the centre section. The inner bulkhead was of 40-mm (1.6-inch) plate. As oil firing was now the norm, the resulting

spaces could be void or used for bunkers. Again, these deep spaces, which offered a 4.5-metre cushion against torpedo explosion, were possible only because of turbine machinery and compact watertube boilers.

Developed power could still be absorbed on three propellers but the centre shaft, intended to be diesel-powered, had also to be given steam turbine powering due to the continued unavailability of the big diesel unit.

At Jutland the Konigs were, at one critical stage, at the tail of the German line, with the Grand Fleet on their quarter. While the Kronprinz escaped damage, her three sisters absorbed a total of 23 heavy hits from 15–, 13.5- and 12-inch projectiles. They survived by a combination of good design and a propensity by British shells to break up on striking armour or to burst prematurely as they penetrated. All three were back in service after 6–7 weeks' repair.

Konig class data:

Displacement, standard	25,595 tons
Displacement, full load	28,380 tons
Length, overall	575.5 feet (175.4 m)
Beam	96.8 feet (29.5 m)

Above: The Konig class were the most powerful battleships in the High Seas Fleet at Jutland, and they survived a succession of heavy shell hits remarkably well. Here, Grosser Kurfurst *steams to surrender in 1918.*

Design draught	29.9 feet (9.1 m)
Complement	1140

Class: *Grosser Kurfurst, Konig, Kronprinz (later Kronprinz Wilhelm) Markgraf.* Completed 1914.

Armament:
Ten 12-in guns (5 × 2)
Fourteen 5.9-in guns (14 × 1)
Six 8.8-cm guns (6 × 1)
Five 19.7-in torpedo tubes

Machinery:
Steam turbines 31,000 shp (23,100 kW)
Three shafts 21 knots.

Armour:
Belt	up to 13.8 in
Bulkheads	up to 7.87 in
Deck	up to 2.4 in
Turrets	up to 11.8 in
Barbettes	up to 11.8 in

Moltke class battlecruisers

The battlecruiser concept was adopted by the Germans soon after the British. It was, perhaps, fortunate that their prototype, *Von der Tann*, was laid down before the *Invincible* was completed, for she thus escaped being influenced by the more extreme and disastrous aspects of the genre. By virtue of steam turbine propulsion, speed was barely inferior to the British ship, but, through a modest increase in displacement and satisfaction with an 11-inch (rather than 12-inch) armament, the *Von der Tann* was adequately protected.

A re-appraisal of the design was made even before the prototype was in the water. An increase in size for the two Moltkes permitted a fifth, superimposed turret aft. The ten guns were of an improved 50-calibre version with a higher muzzle velocity than the *Von der Tann's* 45s. The short forecastle deck of the *Von der Tann* dictated that her casemated secondary armament was set very low. This was rectified in the *Moltkes* by extending the forecastle level to well abaft amidships, tapering it inboard to meet the raised barbette of the superfiring turret.

The British ship, as indicated by the funnel disposition, needed far more space to be devoted to boilers than the German. This further increased the area to be protected. The comparatively high power required a four shaft layout, the fine after run causing problems with long exposed shafts on the inboard propellers and the need for skegs on the outboard screws. Only a centreline rudder could be fitted, so a small auxiliary rudder was added ahead of the main one.

At Jutland, *Moltke* took hits from four 15-inch and one 13.5-inch projectile. Two were contained by the main belt and one by a full coal bunker. The latter caused a secondary magazine flash fire, which progressed no further.

The hunt for the *Goeben*

Moltke class data:

Displacement, standard	22,800 tons
Displacement, full load	25,200 tons
Length, overall	611.9 feet (186.5 m)
Beam	96.8 feet (29.5 m)
Design draught	29.5 feet (9.0 m)
Complement	1050

Class: *Goeben, Moltke*
Completed 1911–1912

Armament:
Ten 11-in guns (5 × 2)
Twelve 5.9-in guns (12 × 1)
Twelve 8.8-cm guns (12 × 1)
Four 19.7-in torpedo tubes

Above: In 1918, Goeben and her consort, the light cruiser Breslau ran on to a British minefield during a sortie from Constantinople, only the battlecruiser surviving.

Machinery:
Steam turbines 52,000 shp (28,800 kW)
Four shafts
Speed: 25.5 knots

Armour:
Belt	up to 10.6 in
Bulkheads	up to .1 in
Decks	up to 2 in
Turrets	up to 9.8 in
Barbettes	up to 9.8 in

German naval presence in the Mediterranean in August 1914 comprised the battle cruiser *Goeben* and the light cruiser *Breslau*, both new ships. On the 2nd they were coaling at Messina when Italy declared neutrality. Anticipating hostilities against France the German admiral, Souchon, sailed immediately to interrupt the repatriation of troops from North Africa. He barely had time to bombard two ports, however, when he received orders to proceed to Constantinople, Germany and Turkey having concluded an alliance. With insufficient fuel aboard, Souchon again made for Messina. En route, he encountered two British battlecruisers which, although not yet at war, turned to track him. The German units separated, out-ran the British and met up again on the 5th at Messina where, as belligerents, they were allowed to stay for no more than 24 hours.

With hostilities declared on the 4th, the CinC, Mediterranean, Admiral Milne, deployed his battlecruisers to set up a patrol line west of Sicily, covering French troop movements from North Africa against a German incursion. Rear Admiral Troubridge, with four armoured and four light cruisers, was to stop any attempt by Souchon to join the Austrians in the Adriatic. Only at 1700 on the 5th did Milne learn that the *Goeben* had returned to Messina, and detached a force to block the strait's northern exit. Souchon, uneasy, requested support from the Austrian fleet. This was refused on political grounds.

As required, the Germans sailed by 1600 on 6 August, and the light cruiser *Gloucester*, alone at the strait's southern exit, signalled that they were heading eastward. *Gloucester* continued to shadow but the *Dublin*, sent to assist her, failed to make contact and joined Troubridge's force. By 1600 on the 7th, Souchon was off Cape Matapan and the *Gloucester*, several times shot at and short of coal, was ordered to return.

At midnight on the 6/7th, sixteen hours before this, Troubridge had concluded that the *Goeben* was not bound for the Adriatic and made to intercept, *Gloucester's* reports indicating the Germans' speed at only 17 knots. Troubridge could manage on 21, which meant a daylight action. The *Goeben's* 11-inch guns could out-range his 9.2s and 7.5s, while her 4-5 knot advantage would allow her to decide the range. Deciding that the Germans were a 'superior force', Troubridge made the decision at 0400 to break off and not seek action. Milne learned of this at 0515 and queried it with a veiled admonition, which Troubridge countered at 0830 with a rambling justification.

At 0035 on 8 August, Milne belatedly sailed his battlecruisers from Malta to seek out Souchon, but was frustrated by a time-wasting series of telegrams from London with ambiguous views on his opening hostilities with Austria. The *Goeben* could still have been intercepted, as she and the *Breslau* hung around the Aegean topping-up with coal while awaiting Turkish permission to enter the Dardanelles, which they did only at 1700 on the 10th.

Subsequent court martial cleared Troubridge, although he never again served at sea. Milne was blamed for not correctly deploying his battlecruisers, and he spent the war on half pay. The real villain was the Admiralty which had first agreed with Milne's supporting the French and had then dithered over the irrelevant question of Austria.

Below: Goeben was 'transferred' to the Turkish navy during World War I, fighting several engagements in the Black Sea against the Russians. She survived until 1971 although she did not put to sea after 1950.

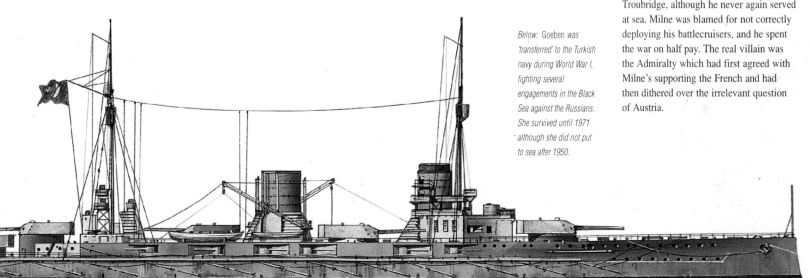

Left: Seydlitz was a lengthened Moltke class battlecruiser, with a short forecastle deck and more powerful engines. She survived tremendous punishment at Jutland.

Later German battlecruisers

Laid down in 1911, the one-off *Seydlitz* was essentially an up-graded *Moltke*, and continued the custom of naming battle cruisers after military heroes. In appearance she was very similar, the major difference being the addition of a short forecastle deck to improve seakeeping and ability to drive at high speed into a sea. Not so apparent was the fourteen-metre increase in length to accommodate a further three boilers. Her beam was actually decreased by a metre, the improvement in lines and a 29 per cent increase in power adding a knot in speed.

She was followed by the three Derfflingers, which were the first German battlecruisers to mount a 12-inch armament. Despite a further increase in size, only eight guns were carried, with superfiring twin turrets forward and aft. The lack of waist turrets permitted a much more compact arrangement of boiler spaces, with the two substantial funnels more closely spaced. There was a distinct space between the superimposed after turrets, the distance between their barbettes bounding the turbine room.

The innovation on the *Seydlitz* of the raised forecastle was not continued probably because of the weight involved. In place of this feature, the forward end was given a long, easy sheerline to effect the required freeboard. Although the casemated secondary armament was now situated in the superstructure, the low freeboard amidships gave them very little extra command.

Above: Hipper's flagship at Jutland, the newly-commissioned Lutzow *sustained fatal damage from British shellfire, and had to be abandoned during the night.*

Because the spaces between the funnels in earlier ships were dominated by the main armament firing arcs, the carriage of the many ship's boats were a major problem. The more logical layout of the Derfflingers created natural space between the funnels. Length was again increased by a greater proportion than the beam, permitted even more fining of the lines and, in spite of a greater displacement, the same speed on an actual reduction in power. Both *Derfflinger* and *Hindenburg* had a new feature in heavy tripod foremasts, to reduce vibration in the fire control station. The completion dates of this class showed a marked slowing down in the rate of German capital ship construction during the war; construction periods were: *Derfflinger* 32 months, *Lutzow* 37 months and *Hindenburg* 47 months.

The culmination of German battle cruiser design would have been the four *Mackensens*. These logically continued the

design process from the Derfflingers but were enlarged further to accommodate heavier 35 cm (13.78-inch) main battery.

The practice of remaining one calibre behind the British and maintaining a moderate speed continued to pay off inasmuch as the class had significant improvements in protection. Although all four were laid down in 1915, only three ever progressed to the launching stage, due to other wartime priorities.

German battle cruisers' capacity for absorbing punishment was remarkable. After Jutland, the *Lutzow* had to be sunk due to progressive flooding following 24 hits by a mix of 12–13.5– and 15-inch shells. *Derfflinger* took 21 hits, more of them of smaller calibre, *Seydlitz*, the older ship, received 22 hits, including seven 15-inch, and a torpedo. She narrowly escaped the fate of the *Lutzow*, getting home with her stemhead barely above water. *Hindenburg* was not completed for another year and was able to incorporate some improvements based on battle experience.

Seydlitz data:

Displacement, standard	24,320 tons
Displacement, full load	26,850 tons
Length, overall	657.8 feet (200.5 m)
Beam	93.5 feet (28.5 m)
Design draught	30.2 feet (9.2 m)
Complement	1070

Class: *Seydlitz*
Completed: 1913

Armament
Ten 11-in guns (5 × 2)
Twelve 5.9-in guns
Twelve 8.8-cm guns
Four 19.7-in torpedo tubes

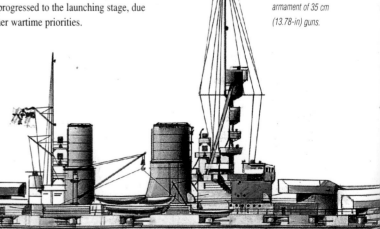

Below: How the Mackensens would have looked had they been completed. They were to have carried a heavier armament of 35 cm (13.78-in) guns.

Machinery:

Steam turbines 67,000 shp (50,000 kW)

Four shafts

Speed: 26.5 knots

Armour:

Belt ....up to 11.8 in

Bulkheads ....up to 5.9 in

Deck ....up to 3.2 in

Turrets ....up to 9.8 in

Barbettes ....up to 9.8 in

Derfflinger data:

Displacement, standard ....26,500 tons

Displacement, full load ....31,000 tons

Length, overall ....690.3 feet (210.4 m)

Beam ....95.1 feet (29 m)

Design draught ....31.5 feet (9.6 m)

Complement 1120

Class: *Derfflinger, Lutzow, Hindenburg*
Completed: 1914–1917

Armament:

Eight 12-in guns (5 × 2)

Twelve 5.9-in guns

Eight 8.8-cm guns

Four 19.7-in torpedo tubes

Machinery:

Steam turbines 63,000 shp (47,000 kW)

four shafts

Speed: 26.5 knots

Armour:

Belt ....up to 11.8 in

Bulkheads ....up to 9.8 in

Deck ....up to 3.2 in

Turrets ....up to 10.6 in

Barbettes ....up to 10.2 in

Mackensen data:

Displacement, standard ....30,760 tons

Displacement, full load ....35,050 tons

Length, overall ....734.9 feet (224.0 m)

Beam ....99.7 feet (30.4 m)

Design draught ....30.5 feet (9.3 m)

Complement 1185

Class: *Mackensen, Prinz Eitel Friedrich, Graf Spee, Furst Bismarck.* None completed

Armament:

Eight 13.78-in guns (4 × 2)

Fourteen 5.9-in

Eight 8.8-cm guns

Five 23.6-in torpedo tubes

Above: Seydlitz's midships turrets were far enough apart to have a reasonable arc of fire on the opposite beam.

Right: With no midships turrets, Derfflinger used the space between her funnels to store the ship's boats.

Machinery:

Steam turbines 90,000 shp (67,100 kW)

Four shafts

27 knots

Armour:

Belt ....up to 11.8 in

Bulkheads ....up to 9.8 in

Deck ....up to 4.7 in

Turrets ....up to 12.6 in

Barbettes ....up to 11.4 in

Admiral Hipper

Stemming from southern Germany, Hipper came from a family with no naval tradition. He joined the navy in 1881 as an eighteen-year-old cadet. Specialising early in torpedoes, the dash of this type of warfare was probably the stimulus to his transferring, as a lieutenant commander, to the reconnaissance wing of the fleet. His promotion to senior rank coincided with the introduction of the battlecruiser and it is as senior officers of the scouting groups that he is chiefly remembered. His leadership was inspirational rather than scientific, and he several times duelled with the battle cruisers of Beatty, his Grand Fleet opposite number, with determination and success. Like Beatty, he was eventually to succeed to command of the whole fleet but, only weeks from the end of the war, he was unable to prevent its slide into mutiny. Disillusioned, he left the service and ennobled, as Franz Ritter von Hipper, died in 1932.

The East Coast Raids

With a numerically-inferior fleet, German naval policy was directed toward reducing British strength by attrition. In the long term, submarines and mines would play their part but, for predictable results, it was

planned to lure British squadrons to sea and ambush them with superior forces. The chosen bait was to be 'tip-and-run' raids on English East Coast towns by Hipper's battle cruisers, which were fast enough to be in and out before the British could respond effectively. Public outrage would demand that the perpetrators be pursued, probably by British battlecruisers, and these would follow the retreating Hipper straight into the arms of the High Seas Fleet, which would be laying back in unsuspected deep support.

Left: Hipper was knighted by the King of Bavaria for his bold leadership of the German battlecruiser squadron.

The tactic involved almost by accident when, in November 1914, German battle cruisers bombarded Yarmouth as a diversion to cover a mine laying sortie. During the following month, when the Germans knew that two British battlecruisers had been detached for the Falklands operation, an attempt was made using a bombardment of Scarborough and Hartlepool. Both sides, however, missed opportunities in unexpectedly atrocious weather conditions.

In April 1916 it was the turn of Lowestoft and Yarmouth, but the intervention of Tyrwhitt's Harwich Force was sufficient to un-nerve Admiral Boedicker, who had brought about the very situation that the Germans had been seeking. Ten weeks after Jutland a plan based on a bombardment of Sunderland went awry after one of Scheer's battleships was torpedoed.

Given the geography of the North Sea and relative fleet strengths, the German policy was sound. It never, however, succeeded in amputating a limb of the Grand Fleet, while two similar feints worked to German disadvantage in bringing about the Battles of the Dogger Bank and Jutland.

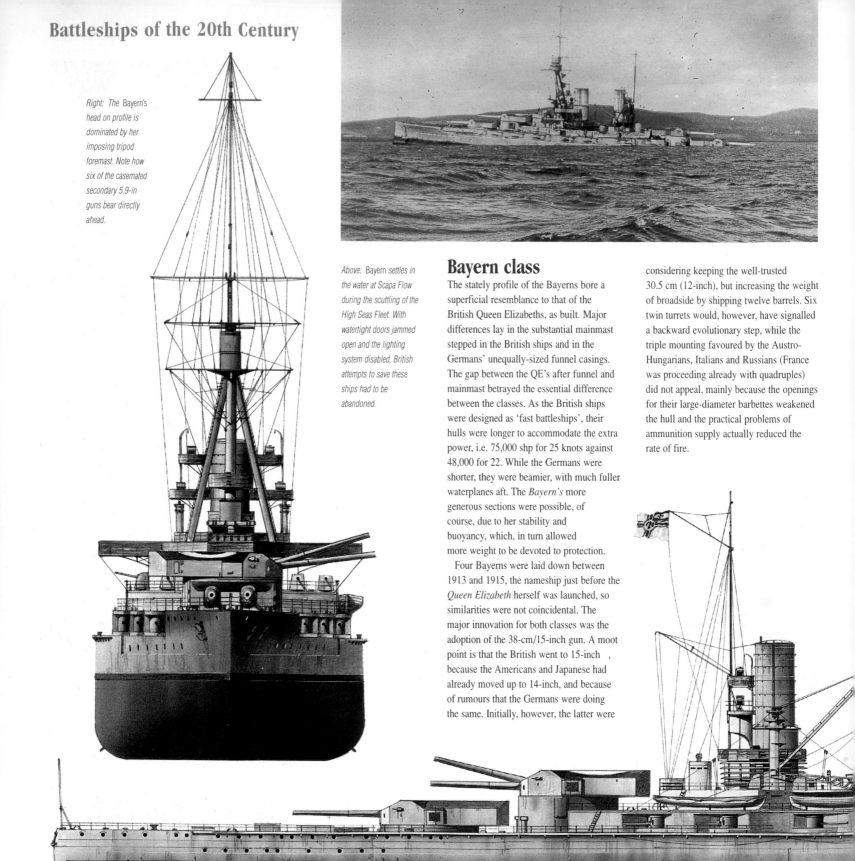

Right: The Bayern's head on profile is dominated by her imposing tripod foremast. Note how six of the casemated secondary 5.9-in guns bear directly ahead.

Above: Bayern settles in the water at Scapa Flow during the scuttling of the High Seas Fleet. With watertight doors jammed open and the lighting system disabled, British attempts to save these ships had to be abandoned.

Bayern class

The stately profile of the Bayerns bore a superficial resemblance to that of the British Queen Elizabeths, as built. Major differences lay in the substantial mainmast stepped in the British ships and in the Germans' unequally-sized funnel casings. The gap between the QE's after funnel and mainmast betrayed the essential difference between the classes. As the British ships were designed as 'fast battleships', their hulls were longer to accommodate the extra power, i.e. 75,000 shp for 25 knots against 48,000 for 22. While the Germans were shorter, they were beamier, with much fuller waterplanes aft. The *Bayern's* more generous sections were possible, of course, due to her stability and buoyancy, which, in turn allowed more weight to be devoted to protection.

Four Bayerns were laid down between 1913 and 1915, the nameship just before the *Queen Elizabeth* herself was launched, so similarities were not coincidental. The major innovation for both classes was the adoption of the 38-cm/15-inch gun. A moot point is that the British went to 15-inch, because the Americans and Japanese had already moved up to 14-inch, and because of rumours that the Germans were doing the same. Initially, however, the latter were

considering keeping the well-trusted 30.5 cm (12-inch), but increasing the weight of broadside by shipping twelve barrels. Six twin turrets would, however, have signalled a backward evolutionary step, while the triple mounting favoured by the Austro-Hungarians, Italians and Russians (France was proceeding already with quadruples) did not appeal, mainly because the openings for their large-diameter barbettes weakened the hull and the practical problems of ammunition supply actually reduced the rate of fire.

Dual coal/oil firing for boilers was retained as, unlike the British, the Germans had no guaranteed oil supply. Practice had also shown the value of well-packed coal bunkers as protection against shell fire.

Secondary armament was increased to sixteen 6-inch, all casemated and at a practical height above normal waterline. Casemates fitted neatly into the flanks of the superstructure but their guns had limited elevation and firing arcs, while their wide separation complicated fire control.

Separated only by bulkheads, each position was at some risk from any explosion in its neighbour, while the problems of ammunition supply (a 6-inch/15-cm shell weighs about 100 lb/45.5 kg) can only be guessed at.

Forward of the boats were sited four high-angle 8.8-cm guns for use against aircraft. The battle cruiser *Derfflinger* had been the first major unit so fitted, but it had become standard practice.

Bayern was completed at the time of Jutland but did not sail with Scheer as she was still 'working up'. A further fleet action in which the *Bayern* would have participated was only narrowly missed in August 1916, resulting from the High Seas Fleet's probe towards Sunderland.

The third and fourth ships of the class launched but never completed. *Baden* survived the mass scuttling at Scapa flow, to be destroyed in 1921 as a gunnery target.

Bayern class data:

Displacement, standard ....28,330 tons
Displacement, full load..................31,950 tons
Length, overall ....590.6 feet (180.0 m)
Beam ....98.4 feet (30.0 m)
Design draught ....30.8 feet (9.4 m)
Complement 1170

Class:
Baden, Bayern (completed 1916)
Sachsen, Wurttemberg (scrapped incomplete).

Armament:
Eight 15-in guns (4 × 2)
Sixteen 5.9-in guns (16 × 1)
Four 8.8-cm guns (4 × 1)
Five 23.6-in torpedo tubes

Machinery:
Steam turbines 48,000 shp (35,800 kW)
Three shafts
22 knots

Armour:
Belt ....up to 13.8 in
Bulkheads ....up to 7.87 in
Decks .... up to 4.7 in
Turrets ....up to 13.8 in
Barbettes ....up to 13.8 in

Admiral Scheer

Born in 1863, Reinhard Scheer, like Hipper, came from a non-naval background. He joined the service as a 15-year old cadet, and also became a torpedo specialist. Serving at the German Admiralty and on the Fleet Staff, he was a vice-admiral in 1914. Within months he was moved from the command of Squadron II's eight pre-dreadnoughts to that of Squadron III, comprising the fleet's latest battleships. In 1916 he succeeded the ailing Admiral von Pohl as CinC of the High Sea Fleet. Although wrong-footed at Jutland, he achieved enough for his fleet to emerge with pride. In August 1918, too late to be of value, he was appointed Chief of the Admiralty Staff, charged with gingering-up its previously lacklustre direction. He died in 1938. His writings reveal an ambivalent attitude towards the Royal Navy, at once envious of its tradition of superiority and deprecating of his perception of its unwillingness to risk it in combat.

Below: The High Seas Fleet painted the turret tops black with white rings as an aerial recognition aid. Like the Derfflinger class battlecruisers, the Bayerns were built with anti-aircraft guns.

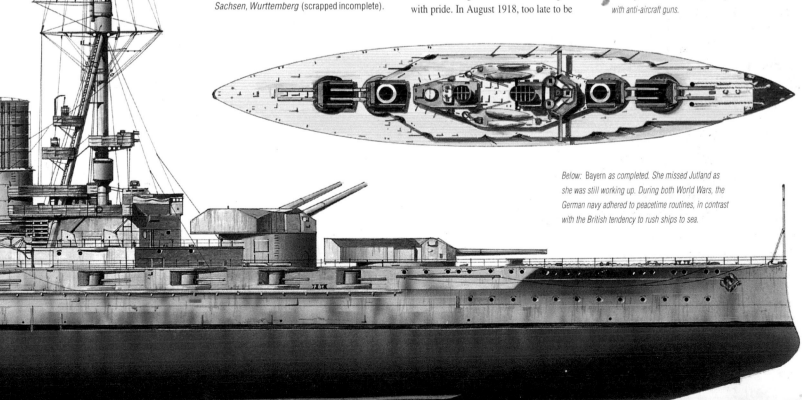

Below: Bayern as completed. She missed Jutland as she was still working up. During both World Wars, the German navy adhered to peacetime routines, in contrast with the British tendency to rush ships to sea.

High seas fleet to Hitler's navy

On June 21, 1919, as the victorious powers interminably debated its ultimate fate, the cream of the Imperial German Navy, interned in Scapa flow, scuttled itself. To the immense, but unvoiced, relief of both Great Britain and the United States ten of the best battleships and five battlecruisers disappeared beyond economic recovery.

The 'old' Reichsmarine was effectively dead. Hostilities had been terminated by armistice, not by surrender, but all that was allowed Germany were six battleships, six cruisers and three flotillas of destroyers, all old. Following their 1918 revolt, all naval personnel had been released from their oaths of allegiance. A new start had to be made.

New construction was permitted only when existing ships reached a specific age and no 'armoured ship' was to exceed 10,000 tons standard displacement. Acquisition of submarines was specifically forbidden.

Between 1919 and 1928 the 'new' navy was headed, first by Admiral Behncke, then Admiral Zenker, both of whom worked actively to rebuild the rump of a fleet into a credible deepwater force, worthy of attracting alliance where it was sought. The means that they adopted were, to a great extent, those that they could get away with.

Behncke, recognising the potency of the U-boat during World War I, was determined to retain and develop existing design skills, supposedly abandoned. Submarine experts were thus 'recruited' to a Netherlands-based design bureau. This would undertake detailed design, oversee construction and conduct trials. As the enterprise developed, funds were channelled through bogus 'front' companies. By the time that Admiral Raeder succeeded Zenker in 1928, what were effectively prototype U-boats were being built in Spain and Finland. These activities thrived with the laxity of the Allied Control Commission, which not only failed its objectives but was formally disbanded in 1926.

Raeder proved adept at managing the navy's affairs despite a cash-strapped and parsimonious Reichstag. In 1929 the keel of the first Deutschland was laid. Her diesel propulsion allowed her theoretically to comfortably undertake a return trip to the Horn without refuelling. Ever mindful of

threats to trade the British Admiralty was alarmed. Over-optimistic that newly-developed ASDIC had solved the submarine problem, it was convinced that surface raiders posed the greater threat. In acting accordingly, it showed considerable misjudgement.

A more confident Germany was, by 1932, demanding equal building rights, with Raeder promoting a five-year plan to expand the fleet by, inter alia, six Deutschlands and, significantly, sixteen submarines. Its approval was overtaken by events when, in January 1933, a National Socialist government was formed. Hitler, the new Chancellor, made unequivocal statements that he wished to avoid war with Great Britain, yet proposed to create a navy "for tasks within the framework of a European continental policy". To replace the vague restrictions of Versailles, he sought the right to build to a total of 35 per cent of the total tonnage operated by the Royal Navy. this would be in each major category of ship except submarines, where 45 per cent was required, extendible to 100 per cent if, "in Germany's opinion (she) needed to avail herself of that right".

With the death of Hindenburg in August 1934, Hitler became both President and Supreme Commander of the Armed Forces. He had already removed Germany from the League of Nations and now, unilaterally, renounced the Versailles provisions. In June 1935 the Anglo-German Naval Agreement was signed, with Britain confident that Germany's plans were beyond her capacity to realise. The programme included two 26,000-ton capital ships, two heavy cruisers, two flotillas of destroyers and twenty-eight submarines of various types. New battleships were planned for 1936 "and the following years", but none "of less than 17,500 tons", (the Deutschland type of which Britain was so sensitive) "until January 1, 1943".

With France already building the Dunkerques, Germany saw the Deutschlands as vulnerable. The two "26,000-tonners" were the Scharnhorsts, whose 28 cm (11-inch) guns were reckoned superior to the French 33 cm (13-inch) weapon. Later units were to be equipped with 38 cm (15-inch) however, to match more usual foreign practice.

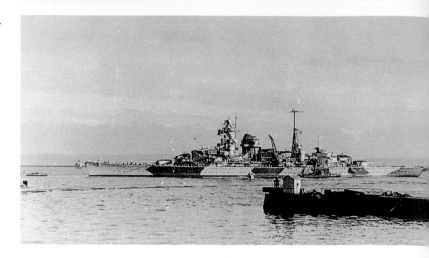

During the mid-thirties, Hitler's view appeared to be that, with Italian help, the French fleet could be contained, war with Britain still not on the cards. By 1938, however, a stronger Germany was adopting a more reckless and provocative foreign policy. Behind the scenes, Raeder was ordered to prepare two, alternative, plans for fleet expansion aimed specifically at hostilities with Britain. The first, based on Deutschland-type surface raiders and submarines, would have been quicker and cheaper, but was thought to have been unable to bring about a decisive result. An alternative, 'balanced fleet' concept was preferred by the Fuhrer. By 1946, under the so-called Z-plan, two surface action groups, each with a carrier, would be constructed to bring commerce to a standstill, while a home defence fleet would tie down the bulk of the Royal Navy in the North Sea.

Top: The heavy cruiser Prinz Eugen *at Brest after her sortie with* Bismarck. World War II *caught the German navy badly unprepared.*

Above: Markfgraf, *one of the magnificent Konig class scuttled at Scapa Flow in 1918. She was one of the battleships never raised.*

In April, 1939, Germany renounced the Naval Agreement, needlessly antagonising Britain further as it was already becoming obvious that the Z-plan could not be implemented before 1948. Germany's 'foreign policy', in general, stirred up such hostility that war with British would occur long before this. With a total change of plan, priority was switched to U-boat production. When war came, the German fleet had the worst of both worlds, with neither expansion programme having reached a mature stage.

The battlecruiser Hindenburg seen with Derfflinger behind on the left and Kaiser on the right. Hindenburg was the last capital ship to be commissioned by the Imperial German navy.

Left: Friederich der Grosse, steams to Scapa Flow in 1918. Subsequent British battleship designs benefitted from experiments carried out on some of the captured vessels.

Above: Seydlitz revealed the incredible strength of German capital ships at Jutland, surviving two burnt out turrets and shipping so much water that her freeboard was just 2.5 metres forward.

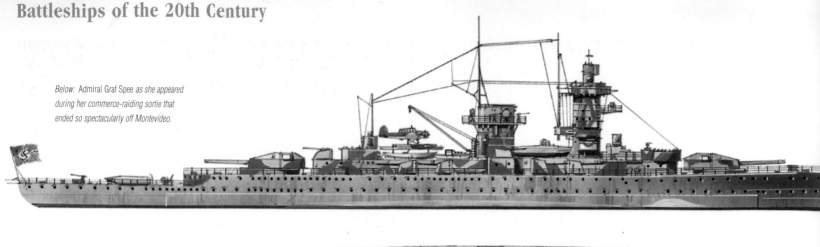

Below: Admiral Graf Spee as she appeared during her commerce-raiding sortie that ended so spectacularly off Montevideo.

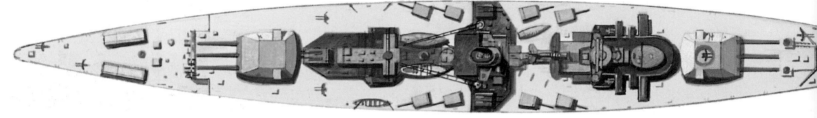

Deutschland class

The German fleet was permitted by the Treaty of Versailles to replace existing obsolete battleships only twenty years after their date of launch, the first opportunity being in 1924. Replacement 'armoured ships' were not to exceed 10,000 tons displacement but, Germany not being a signatory to the Washington Treaties, no limit had been set on gun calibres. Admiral Zenker, who took over the office of naval supremo in 1924, was determined that the fleet would not be relegated to a coast defence force. Neither was he going to replace battleships, however, obsolete, with cruisers. He ordered a study on a series of ships, optimising main battery, protection or speed. Reduced to a short list of four, the options were as follows. Four 38-cm (15-inch) or six 30.5-cm (12-inch) could be allied to a 250 mm (9.8-inch) belt for a modest 18-knot speed. Reducing the protection to 200 mm (7.9-inch) allowed

21 knots. If six smaller 28-cm (11-inch) guns be shipped, and vertical protection pared to 100 mm (3.9-inch) a speed of 26 knots was possible. the best that Zenker could hope for was a vessel that could out-run a more powerful capital ship while being able to out-gun a faster cruiser. The last of the above choices was, therefore, accepted as the basis of what were to become the famous 'pocket battleships'.

Weight saving was critical. Extensive welding (a new technology) greatly reduced hull weight. Tripling the main armament saved considerably more, although the turrets, barbettes and hull were protected only on a scale sufficient to withstand cruiser fire. Despite this, the 20 per cent of displacement devoted to protection was very low, while the 19 per cent for armament was very high. Tenderness was evident by progressive increases in beam, while final displacement exceeded the legal limit by a large margin.

Three were built, each with a different protective scheme. Common to each was

a shallow external belt, seated on an integral bulge and backed by a void space. The inboard boundary of the void was a longitudinal torpedo bulkhead. Both belt and bulkhead were inclined to increase their resistance to penetration. *Graf Spee*, the last unit, had an increased displacement to permit deepening of both belt and bulkhead, together with an extended armoured deck.

Eight 15 cm (5.9-inch) guns comprised the secondary battery, in open mounts to save weight. An original addition of 8.8 cm guns was later up-graded to 10.5 cm (4.1-in). An unusual feature was the two quadruple torpedo tube banks on the low quarterdeck.

For the first time, an all-diesel machinery fit was specified, but then-current technology could do no better than set four, nine-cylinder units to drive each of the two shafts. Great economy and ease of maintenance was possible by simply de-clutching and shutting down unnecessary engines. The diesels proved to be a

Above: A plan view of the Graf Spee. The rectangular shapes at the stern are quadruple 21-in torpedo tubes. Her ill-fated captain was a torpedo specialist before commanding the 'pocket battleship'.

disappointment, however, in being space-consuming, noisy and vibration-prone, the last sufficient to affect the gun directors.

While the three *'panzerschiffe'* were ingenious solutions to a particular set of limitations, they were not influential, inasmuch as no other fleet was bound by the same marriage of limitation and requirement. They did, however, provoke 'responses', notably that of the French Dunkerques.

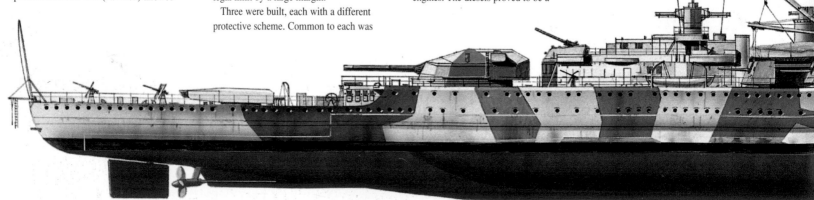

Deutschland class data:

Displacement, standard	13,600 tons
Displacement, full load	15,900 tons
Length, overall	610.2 feet (186.0 m)
	later 616.5 feet (16.9 m)
Beam	67.6 feet (20.6 m)
Design draught	21.3 feet (6.5 m)
Complement	950

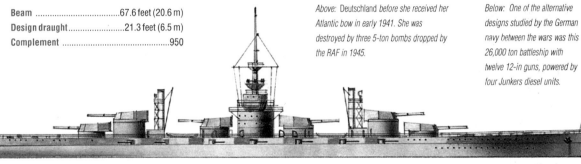

Above: Deutschland *before she received her Atlantic bow in early 1941. She was destroyed by three 5-ton bombs dropped by the RAF in 1945.*

Below: One of the alternative designs studied by the German navy between the wars was this 26,000 ton battleship with twelve 12-in guns, powered by four Junkers diesel units.

Below: Lutzow *(formerly Deutschland) as she appeared when based in Norway during the summer of 1942. She could be distinguished from her sisterships by the location of the catapult between the bridge and funnel.*

Class: *Admiral Graf Spee, Admiral Scheer, Deutschland* (later re-named *Lutzow*)
Completed 1933–1936.

Armament:
Six 11-in guns (2 × 3)
Eight 5.9-in guns (8 × 1)
Six 8.8-cm guns (6 × 1)
Eight 21-in torpedo tubes
Two aircraft

Machinery:
Eight diesel engines 54,000 shp (40,300 kW)
Two shafts 26 knots

Armour:
Belt	up to 2.36 in
Bulkheads	up to 3.15 in
Deck	up to 1.6 in
Turrets	up to 5.5 in
Barbettes	up to 3.9 in

Ocean raiders

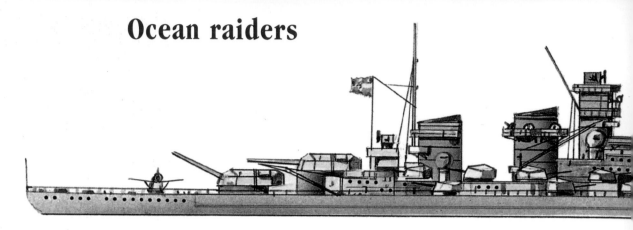

The combination of speed, striking power and endurance of the so-called 'pocket battleships' caused the British Admiralty considerable concern. At the commencement of hostilities in September 1939, two had been pre-positioned – the *Deutschland* south of Greenland and the *Graf Spee* in the South Atlantic. The former caused disruption to convoy cycles and Allied warship dispositions but, in a ten-week cruise, sank only two merchantmen.

The *Graf Spee*, meanwhile, operated in the sparsely-populated South Atlantic. No less than eight hunting groups were formed to catch her, discovering and destroying six German merchant ships in the process. Finally confronted by three British cruisers, she allowed herself to be completely out-fought. Having retreated into Montevideo, she had no chance of ever making the 7,000 miles home, and destroyed herself. History once again showed that raiders rarely long survive interception, and her total 'bag' of nine British merchant ships was a poor return on outlay.

Initially plagued by main diesel problems, the *Scheer* did not begin independent operations until November 1940. On the 5th she encountered a laden, 27-ship Halifax convoy, escorted by the solitary armed auxiliary *Jervis Bay*. *Scheer's* correct approach would have been to use her 26 knots to round up and dispose of the entire convoy. Instead, she was diverted by the dogged sacrifice of the armed liner, which bought sufficient time to allow the convoy to scatter. In failing light, the *Scheer* could locate and destroy only five.

The *Scheer* correctly changed area and cruised in the South Atlantic and Indian Ocean before returning safely in April 1941. Her 46,000 mile operation had netted sixteen ships of about 100,000 grt, but, again, her greatest contribution had been in disruption. Three hunting groups had failed to track her down and all North Atlantic convoys were now expected to be accompanied by a battleship, of which there were insufficient.

Despite this success, the *Scheer* spent most of the remainder of the war in the Baltic and the far north, operating against Soviet forces. She participated in a couple of abortive forays against Arctic convoys but undertook no more independent raiding.

Following her early return to Germany in November 1939, the *Deutschland* was re-

Below: Seen here shortly after completion, Admiral Scheer raided as far afield as the Indian Ocean during her epic sortie in 1940-41.

Below: German naval planning during the late 1930s was based on Hitler's assurance that there would be no war before the mid-1940s. The H41 design was supposed to follow the Bismarcks and were to have carried eight 16-in guns. Two 62,500 ton battleships were laid down in 1939 at Hamburg and Bremen, but both were broken up on the stocks in late 1941.

named *Lutzow*. Involved in the Norwegian campaign, she survived a period of misfortune, during which she was damaged by shore batteries, submarine torpedo, bombing, an aerial torpedo and, finally, grounding.

Until late 1942 she spent most of her time under repair. Her return to activity was only to participate in the poorly-conducted attack on the Arctic convoy JW.51B on the last day of 1942. Accompanied by the heavy cruiser *Hipper* and destroyers, she was fought off by two light cruisers and the close escort. Hitler's enraged response was an 'unalterable resolve' to de-commission all heavy units, which brought about the resignation of Grand Admiral Raeder.

Both *Lutzow* and *Scheer* spent the remainder of their lives in the Baltic until finally immobilised by bombing. Their careers had shown that surface raiding was too ephemeral an occupation to warrant significant outlay on specialised ships.

Hitler's super dreadnoughts

Germany's geographical disadvantage with respect to the British Isles caused Admiral Raeder to specify very long ranges for his Z-plan capital ships. Hence his preference for diesel propulsion. Had these endlessly-delayed engines been available, the two Bismarcks would have been so powered but the first to be built around them would have been the six 55,000-tonners destined for the carrier-supported surface action groups. Twelve diesel engines were to be individually clutched to the gearboxes of three shafts, the centre one of which was of immense length. Despite being up-gunned to 40.6-cm (16-inch) the ships had a marginally thinner belt,

offsetting the weight of thicker horizontal protection. The planned triple bottom followed the precedent set by the Americans in the North Carolinas. Unlike American and British practice, which opted for a single calibre, dual-purpose secondary armament, the Germans still favoured the greater hitting power of the 15-cm (5.9-inch) allied with the high-angle, rapid-fire 105-mm (4.1-inch). These were all grouped in twin mountings in a symmetrical layout reminiscent of allied design practice. Four aircraft were to be housed in hangars flanking 'C' turret, connected by trackways to the single quarterdeck catapult.

For detached commerce raiding the Z-plan included also three, 34-knot versions of the 'pocket battleships' but these needed to be so large in relation to their striking power that the plan was quickly subordinated to that for three battlecruisers. To develop the necessary power in the allotted space, these featured a steam-turbine centre shaft with diesel driven wing shafts. With just the outers operating for cruising, the ship would still have developed 27 knots. The 180 mm belt would probably have defeated an 11-inch shell, had any allied ship been so armed. None of the three was ever laid down.

Planned battleship data:

Displacement, standard	55,450 tons
Displacement, full load	62,500 tons
Length, overall	911.4 feet (277.8 m)
Beam	122.0 feet (37.2 m)
Design draught	32.8 feet (10.0 m)
Complement	2600

Class: Six: only two laid down

Above: Captain Krancke of the Scheer after his successful raid and promotion to Vice Admiral. He took Scheer to sea on 23 October 1940, passing north of Iceland and rounding Cape Horn in February 1941.

Armament:
Eight 16-in guns (4 × 2)
Twelve 5.9-in guns (6 × 2)
Sixteen 4.1-in guns (8 × 2)
Six 21-in torpedo tubes
Four aircraft

Machinery:
Steam turbines 165,000 shp (123,100 kW)
Three shafts
30 knots

Armour:
Belt	up to 11.8 in
Bulkheads	up to 8.7 in
Deck	up to 4.7 in
Turrets	up to 15.2 in
Barbettes	up to 14.4 in

Planned battlecruisers data:

Displacement, standard	31,950 tons
Displacement, full load	35,750 tons
Length, overall	841.5 feet (256.5 m)
Beam	98.4 feet (30.0 m)
Design draught	34.1 feet (10.4 m)
Complement	1960

Class: Three: none laid down

Armament:
Six 15-in guns (3 × 2)
Six 5.9-in guns (3 × 2)
Eight 4.1-in guns (4 × 2)
Eight 37-mm guns
Six 21-in torpedo tubes
Four aircraft

Machinery:
Steam turbines 60,000 shp (44,760 kW)
Diesels 116,000 shp (86,500 kW)
Three shafts
33.5 knots

Armour:
Belt	up to 7.1 in
Bulkheads	up to 3.9 in
Deck	up to 3.1 in
Turrets	up to 8.3 in
Barbettes	up to 7.1 in

Scharnhorst class

Hitler's renunciation of the Versailles limitations coincided with the keel-laying of the *Gneisenau* which, with the *Scharnhorst*, laid down two months later, were said to have been designed to displace 26,000 tons in the standard condition. This, of course, was well in excess of the treaty limit of 10,000 tons, exacerbated by the fact that they were finally completed at nearly 35,000 tons. Under the terms of the soon-to-be signed Anglo-German Naval Agreement, however, their construction suddenly became 'legal'. The reason for the urgency in their building was the rapid French response to the Deutschlands, their Dunkerques (of which the name ship was nearing launching stage) having a marked advantage in speed, armament and protection. In effect, the Dunkerques were to the 'pocket battleships' as battlecruisers were to armoured cruisers in the previous world war.

Due to a combination of haste and a final nod in the direction of foreign sensitivities, the triple 28 cm (11-inch) mounting was again adopted, though the navy would have preferred the 38 cm (15-inch), for which

building experience was still extant. As with Japanese examples of up-gunning, it would later have been possible to mount a twin 15-inch on the same diameter of barbette as the triple 11-inch, provided that structural stiffening was increased.

The Germans felt that the final, unrealised designs of World War I capital ships represented the best that could be achieved on a given size. For that reason the unbuilt *Ersatz Yorck* (or 'Yorck replacement') design provided the basic design parameters. The designers did exceptionally well with improved technologies in fining the hull, yet increasing installed power from the *Yorck's* 90,000 shp for 27.5 knots to 160,000 shp for 31.5 knots, while also improving the protection. The massive increase in machinery output was possible only by remaining with high pressure steam technology, rather than adopting diesels. Protection was a blend of *Graf Spee* and *Yorck*, with a vertical belt, tapering from 350 mm (13.8-inch) to 170 mm (6.7-inch) backed by a cellular void space, whose inboard boundary was a sloped 45 mm (1.8-inch) torpedo bulkhead. An important

addition was the 50 mm (2.0-inch) upper deck. A very unusual feature was the prominent, pedestal-mounted catapult on the after superstructure. The adjacent hangar was always larger in the *Scharnhorst* which, other than for a light pole foremast, was near-identical with her sister as built.

Change in appearance was not long in coming. The original profile showed a very moderate forward sheer, which proved to be insufficient to prevent wetness, made worse by the anchors throwing spray.

In two stages the ships gained 'Atlantic' bows, increasing freeboard with a pleasing sheerline and curved stem, long spray rails and anchor stowage removed to deck edge level. Smoke problems on the bridge were improved by the fitting of prominent clinker screens to the funnel tops. The main-mast, earlier stepped on the after side of the funnel in both ships, was later moved to the after superstructure in the *Scharnhorst* only.

Scharnhorst was finally sunk in a classic gunnery duel but her sister suffered a wrecked forward end during air attack on Kiel. She was never recommissioned, but dismantled in 1943.

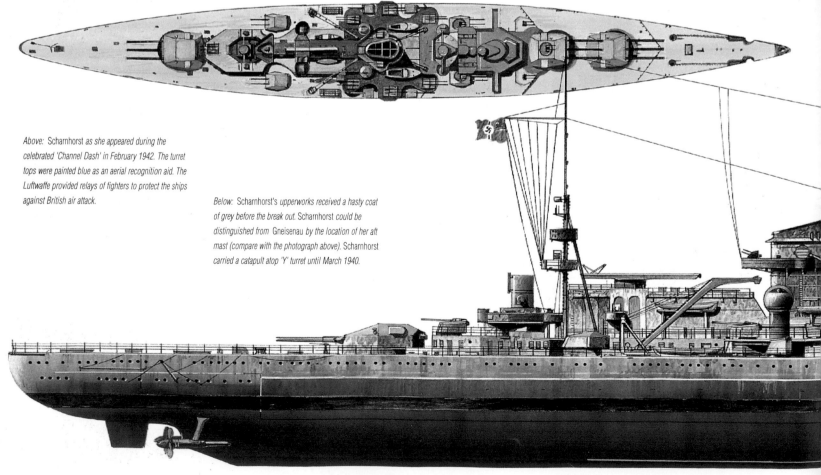

Above: Scharnhorst *as she appeared during the celebrated 'Channel Dash' in February 1942. The turret tops were painted blue as an aerial recognition aid. The Luftwaffe provided relays of fighters to protect the ships against British air attack.*

Below: Scharnhorst's *upperworks received a hasty coat of grey before the break out.* Scharnhorst *could be distinguished from* Gneisenau *by the location of her aft mast (compare with the photograph above).* Scharnhorst *carried a catapult atop 'Y' turret until March 1940.*

Above: Gneisenau *after she received her Atlantic bow in January 1939. Poor sea boats, the aft deck was usually awash, forcing the companionways to be sealed. It was planned to re-arm them with six 15-in guns in 1940-41 when, it was assumed, the war would be over.*

Scharnhorst class data:

Displacement, standard	34,850 tons
Displacement, full load	38,900 tons
Length, overall	770.7 feet (234.9 m)
	with modified bows
Beam	98.4 feet (30.0 m)
Design draught	28.5 feet (8.7 m)
Complement	1670

Class: *Gneisenau Scharnhorst*
Completed 1938–9

Armament:
Nine 11-in guns (3 x 3)
Twelve 5.9-in guns (6 x 2)
Fourteen 4.1-in guns (7. x 2)
Sixteen 37-mm guns (8 x 2)

Six 21-in torpedo tubes
Four aircraft

Machinery:
Steam turbines 160,000 shp (119,400 kW)
Three shafts 31.5 knots

Armour:
Belt	up to 13.8 in
Bulkheads	up to 7.9 in
Deck	up to 2.0 in
Turrets	up to 14.2 in
Barbettes	up to 13.8 in

Above: Scharnhorst *and* Gneisenau *remained very wet at the bows even after modification. 'A' turret was practically unusable in a head sea, a weakness exposed off Norway in 1940 when these two modern battleships fled from HMS* Renown *in the teeth of a gale.*

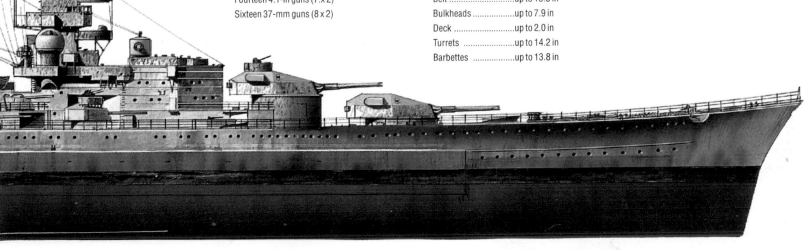

Early war career of the Scharnhorsts

Until March 1941, the *Scharnhorst* and *Gneisenau* were quite successful, operating as a pair and inseparable to the point where the British referred to them as 'Salmon and Gluckstein'.

They gained early notoriety when, in November 1939, they sortied briefly to probe British patrol dispositions in the Iceland-UK gap. Encountering the armed merchant cruiser *Rawalpindi*, an P & O liner with guns, they quickly disposed of her but, apprehensive of the resultant British response, then headed for home.

During the German invasion of Norway in April 1940 they covered a military landing at Narvik but were intercepted at sea by the British battle cruiser *Renown*, which put three 15-inch shells into the *Gneisenau* before their admiral, Lutjens, succeeded in disengaging among numerous snow squalls.

By June, the allied military campaign to save Norway had failed and evacuation was in full swing. On the 8th the two Germans sighted the British carrier *Glorious* which, escorted by two destroyers, was proceeding independently. Inexcusably, she had neither an air patrol aloft nor an armed strike ready to be ranged, and was quickly disposed of by gunfire. In a gallant defence, both of her escorts were also lost, but the *Acasta* succeeded in torpedoing the *Scharnhorst*, putting her in dock for five months. Days later, the *Gneisenau* was similarly damaged by the submarine *Clyde*. Not until January 1941 were the pair again operational.

Breaking out, with some difficulty, into the Atlantic, Lutjens intercepted the loaded eastbound convoy HX 106, but its escort of the battleship *Ramillies* deterred him from attacking. With few means of support, raiders cannot voluntarily risk damage through major combat. Twice more during this foray were the Germans similarly frustrated – by the *Malaya*, protecting SL67 off the west coast of Africa, and by the *Rodney*, in company with another Halifax convoy HX 114.

Unfortunately, outward-bound empty convoys needed to be dispersed well before reaching the north Atlantic in order that ships could head more quickly for their ports of destination. Lutjens, well aware of this, was twice able to intercept convoys soon after dispersal and, in the space of two days, March 15–16th 1941, disposed of sixteen unprotected merchant ships.

Successfully disguising his intentions, he also succeeded in evading the royal Navy, gaining the safety of Brest on 22 March after a two-month cruise that had covered nearly 18,000 miles.

The British, unable to bring the enemy to action had, nonetheless, gained valuable experience in the fusion of intelligence, reconnaissance and rapid fleet re-disposition. It proved indispensable when the *Bismarck* broke out only weeks later.

Below: Gneisenau *opens fire on the British aircraft carrier* Glorious *in June 1940.* Glorious *had no aircraft aloft and none ready to launch.*

Operation 'Cerberus'– the Channel Dash by *Scharnhort* and *Gneisenau*

Following their productive raiding cruise of January – March 1941, the two Scharnhorsts returned to Brest. Determined to keep them there, the British attacked them repeatedly from the air. Over a period of months the ships suffered a total of nine bomb – and one torpedo – hit, and their return to Germany became imperative. In company with the heavy cruiser *Prinz Eugen*, they were to make the passage in February 1942. Inactive for many months, they were ordered to break through the English Channel rather than risk the long, northabout route.

The British had long anticipated such a move but, on the day, the standing aerial watch on Brest and the western Channel was experiencing major technical problems. At about 2300 on 11 February in conditions of low cloud cover, the German squadron, under Vice Admiral Ciliax, slipped out of Brest, rounded Ushant and headed eastward at high speed. They followed a narrow track, swept surreptitiously over previous weeks, and marked at waypoints by anchored patrol craft.

Covered by a rolling Luftwaffe escort, Ciliax incredibly had advanced as far as the Somme estuary and was approaching the Channel narrows before being reported, almost by accident, when British fighters encountered his air cover. By noon, the Germans were off Cap Gris Nez. British shore batteries failed to hit them and a valiant effort to attack by six Fleet Air Arm Swordfish, based at Manston, ended in their being wiped out. Motor torpedo boats from Dover and Ramsgate, elderly destroyers from Harwich and Royal Air Force Beauforts from as far afield as Cornwall and Scotland fared no better.

Fortunately, the RAF had extensively mined coastal shipping lanes and, north of Ostend, Ciliax had his first check

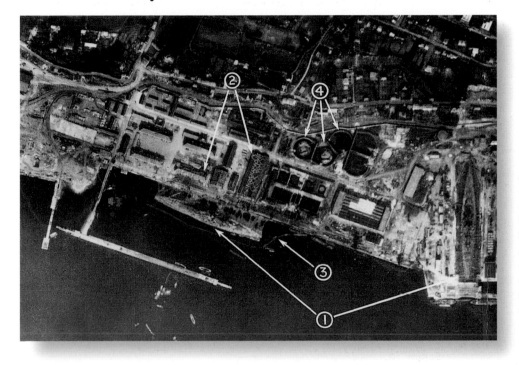

Left: An RAF photo reconnaissance aircraft took this picture of Scharnhorst and Gneisenau at Brest. Repeated attacks by British heavy bombers caused some damage, but the harbour was heavily defended and losses were unacceptably high.

when the *Scharnhorst* touched-off a magnetic mine. She dropped back somewhat, but soon regained about 25 knots.

About 400 bomber stories were flown by the RAF as Ciliax ran up the Dutch coast. In the thick conditions, only one in ten aircraft even sighted the target and seventeen were lost making ineffective low-level attacks.

As the German squadron hauled around to the eastward, off the Dutch island of Terschelling, first *Gneisenau*, then

Scharnhorst triggered mines. This time, the flagship was considerably injured, being obliged to limp in to Wilhelmshaven on one engine and with 1000 tons of water aboard. Her compatriots made the Elbe safely in the small hours of the 13th.

British mortification was absolute. Plans and inter-force co-operation had proved completely inadequate. Ultimately it devolved on the selfless courage of brave men carrying out penny-packet attacks. Strategically, the removal of these powerful potential raiders from Brest was of considerable comfort to the Admiralty. Tactically, however, the Germans had pulled-off a well-planned and resourceful coup.

Below: Scharnhorst during the Channel Dash: what seemed at the time to be a dramatic victory for Germany actually represented an admission of failure. Neither battleship would reach the Atlantic again.

Left: Bismarck was the first true battleship to be commissioned by the Kriegsmarine. Heavily protected and armed with 15-in guns, she was theoretically a match for any other modern battleship.

1939, the maritime powers had adopted this figure, superseding the limit that had been imposed at Washington.

Engineering policy seemed to be confused at the time. Once again, diesels were considered but were unavailable. The next-favoured alternative was turbo-electric drive, previously popular with the Americans. Where the Germans had successfully constructed a few merchant ships with the system, however, it was thought risky to extrapolate the experience by the degree necessary to reliably power a battleship. The Bismarcks were thus steam turbine-propelled.

Bismarck class

The 'pocket battleships' were solutions to a tight set of imposed limitations, while the Scharnhorsts were somewhere between battle cruisers and battleships. As a 15-inch gun design already existed, and was being developed further, the ship design bureau commenced work as early as 1932 on a true battleship, capable of shipping the calibre in a conventional eight-gun main battery. What was purely a paper study gained momentum with the Anglo-German Naval Agreement of 1935. Orders were, in any case, due for replacements for the *Hannover* and *Schleswig-Holstein*, launched in 1905–6. The new rapprochement with Britain, however, enabled the replacements to be up to the agreed Washington maximum of 35,000 tons standard displacement.

A starting point for the protection scheme was the latest previous design, that of the Bayerns, ordered more than two decades earlier. There was no slope either to the main belt or to the torpedo bulkheads but the upper and lower armoured decks were of 50 and 8 mm plate respectively. In profile, the Bismarcks were very much like four-turret versions of the Scharnhorsts but where, in the latter, a continuous line of scuttles indicated the vertical extent of their shallow belt, the long blank shell of the Bismarcks showed that their protection, albeit tapered to 145 mm (5.7-inch), extended right up to the upper deck.

From the outset it was apparent that the heavy armament and protection schemes could not be achieved within the official displacement limits, even though the largest permissible gun, a 40.6-cm (16-inch) had not been selected. To achieve the necessary buoyancy, the length was over one-third greater than that of the Bayerns. Beam was, however, increased by only 20 per cent indicating a finer, faster hull form. The actual 45,000 ton displacement was, however, remarkably prescient for, by the time that the pair were launched in

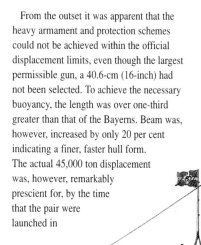

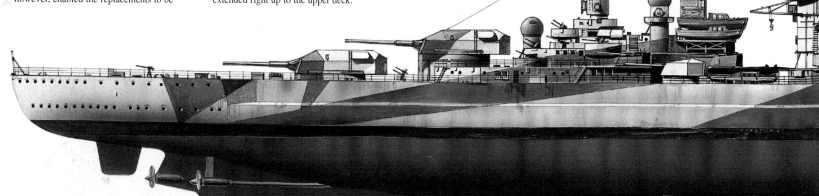

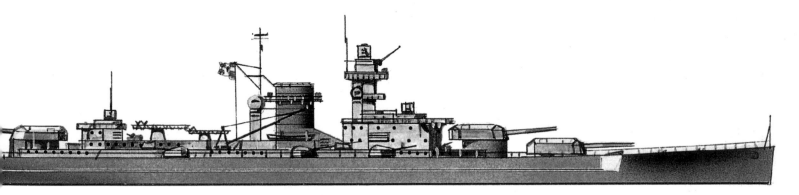

Like the Bayerns, the new ships had three shafts, but where the earlier design had fairly full after waterplanes, the Bismarcks had a much finer run, which meant a greater length of exposed wing shafts. This feature was to prove a problem when she was eventually torpedoed on the port quarter. (Coincidentally, her one-time opponent, HMS *Prince of Wales*, was to suffer similarly).

In keeping with German commerce-raiding tradition, up to six aircraft could be carried, in hangars at the base of the mainmast and flanking the funnel. their catapult ran athwartships in the gap abaft the funnel.

Although the two were very similar in final appearance, the *Tirpitz* could be identified by two further *Wackeltopfe* director housings on the centre-line between the mainmast and 'X' (or 'C') turret.

Bismarck class data:

Displacement, standard	45,200 tons
Displacement full load	50,950 tons
Length, overall	823.5 feet (251.0 m)
Beam	118.1 feet (36.0 m)
Design draught	31.2 feet (9.5 m)
Complement	2100

Class: *Bismarck Tirpitz* completed 1940–1.

Armament:
Eight 15-in guns (4 × 2)
Twelve 5.9-in guns (6 × 2)
Sixteen 4.1-in guns (8 × 2)
Sixteen 37-mm guns (8 × 2)
Eight 21-in torpedo tubes
Four/six aircraft

Machinery:
Steam turbines 138,000 shp (102,950 kW)
Three shafts 29 knots

Above: With a light main mast and straight stem, the original mid-1930s design for the Bismarck class harked back to the Scharnhorst class. Note the absence of scuttles along the armour belt, which extended to the upper deck.

Armour:

Belt	up to 12.6 in
Bulkhead	up to 8.7 in
Decks	up to 3.15 in
Turrets	up to 14.2 in
Barbettes	up to 13.4 in

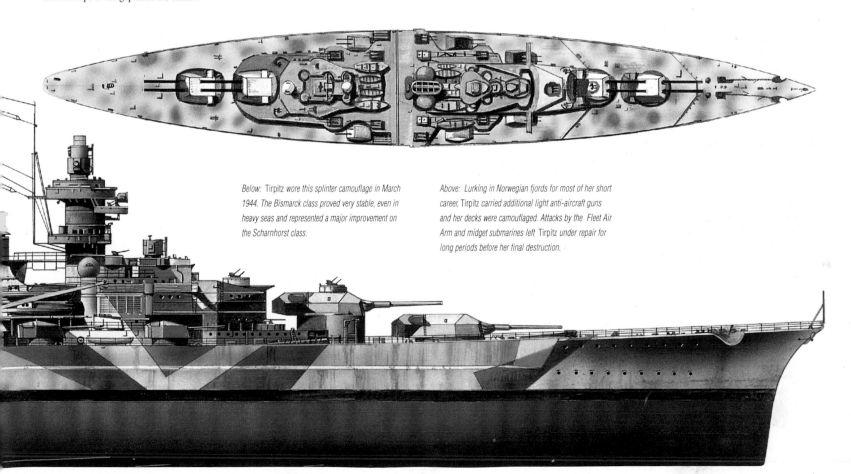

Below: Tirpitz wore this splinter camouflage in March 1944. The Bismarck class proved very stable, even in heavy seas and represented a major improvement on the Scharnhorst class.

Above: Lurking in Norwegian fjords for most of her short career, Tirpitz carried additional light anti-aircraft guns and her decks were camouflaged. Attacks by the Fleet Air Arm and midget submarines left Tirpitz under repair for long periods before her final destruction.

Bismarck – Atlantic raider

Bismarck, the ultimate raider, achieved immortality in an operational career which spanned barely a week and which accounted for not a single merchantman.

In company with the heavy cruiser *Prinz Eugen*, the newly worked-up ship sailed from the Baltic on 18 May 1941. Her function was to engage the battleship with which the British accompanied each homeward convoy, while the cruiser got among the merchant ships. Commanded by Admiral Lutjens, late of the *Scharnhorst*, the pair stopped-over briefly in Norway to await conditions suitable for breaking-out. Here, on the 21st, they were spotted by British reconnaissance.

Admiral Tovey, CinC Home Fleet, was well aware of heightened German reconnaissance activity and tightened the northern cruiser patrols. On the evening of 23 May the *Suffolk* sighted the Germans entering the Denmark Strait (between Iceland and Greenland) from the north. Together with the *Norfolk*, she began to track and report their progress. Their excellent work enabled a heavy British squadron to intercept Lutjens as he emerged from the southern end of the strait early on the 24th.

The battle cruiser *Hood*, wearing the flag of Vice-Admiral Holland, was in company with the new battleship *Prince of Wales*. Having detached his destroyer screen, Holland sighted the Germans at 0535. Because of the *Hood's* vulnerability to plunging, long-range fire, the British admiral sought to close the range quickly, the sharp angle of his approach masking his after turrets. The *Bismarck* quickly found the range and, following several hits, the *Hood* blew up catastrophically at 0600. Already experiencing problems with her new equipment, and now smothered in fire, the *Prince of Wales* broke off the action and joined the cruisers in tracking Lutjens. The latter, damaged, signalled his intention to return to a French port.

Closing from the south-east was Admiral Tovey, with the weight of the Home Fleet while, from the same general direction, came Force H from Gibraltar and the battleship *Rodney*, diverted from convoy duty.

In deteriorating weather, early on the 25th, nine Swordfish from Tovey's carrier *Victorious* attacked the *Bismarck*. A single torpedo hit amidships was insufficient to slow her. Lutjens had already detached the *Prinz Eugen* and now turned from a

southerly to a south-easterly course. For the first time, his shadowers lost touch and, for over thirty anxious hours, the British scoured every likely area.

At 1030 on the 26th a Catalina finally sighted the German, less than 700 miles from Brest. Tovey had no hope of catching her unless she was slowed and, fortunately, Force H was now well placed. Its cruiser *Sheffield* re-established a visual link and Swordfish from its carrier, *Ark Royal*, succeeded, at the second attempt, in torpedoing the *Bismarck* twice. Her steering gear immobilised, the fugitive was harried throughout the following night by destroyers. With daylight, on the morning of the 27th, Admiral Tovey approached with the battleships *King George V* and *Rodney*. Slowly closing the range from a safe 16,000 yards, he pounded the German into a flaming shambles. At about 1015 Tovey ceased fire, leaving the cruiser *Dorsetshire* to finish the task with three torpedoes.

Below: Bismarck *seen from the cruiser* Prinz Eugen *on the eve of their sortie. The camouflage scheme was painted out in Norway, just before she sailed. The plan was for* Bismarck *to attack battleships escorting convoys while* Prinz Eugen *sank the merchantmen.*

Tirpitz in Norway

Left: The 15-in guns of Tirpitz. Reports of her being at sea led to the scattering of convoy PQ17 and its virtual annihilation by air and submarine attack.

With the destruction of the *Bismarck* in May 1941, commerce raiding by regular warships was effectively at an end. *Tirpitz* however, was complete and working up. In November 1941 an introductory Atlantic cruise, in company with the *Scheer*, was cancelled, the ship being sent soon afterward to Norway. Here, with other heavy units, she threatened the flank of the vital convoy route to North Russia. As long as the threat existed, the British Home Fleet needed to keep a disproportionately stronger force available.

Commanded by Admiral Ciliax, *Tirpitz* made her first move in March 1942. In thick, sub-Arctic conditions she narrowly missed both a pair of crossing convoys and a powerful contingent of the Home Fleet. The convoys had been in grave danger but Ciliax had been close to being brought to decisive action, resulting in an order to operate more circumspectly.

In July 1942, reports that she and a supporting force had sailed from Altenfjord were sufficient for the Admiralty to order the convoy PQ17 to scatter. The Home Fleet cover was not able to proceed far enough eastward to cover it and, although the German surface units never came near, the merchantmen fell easy victim to aircraft and submarines.

The battleship fired her main battery on only one occasion against an enemy target, and this was during a bombardment of Spitzbergen in September 1943. With little opportunity to bring her to action by conventional means, the British penetrated her Altenfjord anchorage with midget submarines in the same month. Heavily damaged, she was patched up locally, but her operational usefulness was delayed by a succession of British carrier-based air strikes. Surrounded by nets, the *Tirpitz* could not be torpedoed, while carrier aircraft carried bombs too small to inflict vital damage. Bomber command then took over and, flying from North Russia, Lancasters finished her with the heaviest bombs in the inventory.

Right: Tirpitz with 'B' and 'X' turrets painted pale grey to stand out, making her appear to have only two turrets. The deck is camouflaged.

Below: Aboard the capsized Tirpitz. She went down with over 1200 men on board after being hit by five 5.45 ton bombs dropped by the specially modified Avro Lancasters of 617 squadron.

Left: Tirpitz zig-zags off Norway where British submarines constantly patrolled in the hope of torpedoing her.

Below: Smoke rises from Tirpitz during an attack by British carrier-borne aircraft.

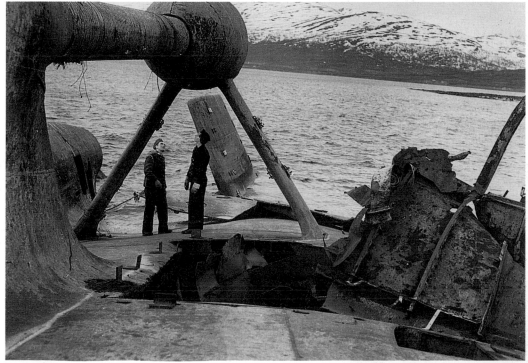

Italy

Italian battleships 1900–1945

The Italian navy was one of the first to advocate the all big-gun battleship, and its chief designer, Vittorio Cuniberti published his ideas in the 1903 edition of *Jane's Fighting Ships*. The Italian navy had a reputation for innovation: designing the first triple turrets, the 'fast battleships' of the Regina Elena class, the first all-metal ships (*San Marco* had no timber fixtures at all) and the first electric gun mounting machinery. Unfortunately, the ingenuity of Italian engineers was not supported by Italian politicians or industry. The pace of construction in Italian shipyards was extremely slow, negating many good ideas and ensuring that some vessels were bordering on the obsolete by the time they were commissioned. For example, although triple turrets were designed in Italy, the first warship completed with triple turrets belonged to the traditional enemy, Austria-Hungary. The *Viribus Unitis* was laid down after *Dante Alighieri* but completed first.

The Italian navy had not seen action since the disaster in 1866 when the Austro-Hungarians scored their dramatic victory at Lissa.

In September 1911 Italy attacked Turkey, seizing control of Tripoli and several islands in the eastern Aegean. The bulk of the Ottoman fleet had made its usual summer cruise to Beirut, but withdrew to Constantinople a few days after the declaration of war, there to stay for the duration of hostilities. The few armed yachts and torpedo boats left in the Aegean were destroyed by Italian warships and Beirut bombarded. Tripoli was annexed and the war concluded in October 1912.

Italy entered World War I in 1915 after a masterly diplomatic offensive that compelled the Allies to promise large territorial concessions at the expense of the Austro-Hungarians and Turks. Italian naval personnel demonstrated their flair for special operations and torpedo boat attacks sinking two Austro-Hungarian dreadnoughts, *Szent István* and *Viribus Unitis* as well as the predreadnought *Wien* and a destroyer. However, the battleships spent most of their war swinging at anchor. Many of the best officers transferred to light forces; morale and efficiency suffered.

Between the wars, Italy discovered a new rival in the shape of France which refused to cede Turkish territory

promised in 1915 and took control of Tunisia. A naval race ensued, with both navies building cruisers, destroyers and submarines in direct competition. Battleship rivalry was checked by the Washington treaties until the 1930s when Italy embarked on the most radical reconstructions of World War I-era dreadnoughts undertaken in Europe. Only some of the Japanese rebuilds matched the ambitious scope of the four-year programmes that converted the Cavour class from elderly veterans to modern fast battleships.

The reconstructions and the splendid Littorio class battleships gave Mussolini a very powerful fleet on the eve of World War II. Unfortunately, the liaison between the Italian navy and air force was even worse than that between the pre-war RAF and the Royal Navy. Italy built no aircraft carriers, and relied entirely on shore-based air cover. The way that the Littorios later carried fighter aircraft on their catapults, not reconnaissance aircraft may give some indication of the fleet's confidence in receiving timely protection from enemy torpedo-bombers.

In November 1940, 20 carrierborne biplanes from the carrier *Illustrious*

Above: Italy reconstructed her dreadnoughts with such thoroughness that they emerged as virtually new ships. The Caio Duilio was converted from an almost obsolete vessel to a modern fast battleship in time for World War II. Italy's battlesquadron had the potential to dominate the central Mediterranean in 1940.

attacked the Italian battleships at Taranto. This audacious raid scuppered more than three battleships: the surprising vulnerability of even the modern ships to lightweight torpedoes, followed by the loss of three cruisers at Cape Matapan in March prevented any serious attempt to intervene in the desperate struggle off Crete the following summer. With neither radar, flashless propellant for night fighting, nor any confidence in land-based air support, the major units of the Italian fleet took little further part in the war. From early 1941 a critical shortage of fuel left much of the fleet immobilised unless the Germans demanded action and supplied the oil.

Ironically, the Italian battleships' last action was against their former ally. As the battlefleet steamed to Malta after the coup against Mussolini, German aircraft finally did appear over the Italian fleet. This time they carried radio-controlled bombs, with which they sank the *Roma*.

Above: One of the reconstructed dreadnoughts fires a salvo. The original 12-in guns were bored out to 12.6-in calibre and fired a substantially heavier shell over a longer range.

Above: Guilio Cesare seen from Andrea Doria in January 1941. The rest of the Italian battleships were out of action after the British air attack on Taranto two months earlier.

Below: Regina Margherita was one of a series of predreadnoughts built at the turn of the century in anticipation of renewed war with Austria-Hungary. Typical of her time, she was armed with guns of four different calibres.

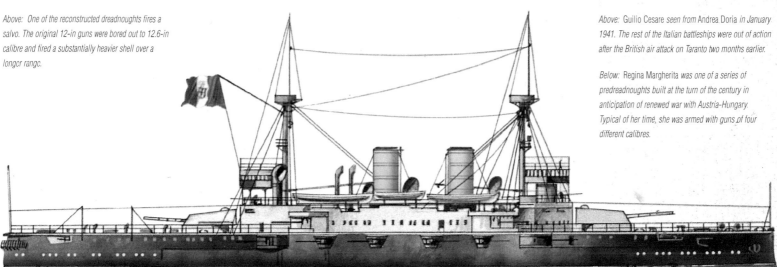

Regina Margherita class

The two Regina Margherita class battleships marked Italy's acceptance of what was becoming a near universal standard in capital ships at the turn of the century. Laid down in 1898 and 1899, they were armed with four 12-inch 40 calibre guns in two turrets. The two previous Italian battleships had been armed with out-moded 10-inch guns, and the three Re Umbertos completed in the early 1890s sported slow-firing and inaccurate 13-inch 30 calibre guns in open barbettes. Original plans gave the Margheritas the same armament as the later Regina Elenas: two 12-inch 'chasers' and a main battery of twelve 8-inch guns. However, after the death of Admiral Brin a more conventional armament was adopted and the second ship given his name. The

Margheritas also carried a mixed battery of four 8-inch guns and twelve 6-inch guns on a modest displacement. With forced draught their triple expansion engines delivered 21,000 ihp for a speed just topping 20 knots. The impressive armament and turn of speed was purchased at the expense of protection: the armour belt (Terni Harvey steel, not Krupp Cemented) was only 6-inch thick over the vitals and tapered to 2-inch at the ends.

Had they been promptly completed, the Margheritas would have compared favourably with the battleships joining the rival Austrian or French navies at the beginning of this century. However, they took nearly three years to be launched, and another three to be completed. Benedetto Brin, laid down in January 1899 was not commissioned until the autumn of 1905. A generation of

better battleships was already in the water, and Dreadnought was only months away from her launch.

Both Margheritas were sunk during the Great War. Benedetto Brin exploded in Brindisi in September 1915 in an early sabotage operation by the Austro-Hungarians; over 450 officers and men were killed. Regina Margherita ran on to mines laid by the German submarine UC-14 in December 1916.

Regina Margherita class data:

Displacement, standard	13,215 tons
Length overall	454 feet 10.5 in (138.65 m)
Beam	78 feet 2.5 in (23.84 m)
Design draught	28 feet 11 in (8.81 m)
Complement	812

Class: Benedetto Brin, Regina Margherita

Armament:
4 × 12-in guns (2 × 2)
4 × 8-in guns (4 × 1)
12 × 6-in guns (12 × 1)
20 × 3-in guns
4 × 17.7-in torpedo tubes

Machinery:
Triple expansion steam engines, 21,790 ihp
2 shafts
20 knots

Armour:
Sides ....6 in
 (Terni Harvey steel)
Decks ....3.1 in
Turrets ....8 in
Battery ....6 in
Conning tower............6 in

Regina Elena class

The Chief Engineer of the Italian navy, Vittorio Cuniberti published plans for an all-big gun battleship in the 1903 edition of *Jane's Fighting Ships*. He was one of several designers whose work helped stimulate the British to build the *Dreadnought*. Cuniberti's own plans for a 17,000 ton battleship with twelve 12-inch guns were not acted upon in his own country, but one of his other designs was adopted, giving the Italian navy a unique class of fast battleships that anticipated the battlecruiser concept pioneered by the Royal Navy. The Regina Elena class, laid down in 1901 were slightly longer than the earlier Margheritas, but 5-feet narrower in the beam. Using the same engines, they achieved a speed of 22 knots yet were protected by a 9.8-inch armour belt.

At 22 knots, the Regina Elenas outpaced all battleships then in service or building, and could probably have forced most armoured cruisers to action. Their standard of protection would have stood them in good stead against any cruiser. However, their speed and armour came at a cost: their effective main armament consisted of twelve 8-inch guns in twin turrets, three each side. The fore and aft turrets housed single 12-inch guns. Useful though they might have been to wing a fleeing enemy cruiser, or perhaps discourage a pursuer, two guns were insufficient for accurate salvo firing.

Italian shipbuilding remained a leisurely business, with the lead ship taking six and half years to complete. The second pair were completed in five years. That they represented a halfway house between fast battleships and cruisers became more obvious with subsequent Italian construction. Four 10,000 ton 22-knot warships followed them into service: classed by the Italian navy as 'second class battleships' but by most subsequent authorities as armoured cruisers. The Pisa and San Georgio classes both featured a main armament of four 10-inch guns and secondary batteries of eight 7.5-inch guns. How far this represented naval policy and how far political expediency is difficult to judge. These were adequate warships with which to challenge contemporary Austro-Hungarian 'battleships' with 9.4-inch main armament; but, above all, they were far cheaper than full-scale predreadnoughts and a 'second class battleship' was politically easier to fund than a battleship proper.

The Regina Elenas took part in the war with Turkey in 1911–12 and survived World War I. Obsolete after 1918, they were scrapped during the late 1920s.

Regina Elena class data:

Displacement, full load	13,774 tons
Length overall	474 feet 5 in (144.6 m)
Beam	73 feet 6 in (22.4 m)
Design draught	25 feet 11.5 in (7.91 m)
Complement	742

Class: *Napoli, Roma, Regina Elena, Vittorio Emanuele*

Armament:
2 × 12-in guns (2 × 1)
8 × 8-in guns (4 × 2)
16 × 3-in guns
2 × 17.7-in torpedo tubes

Machinery:
Triple expansion steam engines, 19,299 ihp
2 shafts
21 knots

Armour:
Belt	9.45 in
Deck	5.5 in
Turrets	up to 13 in
Conning tower	10.6 in

Below: The Regina Elena class were ahead of their time. Fast, and armed with a single 12-in gun fore and aft and turreted 8-in guns amidships, they were effectively predreadnought battlecruisers.

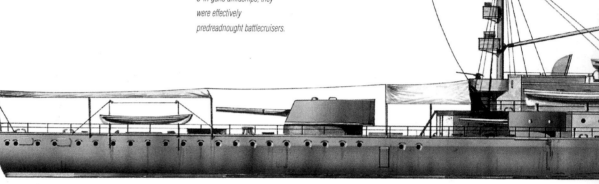

Dante Alighieri

In 1909 an effective four year moratorium on battleship construction was ended by the Italian parliament and permitted the Italian navy to lay down its first dreadnought. *Dante Alighieri* was the first battleship designed to carry her main armament in triple turrets. Cuniberti distrusted superfiring arrangements, so the four turrets were on the centre line: one on the forecastle, two amidships between the two pairs of funnels, and one aft. The arcs of fire were very wide, even if the turret arrangement gave them a very unusual appearance. The turret layout dictated everything else, with the turbines located between the two midships turrets and the boilers in two groups, one behind the forward turret and one in front of the aft turret.

The 3.9-inch secondary armament was divided into two six-gun casemated batteries either side, but eight guns were disposed in armoured twin turrets abreast of the end 12-inch turrets. The guns in the casemates were difficult to work in a seaway, a common problem with this period. However, the use of twin turrets for the secondary armament was ahead of its time.

Much was made of the *Dante's* speed, claimed as 23 knots, and she is often described as the fastest battleship in the world at the time of her completion. She made 24.2 knots on her trials at 35,000 shp. She survived World War I, although her only real action was the bombardment of Durazzo in 1918. She was scrapped in 1928.

Above: Vittorio Emanuele at Taranto in 1917, by which time there was not much for the big surface ships to do. The Adriatic was infested with mines and enemy submarines.

Dante Alighieri data:

Displacement, standard	19,500 tons
Displacement, full load	21,800 tons
Length overall	551 feet 6 in (168.1 m)
Beam	87 feet 3 in (26.59 m)
Design draught	31 feet 10 in (9.7 m)
Complement	970

Below: Dante Alighieri as completed. During reconstruction in 1923 her pole foremast was replaced by a tripod mast and the fore funnel raised.

Class: Dante Alighieri

Armament:
12 × 12-in guns (4 × 3)
20 × 4.7-in guns (4 × 2, 12 × 1)
16 × 3-in guns
3 × 17.7-in torpedo tubes

Machinery:
3 Parsons geared turbines, 32,000 shp
4 shafts
23 knots

Armour:
Belt	up to 9.8 in
Turrets	9.8 in
Secondary turrets and casemates	3.9 in
Decks	up to 1.2 in
Conning tower	11 in

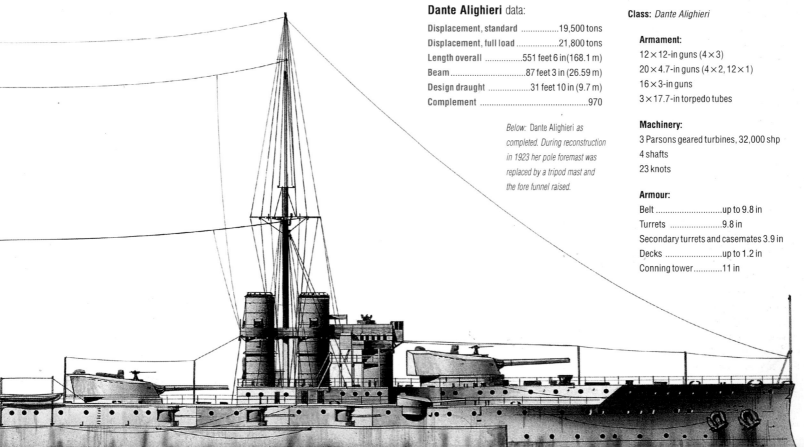

Francesco Caracciolo class

In 1913 it was decided to construct a new class of 'super dreadnought' that would match the 14– and 15-inch fast battleships now under construction in some foreign yards. Early designs envisaged a 29,000-ton battleship armed with nine 15-inch guns. In the final design, they resembled the British Queen Elizabeths. Flush-decked, they carried eight Armstrong-designed 15-inch guns in twin centre-line turrets, two fore and two aft. Their intended speed of 28 knots would trump the Austro-Hungarian Ersatz Monarch class then building. This was achieved by using thinner armour than on the latest foreign battleships.

Four Caracciolos were ordered in April 1914, but Italy declared war only a year later and construction was soon halted in favour of torpedo boats and destroyers that could be completed in time to see action. Work on *Francesco Caracciolo* began again in 1919, initially to clear the slipway, then in the hope that she might be used either as an aircraft carrier or a fast freighter. Neither plan came to pass and the hull was scrapped in 1921.

Francesco Carraciolo class data:

Displacement, standard	32,800 tons
Displacement, full load	34,000 tons
Length overall	695 feet 11 in (212.1 m)
Beam	97 feet 1 in (29.6 m)
Design draught	31 feet 2 in (9.5 m)
Complement	Not known

Class: *Cristoforo Colombo, Francesco Caracciolo, Francesco Morosini, Marcantonio Colonna*

Armament:
8 × 15-in guns (4 × 2)
12 × 6-in or × 4.7-in guns
12 × 40-mm guns

Machinery:
4 Parsons geared turbines, 105,000 shp
  forced draught
4 shafts
28 knots

Armour:

Belt	up to 11.8 in
Turrets	15.7 in
Barbettes	11.8 in
Casemates	5.9 in
Deck	1.4 in
Conning tower	13.4 in

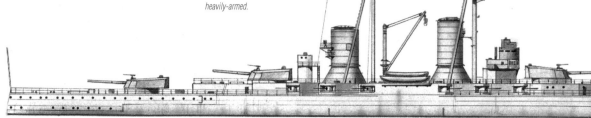

Below: Italy's first 'super dreadnoughts', the Francesco Caracciolos were planned to be even faster than the British Queen Elizabeth class fast battleships, and just as heavily-armed.

Conte Di Cavour class

Laid down in 1910, the three Cavour class dreadnoughts had the unusual total of thirteen big guns. Having overcome the doubts about superfiring turrets that led to the design of the *Dante Alighieri*, the Italians were still reluctant to superimpose triple turrets. So the Cavours were built with a triple turret in the 'A' and 'Y' positions, each with a superfiring twin turret. A fifth twin turret was fitted amidships. The *Dante's* partly turreted secondary armament was not repeated, and the 18 4.7-inch guns were disposed in casemates. However, they were one deck higher, enabling them to be worked in a seaway.

Armour protection was not improved on the Dante design, and was light by comparison with the latest battleships entering service with most other major navies. Yet again, the slow pace of construction in Italian yards ensured that these 1908 designs did not enter service until 1915. Britain, Japan and the USA were already a generation ahead by then, with fast battleships armed with 14– and 15-inch guns.

Conte di Cavour and *Giulio Cesare* were followed by *Leonardo da Vinci*, the only battleship to have been named after an artist rather than the usual statesman, battle or mythological figure. This third unit differed slightly from her sisters: she had a different bridge structure and four derricks attached to the support legs of the tripod masts rather than two attached to the masts themselves.

In August 1916 *Leonardo da Vinci* exploded and sank in Taranto harbour in what is generally assumed to have been another sabotage operation by Austro-Hungarian agents. However, the Italian navy used British cordite charges which were responsible for catastrophic accidents like the loss of the battleship *Vanguard*. The Japanese used them too, and also lost warships to mysterious magazine explosions. The capsized battleship was brought into dock, her keel still uppermost, but damage was too extensive to warrant repair.

Her two sisters underwent a comprehensive reconstruction 1933–7, emerging almost as new ships. The superstructure, midships turret, engines and boilers were removed. An additional 33-feet hull section was added at the bow and the new machinery, delivering three times as much power, increased their speed to 28 knots. Their 12-inch guns were bored out to 12.6-inch calibre, enabling them to fire a heavier round to 31,000 yards.

Their new profile was extremely graceful, and these modernised battleships provided Mussolini's fleet with a core of fast, powerful units capable of dominating the central Mediterranean. Both were in action within weeks of the Italian declaration of war,

Below: The Cavour class as completed. Compare this profile with the profile of Duilio *on p60. The foremast was changed to a four-legged affair with a fire control position before their reconstruction in the 1930s.*

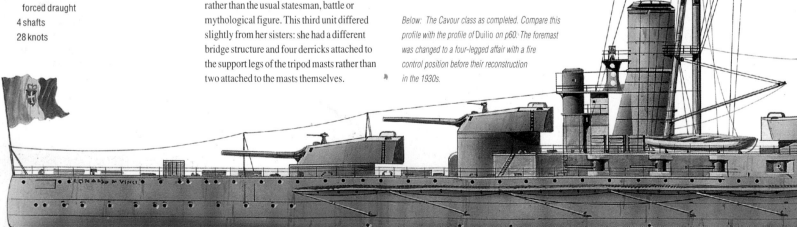

although they withdrew after HMS *Warspite* scored a hit with one of her 15-inch shells at extreme range. *Cavour* was sunk at Taranto by a single 18-inch torpedo which blew a large hole below the armour belt. Raised in 1941, she was still under repair at Trieste in 1943 when US bombers destroyed her.

Mystery surrounds the ultimate fate of the *Cesare*. Surrendered to the Allies in 1943, she was allotted to Russia as war booty and delivered in 1949. Renamed *Novorossiysk*, she became part of the Black Sea fleet but was reportedly broken up or sunk in November 1955. Conflicting reports suggest she either hit a mine or suffered an internal explosion.

Conte di Cavour class data:

Displacement, standard	23,088 tons
Displacement, full load	25,086 tons
	(29,000 tons after 1937)
Length overall	577 feet 9 in (176.1 m)
Beam	91 feet 10 in (28 m)
Design draught	30 feet 10 in (9.4 m)
Complement	1,197

Class: *Conte di Cavour, Giulio Cesare, Leonardo da Vinci*

Armament:
(A) As built:
- 13 × 12-in guns (3 × 3, 2 × 2)
- 18 × 4.7-in guns
- 13 × 3 in QF
- 3 × 17.7-in torpedo tubes

(B) From 1937:
- 10 × 12.6-in guns (2 × 3, 2 × 2)
- 12 × 4.7-in guns
- 8 × 3.9-in guns
- 12 × 37-mm guns

Machinery:
(A) As built:
3 Parsons turbines, 31,000 shp
4 shafts
21.5 knots

(B) From 1937:
Steam turbines, 93,000 shp
2 shafts
28 knots

Armour:
Belt	9.45 in
Deck	5.5 in
Turrets	up to 13 in
Conning tower	10.6 in

Torpedoed at Taranto

British opposition to the Italian attack on Abyssinia in 1935 created the prospect of war between the former allies. At the time of the crisis there was some discussion within the British Mediterranean fleet about a possible airstrike on the Italian battle squadron based at Taranto. Mussolini's support for the Nationalists in the Spanish Civil War included the loan of four submarines and led to the first clash with the Royal Navy. In 1938, the crisis over Czechoslovakia brought Europe to the brink of war, and further planning was done aboard the carrier *Glorious*. So when in June 1940, Mussolini declared war on Britain and France, the Royal Navy's informal ideas were soon translated into an operational plan.

With no effective carrierborne fighters, the elderly Fairey Swordfish torpedo-bombers aboard the British aircraft carriers were hopelessly vulnerable to modern interceptors. But, as the Italian chief of naval staff, Admiral Domenico Cavagnari had already complained to Mussolini, liaison between the fleet and the Italian air force was poor. British reconnaissance flights over Taranto suggested some form of attack might be planned, and on the night the attack the Italian battleships were at partial readiness, with some of the anti-aircraft armament already manned.

The British attack was postponed after a fire aboard the carrier *Illustrious* but on the night of 11 November 1940, two flights of Fairey Swordfish took off. The initial wave comprised 12 aircraft, the second was of nine (although one was forced to return to the carrier) and only 12 aircraft actually carried torpedoes. The rest carried flares and bombs, partly to divert the anti-aircraft defences and partly because there was little space for torpedo-launching. Lt.-Commander Williamson, CO of 815 Squadron led the first wave, weaving his way past the barrage

balloons to torpedo the *Conte di Cavour* just aft of 'B' turret. Brought down by machine gun fire moments after dropping his torpedo, he and his observer survived the crash and were taken prisoner. Two other aircraft attacked the *Cavour*, but both missed. *Littorio* was hit soon afterwards, the first torpedo impacting by 'A' turret, the second on the port quarter. A third torpedo aimed at her struck the bottom and exploded by the battleship's starboard quarter.

Five torpedoes were released by the second wave. One hit *Littorio* on the starboard bow, causing her to settle rapidly. In deeper water, she would undoubtedly have been lost. A fourth hit struck her stern but failed to detonate. *Caio Duilio* was hit by 'B' turret, flooding her forward magazine and eventually sinking her on the harbour bottom.

For the loss of only two aircraft, the Fleet Air Arm had halved the battleship strength of the Italian fleet. Air pursuit of the British during their withdrawal was unsuccessful: directed by radar, the Fulmar fighters aboard *Illustrious* shot down three flying boats sent to locate the British squadron before they could report.

Conte di Cavour could not be saved. The flooding progressively worsened and she was towed towards the shore to save her. The crew abandoned ship six hours after the torpedo struck and she eventually settled on the bottom, with her decks awash, turrets just clear of the water. Although refloated eight months later, she was never to be repaired. *Littorio* was pumped out and repaired within four months and *Duilio* was returned to service by July 1941, but the absence of these ships occurred at a critical time for the Mediterranean campaign.

The repercussions within the Italian armed forces were significant, with the air force blamed for not detecting the attack and the navy criticised for its lax anti-torpedo defences. The battleships proved terribly susceptible to underwater damage. The attack also revealed just how vulnerable capital ships could be to air attack, even by a modest number of effectively obsolete aircraft. The Japanese navy certainly took note.

Andrea Doria class

Andrea Doria and *Caio Duilio* were virtual repeats of the three Cavours, commissioned in 1914–15. Italian practice at the time involved grouping the superstructure in two compact groups around two side-spaced funnels and masts. This increased survivability through the wide separation of machinery spaces but, by dividing the main armament forward, amidships and aft, caused protection to be lighter.

As Italy was not over-strength in capital ships, both classes survived the Washington treaties. Between 1933 and 1940 the *Doria* and *Duilio* were also taken in hand for modernisation. The hull was lengthened by nearly eleven metres by fitting an elegant new bow, with anchors stowed at the deck edge. The centre turret was removed and new, more compact machinery installed, powering two shafts in place of the previous four. The remaining ten guns were re-bored and re-chambered to take a larger 32 cm round (an increase from 12 to 12.6 inches in calibre, the new round weighing 1157-lb against the 996-lb of the 12-inch gun). The total weight of the broadside was still reduced (from 13,391-lb to 11,865-lb), but weight and space needed to be saved for the vastly more powerful machinery that increased their speed by over five knots.

Sixteen 6-inch guns were removed together with their casemates. They were replaced by twelve 5.3s in a pair of superfiring triple turrets on either side. A distinctive row of five single 90-mm high angle guns occupied either side of the waist. The anti-aircraft armament looked impressive, but proved unable to inflict serious losses on the obsolete bi-planes with which the British crippled the Italian battleships at Taranto.

No aircraft or arrangements were embarked. Both units survived the war, both being inactive, due to fuel shortages, for the final 18 months to the armistice. Surrendered at Malta, they returned to join the post-war Italian navy, serving until 1956.

Andrea Doria class data:

Displacement, standard	22,694 tons
Displacement, full load	25,200 tons
	(29,000 tons after 1940)
Length overall	577 feet 9 in (176.1 m)
Beam	91 feet 10 in (28 m)
Design draught	29 feet 2 in (8.9 m)
Complement	1,233

Class: *Andrea Doria, Caio Duilio*

Armament:

(A) As built:
- 13 × 12-in (3 × 3, 2 × 2)
- 16 × 6-in guns
- 18 × 3-in guns
- 3 × 17.7-in torpedo tubes

(B) From 1940:
- 10 × 12.6-in guns (2 × 3, 2 × 2)
- 12 × 5.3-in guns
- 10 × 3.5-in guns
- 15 × 37-mm guns
- 16 × 20-mm guns

Machinery:

(A) As built:
- 3 Parsons turbines
- 20 Yarrow boilers
- 4 shafts
- 32,000 shp
- 21.5 knots

(B) From 1940:
- 2 steam turbines, 87,000 shp
- 2 shafts
- 27 knots

Armour:

Belt	up to 9.8 in
Turrets and barbettes	9.4 in
Casemates	5 in
Decks	1.6 in
Conning tower	12.6 in

The battle of Cape Matapan

Unknown to the Italian navy, its codes had been broken by British intelligence, and its movements were frequently betrayed by intercepted signals. In March 1941 British army units were being shipped from Egypt to Greece as part of an ill-fated attempt to save another ally from German invasion. An Italian sortie, intended to disrupt these convoys, if not snap up some British light forces was planned for 26 March. It became known to the Royal Navy in time for the British to divert the troopships and deploy all available heavy units to meet the threat.

Flying his flag in *Vittorio Veneto*, Admiral Angelo Iachino put to sea escorted by four destroyers. Probing further towards Crete, where British aircraft were now based, were two cruiser squadrons; one of three 8-inch gun heavy cruisers and three destroyers, the other of three 8-inch heavy cruisers, two 6-inch light cruisers and six destroyers.

The most recent Italian reconnaissance flights over the British fleet base at Alexandria had shown all three battleships of the Mediterranean fleet at anchor. In fact, the orders to sail had already been issued. The impression of inactivity, compounded by party invitations and Admiral Cunningham's afternoon round of golf was all for the benefit of Italian agents in Egypt – not least the Japanese consul who reported all shipping movements to his future ally. The fleet sailed at dusk, only three hours after Iachino left port himself.

By dawn on 28 March, *Warspite*, *Valiant*, and *Barham* were 150 miles south of Crete, having joined with the carrier *Formidable* and nine destroyers. Thirty miles south of the eastern tip of Crete were four British 6-inch light cruisers and four destroyers, ordered down from the Aegean to rendezvous with the main force. British shore-based aircraft discovered the three Italian heavy cruisers, but not the presence of the *Veneto* some ten miles astern. Reconnaissance flights from *Formidable* detected both Italian cruiser squadrons. Aboard the *Veneto*, Admiral Iachino was re-assured when the intercepted British signals revealed their ignorance of his battleship's presence.

The British light cruisers encountered the Italian cruisers *Trieste*, *Trento* and *Bolzano*. The Italians carried 8-inch guns to the British 6-inch and were also faster. This was just the situation for which the Italian cruisers were designed and they opened fire from beyond the effective range of their opponents. Iachino hesitated to press on since the promised German air support had failed to arrive, and there was an obvious danger of British air attack. However, he faced the prospect of catching the four British cruisers between his heavy cruisers and the *Veneto*. Working up to full speed, he brought the British under fire with his 15-inch guns but was prevented from developing the situation by the timely arrival of a British airstrike. Six Fairey Albacore bi-planes launched torpedoes: none hit, but it was enough to cause Iachino to reverse course. Taranto had exposed just how vulnerable the Italian battleships were to underwater attack.

An attack by Swordfish based on Crete achieved no hits, and a level-bombing attack by a squadron of Blenheims hit nothing either.

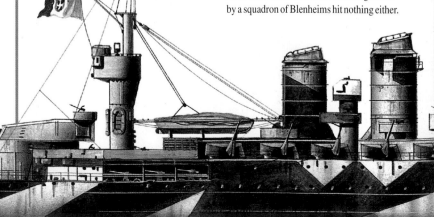

Left: Caio Duilio *seen at Malta in September 1943. The Italian fleet sailed there after the armistice, attacked en route by their former German allies.*

Below: Andrea Doria *and* Caio Duilio *underway before their reconstruction. Note the quick-firing anti-torpedo boat armament atop the aft turrets.*

Above: Gunnery exercises off Sardinia in 1940. Italian surface ships presented a grave threat to the convoys sustaining British control of Malta.

However, as the Italian gunners concentrated on the Blenheims, a second strike arrived from *Formidable*. In a text book attack, two aircraft launched torpedoes at the battleship's port side, and three at the starboard. *Veneto* was hit by her port propellers, putting the port shafts out of action and flooding the after pump room. Stopped in the water, she took on 4000 tons of water. A near-miss from one of the Blenheims struck the sea by her stern, damaging the steering gear. Damage control parties managed to stop the flooding and

restore power to the starboard shafts, getting *Veneto* up to 10 knots. By the time a third airstrike arrived at dusk, the battleship was making a good 15 knots, surrounded by both cruiser squadrons and all their destroyers. The battleship survived further damage, but the 8-inch gun cruiser *Pola* was hit and stopped.

Although intercepted British signals suggested that the Italians were being followed, Iachino mistakenly assumed these were only light forces. Iachino detached *Pola*'s sisterships *Fiume* and *Zara* to shepherd the damaged cruiser home while the rest of his ships made port. Thus it was, 25 years after the

Royal Navy let the German High Seas Fleet escape during the night after Jutland, that Cunningham's battlesquadron steered through the darkness to attack. Locating their prey by radar, and engaging with flashless propellant, the three battleships (two of them Jutland veterans) opened fire on the cruisers at only 4,000 yards, sinking them in minutes.

Below: Andrea Doria *and* Caio Duilio *were not just rebuilt into modern fast battleships – their redesign incorporated all the style and elegance of 1930's Italian warship design. Note the row of 90-mm anti-aircraft guns amidships and the pair of 5.3-in turrets below the bridge structure.*

Vittorio Veneto class

Under the terms of the Washington Treaty, France was allowed to build two 35,000-ton battleships in 1927–29 but did not take up the option until 1932. By then the Italians were under an increasingly belligerent leadership, which was not signatory to the London Naval Treaty of 1930, that extended 'construction holidays'. The two Dunkerques thus triggered the construction not only of the German Scharnhorsts but also the first two Littorios. However, while the French ships had 13-inch guns and the Germans 11-inch, the Italians opted for 15-inch. Officially 35,000 ton ships, they had an actual standard displacement of that exceeding 41,000 tons.

In appearance they were unmistakably Italian, although the later American South Dakotas bore more than a passing resemblance. A most unusual feature was the high exposed barbette of the after turret which set all three turrets at different heights above the waterline. As the quarterdeck was depressed one level, the after turret became a dominating feature. Another 'American' feature was the quarterdeck aircraft catapult and handling crane, the vulnerability of which to blast damage was the original reason for siting the aft turret so high. Although floatplanes were originally shipped, the battleships later carried two Reggiane Re 2000 fighters which had to find a land-base on which to put down, rather like the Hurricanes launched from the British CAM ships.

Their torpedo protection was unusual in that, outboard of the longitudinal bulkhead was a cylinder (nearly four metres in maximum diameter) which was designed to absorb the explosion of a hit, through giving the gases room in which to expand. The *Littorio*, however, was hit by three 18-inch aerial torpedoes during the Taranto raid and would have sunk by the bows had she not been in shallow water. *Vittorio Veneto* was also torpedoed by British carrier aircraft, hit twice by Swordfish from HMS *Formidable* at Cape Matapan, she escaped back to Taranto although shipping some 4000 tons of water.

Two further units, *Impero* and *Roma*, were laid down in 1938. The former was never completed, while the latter, finished in November 1942, became fleet flagship. Her only accomplishment of note was to be first major warship to be destroyed by air-to-surface missiles. Steaming to join the Allies at the armistice, she was hit by two FX 1400 glider bombs on 9 September 1943 and sank with the loss of over 1200 of her crew. *Littorio*, re-named *Italia* by the new Italian regime was also hit, but the bomb passed through the ship to explode in the sea.

Vittorio Veneto class data:

Displacement, standard	41,377 tons
Displacement, full load	45,752 tons
Length overall	778 feet 8.5 in (133.81 m)
Beam	107 feet 9.5 in (24.26 m)
Design draught	31 feet 5 in (8.41 m)
Complement	1,861

Class: *Vittorio Veneto, Littorio, Roma, Impero*

Armament:
9 × 15-in guns (3 × 3)
12 × 6-in guns (4 × 3)
4 × 4.7-in guns
12 × 3.5-in guns
20 × 37-mm guns
16 × 20-mm guns

Machinery:
4 Belluzzo geared turbines, 134,616 shp
4 shafts
30 knots

Armour:
Belt ....up to 13.8 in
Decks ....up to 8.1 in
Barbettes ....13.8 in

Above: Vittorio Veneto *in the splinter pattern camouflage she wore in 1943 during the voyage to Malta. She was lucky to survive a hit from a German radio-controlled bomb during the Luftwaffe attacks. Her sistership* Roma *was not so fortunate.*

Turret .... up to 13.8 in
Secondary turrets ......up to 5.9 in

Right: Littorio *ready for sea trials in December 1939. She still lacks her 90-mm aircraft armament guns, fire control systems and catapult.*

Above: The dramatic bow view presented by the Littorios, with 90-mm anti-aircraft guns elevated and splinter pattern applied.

Below: Aerial recognition markings were intended to identify Italian warships to their own air force. Veneto carried these red and white stripes during 1942.

Right: On its high barbette, the aft 15-in turret loomed over the quarterdeck. This was intended to protect the aircraft from blast damage when the main armament was fired.

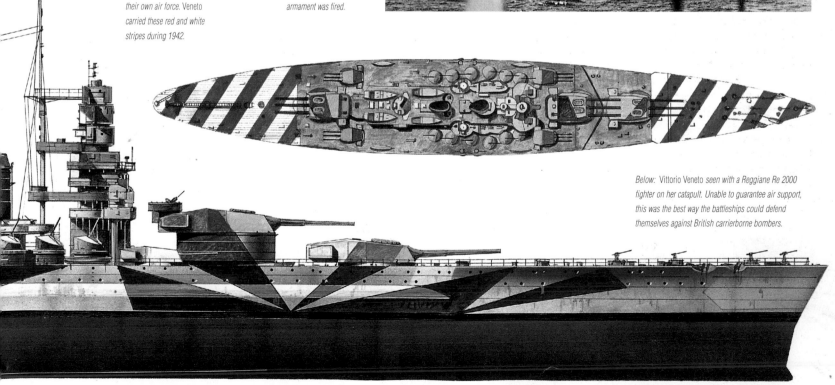

Below: Vittorio Veneto *seen with a Reggiane Re 2000 fighter on her catapult. Unable to guarantee air support, this was the best way the battleships could defend themselves against British carrierborne bombers.*

Japan

The Imperial Japanese Navy

Left: Camera teams at work on the quarterdeck of one of the Fuso class battleships during gunnery training. Although built in Japan, early Japanese dreadnoughts relied on imported British and US engines, armour and guns.

Right: USS Ticonderoga burns after being hit by a kamikaze aircraft off Formosa. Unable to admit defeat by 1945, the Japanese resorted to suicide tactics with both aircraft and warships.

Left: The Russian battleship Peresviet at Port Arthur in 1905. Japan's victory stunned the World.

Two years before Germany embarked on its infamous 1898 naval programme, the challenge to British maritime power that led ultimately to World War I, an arms race had begun in the Far East. In 1896 Japan declared a ten year expansion programme, intended to challenge Russian influence in China and Korea. The fruits of Japan's 1895 victory over China had been denied by Russia (with the support of France) and Port Arthur turned into a Russian naval base that could dominate the Yellow Sea.

Japan transformed itself from a virtually medieval state to a modern industrial power in the space of only four decades. British naval advisors were invited to Japan in the 1870s. Who better to advise a newly-created fleet than the world's premier naval power? In 1902, Britain signed a treaty of mutual defence with its new-found friend, enabling more British units to be concentrated in home waters to meet the threat from Germany.

The navy with which Japan defeated Russia in 1904–5 was based around six battleships and nine armoured cruisers. All the battleships and five of the cruisers were British-built.

However, Japan was not content to import her armaments indefinitely. Japanese companies began to manufacture modern armour plate, boilers, engine parts and heavy artillery. Japanese shipyards had already built several light cruisers and in May 1905, two weeks before Admiral Togo defeated the Russian fleet at Tsushima, the Kure Navy Yard laid down its first battleship.

In the night of 8 February 1904, the Japanese navy launched a surprise attack on the Russian base at Port Arthur. The material damage was not great, despite hits on two of the seven Russian battleships in the harbour.

However, it delayed the Russian response sufficiently for the Japanese to land in Korea. While the Japanese and Russian armies clashed in Manchuria, Japanese forces were able to invest Port Arthur and it was only a matter of time before the Russian fleet's anchorage would be within the range of the Japanese army's siege guns. The first Russian sortie ended in disaster, the Russian flagship *Petropavlovsk* hit a mine and sank; but in May two of Japan's six battleships were lost on a minefield outside Port Arthur. Fortunately for the Japanese, the Russians did not realise that they now enjoyed a 6:4 advantage and they

did not risk a fleet action until the progress of the siege left them no choice. On 10 August, the Russians broke out, fought an indecisive gunnery duel which left most of their battleships damaged, and returned to Port Arthur where they were duly sunk by Japanese howitzers a few months later.

The destruction of the Russian Baltic fleet the following May was regarded at the time as a twentieth century Trafalagar. The enemy had not just been beaten, but annihilated. Admiral Togo had led his fleet into battle, flying a consciously Nelsonic flag signal. 'The fate of our Empire rests on this action. Let every man do his utmost.' Subsequent triumphalism disguised the fact that the Japanese had scored lucky hits in most of the naval actions of the war, that Togo's fleet nearly failed to intercept the Russians at Tsushima and that the Russian navy's leadership had been poor since the death of Makarov aboard the *Petropavlovsk*.

In accordance with its treaty obligations, and scenting rich pickings in German colonial possessions, Japan

Above: Japan's run of victories came to a sudden end in June 1942 at the battle of Midway. Here the fleet carrier Hiryu blazes out of control.

declared war on Germany on 23 August 1914. An ultimatum the week previously, demanding the immediate surrender of Kiao-chau had been rejected by the Germans. Japanese and British warships landed a joint expeditionary force to besiege the German naval base at Tsingtao, China, and Japanese cruisers sailed in search of the German East Asiatic squadron which fled to the south Pacific and thence to its destruction off the Falkland islands. Japanese destroyers served in the Mediterranean in 1917.

The proportion of foreign parts in Japan's dreadnought battleships steadily diminished as Mitsubishi and Kawasaki obtained licenses to build British and American turbines. British influence in Japanese battleship design was still strong: compare the Nagato class to the Queen Elizabeths. However, Japan's ambitious plans for a post-war fleet were soon checked. The USA opposed the Japanese advance into Russia during the Allied intervention against the Bolsheviks, and soon transferred most of its battleships to the Pacific. Japan's

bloated naval budget already consumed some thirty per cent of GNP and a renewed naval race was politically and economically impossible.

In the wake of the 1929 economic crisis, the reins of power were seized by the most bellicose nationalist elements of the Japanese army. Preparations for the anticipated war with the western powers involved the most comprehensive modernisation of Japan's dreadnought fleet, turning them into fast battleships with a high degree of vertical protection. New construction was planned under cover of the strictest secrecy. Japan withdrew from the 1936 London Naval

Conference, already set on the construction of four Yamato class battleships that would be the largest ever built. If Japan could not outbuild the US in quantity, it was hoped that these gigantic battleships would achieve such a qualitative advantage that a successful fleet action would still be possible.

The Japanese battleships of World War II carried the most powerful guns ever taken to sea and their armour protection was the result of exhaustive gunnery tests against the incomplete Tosa class battleship hull. Their optical range-finding equipment was good and the training of their personnel,

especially for night-fighting was brutally effective. However, Japanese radar was in its infancy: the sets fitted to Japanese battleships in 1944 were primitive and unreliable. An almost wilful neglect of anti-submarine technology and tactics led to the annihilation of the Japanese merchant fleet and thus a critical shortage of (imported) fuel oil for the warships.

The Yamato was completed on 16 December 1941, a week after Japanese land-based aircraft had sunk Prince of Wales and Repulse off Malaya. These were not taken by surprise at anchor, but manoeuvring in the open sea, but it made no difference. Husbanded for the climactic surface action that never came, the world's greatest battleships spent most of their time at Truk lagoon while aircraft carriers dictated the pattern of the war. Ironically, in the Leyte Gulf actions in 1944, the largest naval engagement in history, the giants were driven off by air attack with the loss of Musashi, and it fell to the two modernised Fusos to fight and lose the last action between battleships in Surigao strait.

Battleships of the 20th Century

Fuji class

The acquisition by China of two German-built battleships in 1885 led the Japanese navy to trump them with two far superior British-built predreadnoughts, based on the design of the Royal Sovereign class. In the event, Japan disposed of the Chinese 'threat' before the two Fuji class were even launched: one of the Chinese ships was sunk by torpedo boats, and the other one was captured. Constructed by Armstrong Whitworth and the Thames Iron Works respectively, the *Yashima* and *Fuji* were laid down in 1894, launched in 1896 and commissioned in 1897. It is instructive to compare these building times with the work of contemporary French and Italian yards.

The Japanese adopted the Armstrong 12-inch 40 calibre gun for their main armament: a more powerful weapon than the lower velocity 13.5-inch of the Royal Sovereigns. The secondary armament consisted of ten 6-inch guns, four in casemates and six behind shields on the upper deck. One 18-inch torpedo tube was fitted in the bow, with four more submerged tubes located below the main turrets. These could not be operated at speeds above 14 knots. Anti-torpedo boat armament originally consisted of 3-pdr guns, but these were replaced by 12-pdrs in 1901 apart from four in the fighting tops.

Yashima was an early casualty in the Russo-Japanese war, foundering after striking a mine off Port Arthur on 15 May 1904. The Japanese endeavoured to get her back to Sasebo, but she capsized under tow. *Fuji* took part in the battle of Tsushima and served in World War I. Disarmed for use as a training ship in the 1920s, she was sunk by air attack in July 1945 and scrapped in 1948.

Fuji class data

Displacement, standard	12,320 tons
Displacement, full load	12,533 tons
Length overall	412 feet (125.5 m)
Beam	73 feet 9 in (22.4 m)
Design draught	26 feet 6 in (8 m)
Complement	637

Class: *Fuji, Yashima*

Armament:
4 × 12-in guns (2 × 2)
14 × 6-in guns
20 × 12-pdr guns
4 × 3-pdr guns
5 × 18-in torpedo tubes

Machinery:
Triple expansion steam engines, 14,500 ihp
2 shafts
18 knots

Armour: (Compound)

Belt	18 in
Deck	2.5 in
Barbettes	9–14 in
Casemates	up to 6 in
Conning tower	up to 14 in

Shikishima class

In 1896 the Japanese government ordered an ambitious Ten Year Naval Expansion Programme, designed to provide the Imperial navy with a powerful squadron of capital ships to complement its cruiser and torpedo boat forces. While Japanese shipyards were expanded, the two Shikishimas were ordered from Britain.

Designed by G.C. Macrow, the basic layout followed that of the Royal Navy's Majestic class. Armed like the preceding Fujis, their machinery was similar too. An interesting development was the provision of 261 watertight compartments and a double bottom amidships. Extra protection was added by the type of curved armour deck pioneered in the *Renown*: the curved deck started at the lower edges of the belt and sloped upwards, rather than resting flat on the top of the belt. This afforded greater protection against plunging fire, which would have to penetrate the belt and the deck before reaching the machinery and magazines.

Shikishima took part in the blockade of Port Arthur in 1904, and fought at the Battles of the Yellow Sea and Tsushima. In 1921 she was reclassified as a coast defence vessel, and disarmed and stripped of her machinery two years later. She survived as a training ship until the end of World War II when she was scrapped.

Hatsuse was built by Armstrong Whitworth at Elswick and completed in 1901. She was with the battle squadron when it ran into a minefield off Port Arthur on 15 May 1904. Like the similarly-damaged *Yashima*, *Hatsuse* was taken under tow, but she struck a second mine which touched off her magazine.

Asahi differed from her sisterships by only having two funnels. Internally, the subdivision was more extensive with 288 watertight compartments. Slightly damaged by grounding on Southsea beach on her way to Japan, she took part in the Russo-Japanese war. She survived serious damage from a mine in October 1904 but was repaired in time for Tsushima. Used as a training ship after World War I, in 1938 she

Above: Asahi *differed from the other two* Shikishimas *in only having two funnels. She was built at Clydebank from 1898-1900.*

was converted to a repair ship capable of some 12 knots. In May 1942, she was torpedoed and sunk by the US submarine *Salmon* off the Vietnamese coast.

Shikishima class data:

Displacement, standard	14,850 tons
Displacement, full load	15,453 tons
Length overall	438 feet (133.5 m)
Beam	75 feet 6 in (23 m)
Design draught	27 feet 6 in (8.38 m)
Complement	836

Class: *Hatsuse, Shikishima, Asahi*

Armament:
4 × 12-in guns (2 × 2)
14 × 6-in guns
20 × 12-pdr guns
6 × 3-pdr guns
5 × 18-in torpedo tubes

Machinery:
Triple expansion steam engines, 14,500 ihp
2 shafts
18 knots

Armour: (Harvey nickel steel)

Belt ....9 in
Upper belt ....6 in
Deck ....up to 4 in
Barbettes ....up to 14 in
Casemates ....up to 6 in
Conning tower............up to 14 in

Right: Fuji was built at the Thames Iron Works, Poplar and survived until 1945.

Kashima class

Japan continued to buy battleships from British yards during the Russo-Japanese war. The two Kashimas followed the trend towards heavier secondary armament pioneered by the King Edward VII class. Whereas the British added four 9.2-inch guns to complement the four 12-inch guns of the main armament, the Japanese opted for four 10-inch guns. The 6-inch battery was increased from ten to twelve guns, but armour was slightly reduced to compensate. In every respect, the Kashimas were the final expression of the predreadnought battleship design. The guns could be loaded at any angle of traverse, and could be manoeuvred electrically or hydraulically, or even by hand. During eight hours of full power steaming on trials, *Kashima* topped 19 knots and *Katori* registered 20.2.

After service during World War I, both were scrapped in the 1920s.

Kashima class data:

Displacement, standard ....15,950 tons
Displacement, full load.................16,663 tons
Length overall ....456 feet 3 in (139.08 m)
Beam ....78 feet (23.77 m)
Design draught ....27 feet (8.23 m)
Complement 980

Class: *Kashima, Katori*

Armament:
4 × 12-in guns
4 × 10-in guns
12 × 6-in guns
14 × 3-in guns
5 × 18-in torpedo tubes

Machinery:
Triple expansion steam engines, 15,600 ihp
2 shafts
18.5 knots

Armour:
Belt ....9 in
Turrets ....9 in
10-in gun turrets ....8 in
Conning tower...........9 in
Barbettes ....5–12 in

Above: Katori was built by Armstrong Vickers: compare her to the King Edward VII class battleship Hibernia on page 65. Both carried an intermediate calibre secondary battery.

Battleships of the 20th Century

Mikasa class

The *Mikasa* was the last battleship laid down under the 1896 Ten Year Naval Expansion programme. The design was very similar to the *Asahi*, but much better protected because of the use of KC (Krupp Cemented) armour rather than Harvey nickel steel. Main armament was unchanged from the preceding classes, with four 12-inch Armstrong guns. The secondary battery was also the same, but was better protected: ten of the 6-inch guns were placed in a main-deck battery rather than in upper-deck casemates. The battery was also protected from end-on fire by an extension of the bulkhead armour upwards to the upper deck.

Mikasa flew the flag of Vice-Admiral Togo during the Russo-Japanese war. She was hit at the battle off Port Arthur in February 1904 and badly damaged during the battle of the Yellow Sea in August, suffering 32 dead and 78 wounded from at least four heavy shells. At Tsushima, she suffered six hits from heavy shell and her upperworks were peppered with splinters and light calibre hits. In September 1905 *Mikasa* sank as a result of a magazine explosion whilst at anchor at Sasebo, but was refloated in August 1906. In 1921 she was reclassified as a coast defence ship but retired in 1923 to become a national monument at Yokosuka. *Mikasa* remains the last surviving battleship of her era.

Mikasa class data:

Displacement, standard ....15,140 tons
Displacement, full load...................15,179 tons
Length overall ....432 feet (131.7 m)
Beam ....76 feet (23.23 m)
Design draught ....27 feet (8.28 m)
Complement 830

Class: *Mikasa*

Armament:
4 × 12-in guns (2 × 2)
14 × 6-in guns
20 × 12-pdr guns
8 × 3-pdr guns
4 × 2.5-pdr guns
4 × 18-in torpedo tubes

Machinery:
Triple expansion steam engines, 15,000 ihp
2 shafts
18 knots

Armour:
Belt ....9 in
Upper belt ....6 in
Bulkheads ....12 in
Deck ....up to 3 in
Barbettes ....up to 14 in
Casemates ....up to 6 in

Satsuma class

Satsuma was the first battleship to be built in Japan. Laid down before Dreadnought and intended to carry twelve 12-inch guns, she should have been completed as the world's first all big gun battleship. However, there were not enough Armstrong 1904 pattern 12-inch guns available and 10-inch guns had to be substituted for all but four of the weapons. Thus it was that future all big gun capital ships were to be called 'dreadnoughts' and not 'satsumas'. Nevertheless, this Japanese-designed and built battleship was the largest warship in the world the time of her launch in November 1906.

The original armament layout was for 12-inch twin turrets on the centre line fore and aft, plus another four 12-inch guns on each beam in one twin and two single turrets. In the event, three twin 10-inch turrets were mounted on either beam. Twelve 4.7-inch quick-firers were mounted singly in casemates, although their value in a seaway was dubious.

While *Satsuma* was powered by the usual reciprocating engines, *Aki* had American turbines fitted and was capable of 20 knots. She had three funnels to her sister's two.

These fast predreadnoughts deployed in the hunt for the German East Asiatic squadron in 1914, but Admiral von Spee wisely withdrew from the north Pacific and they did not see action. Both were expended as targets after World War I.

Satsuma class data:

Displacement, standard ....19,372 tons
Displacement, full load...................19,700 tons
Length overall ....482 feet (146.91 m)
Beam ....83 feet 6 in (25.5 m)
Design draught..........27 feet 6 in (8.38 m) mean
Complement 887

Class: *Satsuma, Aki*
Completed 1911 and 1909

Armament:
4 × 12-in guns (2 × 2)
12 × 10-in guns (6 × 2)
12 × 4.7-in guns (*Aki* 8 × 6-in)
4 × 3-in guns (*Aki* 12 × 3-in)
5 × 18-in torpedo tubes

Machinery:
Satsuma:
Triple expansion engines, 17,300 ihp
Two shafts
18.5 knots
Aki:
Two Curtis turbines, 24,000 shp
20 knots

Armour:
Belt ....9 in
Upper belt ....7 in
Belt ends ....up to 6 in
Deck ....2 in
Turrets ....up to 9 in
Secondary turrets ......7 in
Battery ....5 in

Kawachi class

Although the Satsumas were Japanese-built, most of the parts were imported from Britain. With the two Settsu class, Japanese shipbuilding took another step forward. They were proper dreadnoughts and only 20 per cent of the parts were imported. The twelve 12-inch guns were arranged in the same way as the German Helgolands, two turrets fore and aft and two on either beam. However, financial problems forced the Japanese to use two different 12-inch guns on the same class of ship. The four beam turrets carried the usual Armstrong 1904 pattern 12-inch 45 calibre gun, but the fore and aft turrets had barrels 50 calibres long. Trajectory was thus different, and performance at longer ranges conspicuously so. The ships were probably restricted to firing 4-gun salvos from wing and centreline turrets in turn.

In July 1918, an explosion in the magazine sank *Kawachi* in Tokuyama Bay with the loss of some 700 men. This was not the only Japanese warship to be lost to British-style propellant charges with their unfortunate safety record. *Settsu* was used as a radio-controlled target ship, armoured to survive 8-inch gunfire and 30 kg training bombs. At Kure in July 1945, she was damaged by US aircraft and had to be beached. She was broken up in 1947.

Kawachi class data:

Displacement, standard ....20,823 tons
Length overall ....526 feet (160.32 m)
Beam................................84 feet 3 in (25.68 m)
Design draught ....27 feet (8.2 m)
Complement 999

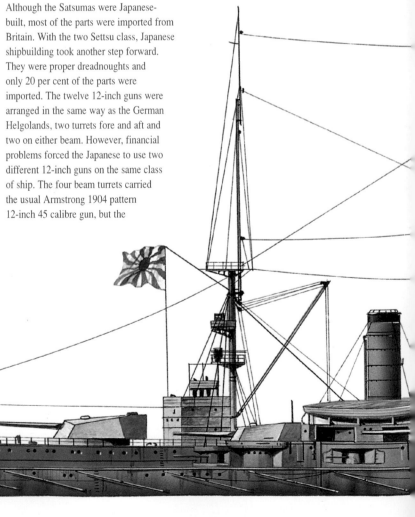

Class: *Kawachi, Settsu*
Completed 1912

Armament:
12 × 12-in guns (6 × 2)
10 × 6-in guns
8 × 4.7-in guns
12 × 3-in guns
5 × 18-in torpedo tubes

Machinery:
2 Curtis turbines, 25,000 shp
2 shafts
20 knots

Armour:
Belt .... 12 in
Turrets .... 11 in
Casemates .... 6 in
Deck .... 2 in
Conning tower .... 10 in

Right: Settsu *as converted to a target ship. She was steered remotely, via radio signals from the destroyer* Yakaze. *The pilots who attacked Pearl Harbor trained against her with practice bombs.*

Right: Mikasa *was Admiral Togo's flagship at the battle of Tsushima. She is the only surviving predreadnought battleship, preserved at Yokosaka as a national monument since 1923.*

Left: Satsuma *was the first battleship built in Japan. Laid down at Kure five months before HMS* Dreadnought, *she was originally intended to be armed with twelve 12-in guns.*

Kongo class

Although Japan was now able to construct capital ships in her own yards, developments in Britain were closely monitored. When Japan decided to build its first battlecruiser, the lead ship was ordered from Vickers. Designed by Sir George Thurston as a modified version of the battleship he built for Turkey (*Reshadieh*, later taken over by the British as HMS *Erin*), *Kongo* was followed by three Japanese-built ships.

Kongo was a great improvement over the British Lion class battlecruisers, both in terms of protection and firepower. The 8 inch by 12.5 feet deep main belt, running from the 'A' turret barbette to that of 'Y' turret, and the 6-inch upper belt extending up to the forecastle deck were closed by bulkheads fore and aft to form a central citadel. Internal compartmentation was extensive. *Kongo* was the first warship to carry a 14-in main armament. The turret and machinery layouts were superior to the Lions and the influence can be seen in the next British battlecruiser *Tiger*.

In 1917, *Haruna* was damaged on a mine in the south Pacific, probably laid by the German raider *Wolf*. All but *Hiei* were modernised at the end of the 1920s, *Hiei* being demilitarised as a training ship due to the Treaty of London in 1930. However, she joined her sisters in a second, radical bout of reconstruction during the 1930s. The Kongos emerged as fast battleships, destined to play a major role in the war in the Pacific. Length was increased by 26 feet aft; funnels were reduced from three to two; armour weight rose from 6,500 tons to over 10,000 tons with horizontal protection substantially improved. Towering 'Pagoda' foremasts were added, torpedo tubes were removed, and new engines and boilers increased their speed to 30 knots. Normal displacement rose to 31,720 tons.

The elevation of the 14-inch guns was increased to 43 degrees.

All four Kongos were lost in action. *Hiei* and *Kirishima* were sunk off Guadalcanal in November 1942. *Kongo* was sunk by the US submarine *Sealion* off Formosa, 21 November 1944. *Haruna*, despite acquiring about 100 25-mm anti-aircraft guns was sunk by US aircraft off Kure in July 1945.

Kongo class data:

As built:

Displacement, standard	27,500 tons
Displacement, full load	32,200 tons
Length overall	704 feet (214.58 m)
Beam	92 feet (28.04 m)
Design draught	27 feet 6 in (8.38 m)
Complement	1,221

Armament:
8 × 14-in guns (4 × 2)
16 × 6-in guns
16 × 3-in guns
8 × 21-in torpedo tubes

Machinery:
4 Parsons turbines, 64,000 shp
4 shafts
27.5 knots

Armour:

Belt	8 in
Turrets	9 in
Barbettes	10 in
Battery	6 in
Bulkheads	up to 9 in
Decks	2.75 in

As reconstructed:

Displacement, standard	31,720 tons
Displacement, full load	36,600 tons
Length overall	720 feet 6 in (219.61 m)
Beam	92 feet (28.04 m)
Design draught	31 feet 11 in (9.72 m) max
Complement	1,437

Class: *Hiei, Karuna, Kirishima, Kongo*
Completed 1912–15

Armament:
8 × 14-in guns (4 × 2)
14 × 6-in guns
8 × 5-in guns
4 × 40-mm guns
Up to 100 × 25-mm guns
(*Kongo* and *Haruna* 1944)

Machinery:
4 Parsons turbines, 136,000 shp
4 shafts
30.5 knots

Armour:

Belt	8 in
Turrets-	9 in
Barbettes	10 in
Battery	6 in
Bulkheads	up to 9 in
Decks	4.7 in

'Ironbottom Sound'

In early 1942 the Japanese navy landed troops on the island of Guadalcanal in the eastern Solomons, and established a seaplane base in the splendid anchorage of Tulagi on nearby Florida island. Construction teams began to build an airfield on Guadalcanal itself. If they had been able to complete it, Japanese aircraft would have able to menace communications between Australia and the USA, but in August the 1st division of the US Marine Corps landed on both Guadalcanal and neighbouring Tulagi. The American counter-offensive in the Pacific had begun.

Only ten days after the US landings, Rear-Admiral Raizo Tanaka landed 1000 Japanese troops from six destroyers that steamed down 'the slot' of the Solomons chain during the night. His operations were always timed to clear Guadalcanal well before dawn, so his squadron was out of range of the US aircraft

now based on the island. The 'Tokyo Express' as it was dubbed, continued to land troops and supplies for the next three months as the land battle for Guadalcanal intensified. Unfortunately for the Japanese, the navy underestimated the number of US troops ashore, and the Japanese army was reluctant to divert reinforcements from its offensive in New Guinea. Japanese forces on the island were actually outnumbered by the Americans they were trying to eject.

Despite regular attacks from Japanese bombers based at Rabaul, the 'Cactus Air Force' flying from the newly-christened Henderson Field dominated the waters around Guadalcanal by day. Successive Japanese army attacks failed with appalling losses exacerbated by the unforgiving climate and inadequate medical support. Casualties were also heavy in frequent night actions off the island; the waters between Savo and Guadalcanal being dubbed 'Ironbottom Sound'.

Henderson Field was the key to the campaign, and in November the Japanese navy despatched two Kongo class battlecruisers to bombard the airfield. *Hiei* and *Kirishima*, supported by a light cruiser and six destroyers passed Savo island at 1.00 am on 13 November. Patrolling the sound were five US cruisers with four destroyers ahead and four more astern. USS *Helena* detected the Japanese on radar, but the Japanese navy's intensive training in night-fighting paid off as usual. The US commander, Rear-Admiral Daniel J Callaghan died aboard the *San Francisco*, which was lucky to survive a hail of 14-inch gunfire and torpedoes. Four US destroyers and the cruiser *Juneau* were sunk. But the Japanese battlecruisers' armour was vulnerable to 8-inch gunfire in the sort of point blank range melee that

Top: Haruna *seen in 1934, on trials after her reconstruction. Note the 'Pagoda' foremast.*

Above: Kirishima *was sunk off Guadalcanal in action with* South Dakota *and* Washington.

followed. *Kirishima* escaped serious damage, but *Hiei* was struck by an estimated fifty 5-inch and 8-inch rounds and discovered just a few miles north of Savo island in the morning. US aircraft sank her with four torpedo hits.

Kirishima returned the next night, with three cruisers and six destroyers; another cruiser and two destroyers probed ahead to locate the US patrols. Admiral Lee's Task Force 64 detected the Japanese on radar and the battleships *South Dakota* and *Washington* prepared for action. *South Dakota's* secondary armament opened fire with starshell, to illuminate the enemy for her 16-inch guns, but her electrical power systems malfunctioned, closing down her radar and leaving her weapons silent. *Kirishima* opened fire immediately, but failed to see the *Washington*, which overwhelmed the battlecruiser in a few minutes' rapid fire.

The battlecruiser concept 'speed is armour' made sense in theory: with a substantial speed advantage, they could control the range of an action, and destroy hostile cruisers from beyond the reach of cruiser armament. However, as in World War I, the battlecruisers' size and battleship armament inevitably led them to be used as battleships. The Kongos' speed enabled them to join cruiser forays to Guadalcanal with every chance of getting out of aircraft range beyond dawn. But at 3000 yards, even their 8-inch armour belt could be penetrated by the guns of the US cruisers.

After the loss of *Hiei* and *Kirishima*, the Japanese refused to hazard any more capital ships off Guadalcanal. Destroyers shuttled in supplies and eventually took off the surviving soldiers when the campaign was abandoned in February 1943.

Fuso class

Laid down in 1912–13, with two further ships in the class planned, the Fusos out-gunned the US Navy's *Texas* and *Oklahoma* and matched the Pennsylvanias. They were also appreciably faster, their American turbines giving a top speed of over 22 knots. However, they were less well protected, their main armament in twin turrets throughout, entailing much greater length.

The Fuso class were armed with Japanese-made 14-inch guns, disposed in an unusual manner: the third turret was carried at forecastle deck level between the funnels and the fourth turret abaft the second funnel, one deck higher. The secondary armament was entirely conventional: sixteen 6-inch guns in casemates at main deck level.

In a 1927–28 refit the Fusos were given rebuilt foremasts and 2×3.1-inch anti-aircraft guns were added. Both were extensively rebuilt in the early 1930s, with imposing 'Pagoda' type fore masts replacing the fore funnel and improved deck and underwater protection. Armour weight increased from 8,588 tons to 12,199 tons; and hulls lengthened aft to 698 feet overall. New machinery was fitted: 4-shaft Kampon geared turbines replaced the Brown-Curtis ones and six

they had been part of the Aleutians diversionary force, it was proposed to convert the Fusos to battleship-carriers like *Ise* and *Hyuga*, but the plan was abandoned after the catastrophic losses of aircraft and pilots in the Battle of the Philippine Sea, June 1944. Both *Fuso* and *Yamashiro* were sunk during the last action in which battleship fired on battleship in Surigao Strait, Leyte Gulf, on 25 October 1944.

Fuso class data:

Displacement, standard	30,600 tons
Displacement, full load	35,900 tons
Length overall	673 feet (205.1 m)
Beam	94 feet (28.65 m)
Design draught	28 feet 3 in (8.6 m)
Complement	1,193

Class: *Fuso, Yamashiro*
Completed 1915–17

Armament:
12 × 14-in guns (6 × 2)
16 × 6-in guns
4 × 3.1-in guns
6 × 21-in torpedo tubes

Below: Fuso as she was completed in 1915. Note that the third turret is at forecastle deck level, with the fourth and fifth turrets one deck higher.

Above: Fuso in dock at Kure Navy Yard, April 1933, after the completion of her first reconstruction. The towering 'Pagoda' bridge structure became a distinctive feature of the modernised Japanese battleships.

oil-fired boilers replaced 24 coal-fired ones to provide 75,000 shp at 24.77 knots and increased radius to 11,000 miles. *Yamashiro* had been used to test the first Japanese flying-off platform and both were fitted for three aircraft during the first refit.

Too slow to support the aircraft carriers, the Fusos spent much of their time in home waters during World War II and never acquired the massed anti-aircraft guns fitted to other Japanese battleships. After the US victory at Midway, during which

Machinery:
4 Brown-Curtis turbines, 40,000 shp
4 shafts
22 knots

Armour:
Belt and bulkheads	12 in
Turrets	12 in
Barbettes	8 in
Casemates	6 in
Deck	up to 2 in
Conning tower	13.75 in

Surigao Strait: the last battleship fight

On 20 October 1944, US forces landed in the Philippines. The Japanese riposte was to concentrate all available naval units for one final battle, in the vain hope that they could reverse the course of the war. The plan was code-named operation *Sho* (victory). After all, as vice-Admiral Kurita remarked, 'there are such things as miracles'. Although the Combined Fleet could still muster a very powerful surface group, including the two Yamato class battleships, there was no air cover. Three months earlier, the Japanese carrier force had been destroyed in the Philippine sea when its novice pilots, flying obsolete aircraft had been defeated so rapidly, it became known as 'the great Marianas turkey shoot'. Next, the Japanese air force units on Formosa and the Philippines were wiped out by the US carrier fleets. To round-off the disaster, most of the fleet's scouting aircraft had been sent forward to join the 5th Air Force on the Philippines and had already been destroyed before Operation *Sho* began. The battle fleet was blind.

Operation *Sho* involved a complex series of manoeuvres by widely separated forces in the usual tradition of the Japanese navy during World War II. In essence, three

surface groups were to attack from the west of the Philippines while the surviving Japanese carrier fleet, including the two hybrid battleship/carriers *Ise* and *Hyuga* approached from the east. The carriers were nothing more than bait: they were almost empty of aircraft, but since they had always been the prime objective of their US counterparts, it was

Below: *After her final reconstruction, the Fuso's profile is dominated by the new bridge structure. The six centreline turrets divide the superstructure into three distinct masses. The floatplane on the third turret is a Nakajima Type 95.*

hoped that Admiral Ozawa could lure the US carriers into a separate fight, leaving the way clear for the battleships to attack the amphibious forces off the beachheads.

Admiral Kurita's squadron included the battleships *Yamato*, *Musashi* and *Nagato* plus the battlecruisers *Kongo* and *Haruna*. *Musashi* succumbed to air attack, but the others attacked US escort carriers off Samar, after the main US carrier force chased after Ozawa, accompanied by Admiral Lee's fast battleship squadron.

Meanwhile, *Fuso* and *Yamashiro* led Admiral Nashimura's squadron into the Surigao strait. This was guarded by TF77.2: six older battleships assigned to provide gunfire support for the landings. The squadron was commanded by Rear-Admiral Jesse B Oldendorf, flying his flag in the

Above: *Fuso's new turbines delivered nearly twice the power of her old ones, increasing her speed by three knots despite her increased dimensions. The catapult was moved from 'C' turret to the quarterdeck just before World War II.*

Mississippi; all five others battleships were survivors of Pearl Harbor. The Japanese fought their way up the strait, driving off US PT-boats with their secondary armament, but a destroyer attack hit the *Fuso* twice shortly after 3 am and she lost speed. She limped back into the darkness and sank after about 90 minutes. Although hit by torpedoes *Yamashiro* pressed on. At 03.51, *Tennessee* and *West Virginia* opened fire, followed by *Mississippi* and *Maryland*, their "arched line of tracers in the darkness looked like a continual stream of lighted railroad cars going over a hill" according to one eye-witness. Within minutes she was all but dead in the water, only a few guns still firing. Blazing from stem to stern, she sank after about 30 minutes. There were no survivors.

Ise class

The Ise class were built in private Japanese yards like the Kongos. The design was clearly a development of the Fusos with the main armament layout improved: 'P' and 'Q' turrets were superimposed and sited abaft the boiler rooms. The two funnels were accordingly more closely spaced. Since the 1890s, Japanese battleships had followed the British practice of fitting 6-inch guns as secondary armament: the largest gun for which ammunition could be loaded by hand. The Ise class introduced a new calibre: a 5.5-inch gun of Japanese design. The casemates were farther forward than in the Fusos, although the two foremost guns, beneath the forecastle, were inoperable in a seaway. Armour protection was similar to the Fuso class. The armoured deck sloped down to meet the bottom of the armour belt over the magazines and boilers. Splinter protection was improved. Powered by Curtis turbines, the Ise made 23.6 knots on trials.

Both received aircraft in the 1920s, with flying-off platforms added to 'X' turret. From 1934–6, Hyuga was comprehensively modernised along the same lines as the Fuso class. Ise was similarly reconstructed during 1935–7. Despite the addition of another 3000 tons of armour, the new Japanese powerplant delivered 80,000 shp for a

maximum speed of 25 knots. Two of the 5.5-inch guns and all the torpedoes were landed. Eight 5-inch dual purpose guns were added plus twenty 25-mm anti-aircraft guns.

After the loss of four aircraft carriers at Midway, in June 1942, all manner of measures were suggested to replace them. Eventually, Ise and Hyuga were converted to hybrid battleship-carriers. Work began on Ise in March 1943 and took seven months; Hyuga's conversion took place between July and November. The two after turrets were replaced by a hangar intended to house 22 dive-bombers or seaplanes. A lift was installed in the centre of the deck and catapults fitted to port and starboard, just forward of the flight deck. The flight deck was too short to permit the

aircraft to land, so the seaplanes would be recovered by crane. Ise received a Type 21 radar set, Hyuga a Type 22, both sited atop the bridge structure. The 5.5-inch secondary armament was landed in favour of extra

5-inch dual purpose weapons and a greatly augmented battery of light automatic anti-aircraft guns. Final armament was eight 14-inch, sixteen 5-inch, 57 (later over 100) 25-mm AA. Six 28-barrel 5-inch anti-

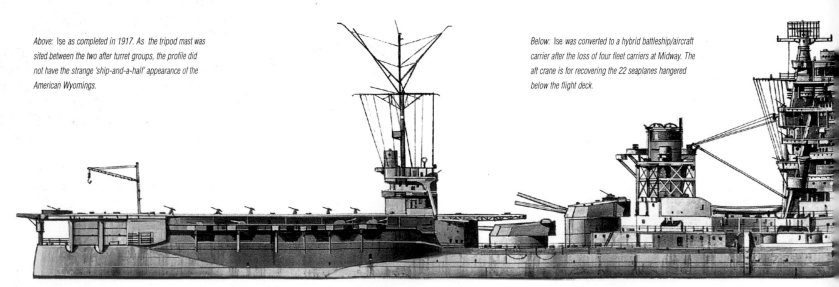

Above: Ise as completed in 1917. As the tripod mast was sited between the two after turret groups, the profile did not have the strange 'ship-and-a-half' appearance of the American Wyomings.

Below: Ise was converted to a hybrid battleship/aircraft carrier after the loss of four fleet carriers at Midway. The aft crane is for recovering the 22 seaplanes hangered below the flight deck.

Left: Ise defends herself against US carrier aircraft with incendiary shrapnel rounds from her forward 14-in guns off Cape Engano.

Right: Ise off Satu Point in August 1943 with an aircraft on her flight deck. When she finally saw action in her new role, there were no aircraft available and she served merely as a decoy.

Below right: Hyuga as she appeared at the end of 1940.

aircraft rocket launchers were added in September 1944.

Ironically, it was decided to remove the catapults in October 1944 to give 'C' and 'D' turrets a better arc of fire. There were no aircraft (or trained pilots) available for these unusual hybrid warships to carry. When they joined Ozawa's aircraft carriers for the battle of Leyte Gulf, they became part of his decoy force which successfully lured away Admiral Halsey and TF38, leaving the invasion beaches open for Kurita's battleships. American air strikes sank all four of the 'proper' aircraft carriers with the Ises, but the hybrid battleship-carriers escaped. Both ended their careers out of fuel at Kure where, in July 1945, they were sunk by air attack.

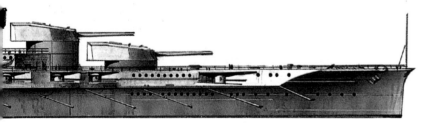

Ise class data:

Displacement, standard ....31,250 tons
Displacement, full load.................36,500 tons
Length overall ....674 feet (205.7 m)
Beam ....94 feet (28.65 m)
Design draught............29 feet 1 in (8.86 m) max
Complement..1,360

Class: Hyuga, Ise
Completed 1917–18

Armament:
12 × 14-in guns (7 × 2)
20 × 5.5-in guns
6 × 21-in torpedo tubes

Machinery:
4 Brown-Curtis turbines, 45,000 shp
4 shafts
23.5 knots

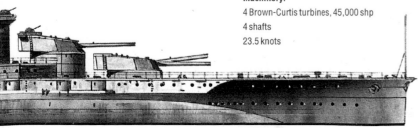

Armour:
Belt ....up to 12 in
Turrets ....up to 12 in
Barbettes ....12 in
Casemates ....6 in
Deck ....up to 2 in
Conning tower............up to 12 in

Above: Ise as she appeared from 1937-43. Together with the two Fuso class battleships, the Ise class formed the second division of the 1st Battlefleet in December 1941.

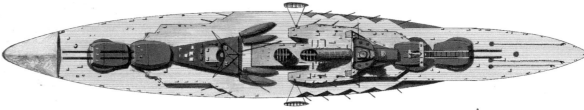

Nagato Class

Within twenty years of ordering their first modern battleships from Great Britain, Japan designed and built a class of battleships superior to any possessed by any of the traditional naval powers. The two units of the Nagato class introduced the 16-inch gun, were extremely well protected, and were even faster than the British 15-inch gun Queen

Top: Nagato on trials. In 1920, she was the most powerful battleship in the world.

Above: Nagato's forecastle deck was swept back to give the maximum arc of fire to 'Y' turret.

Left: Nagato's tripod mast dominated her profile until it vanished beneath the Pagoda style structure added in the early 1930s.

Elizabeth class fast battleships. The hull design was modelled on that of the Ise class, but the Nagatos' eight 16-inch guns delivered the same weight of shell as the *Ise's* twelve 14-inch guns, and the 16-inch shells could penetrate substantially thicker armour. The secondary battery was made up of ten 5.5-inch guns on each beam, seven in casemates along the upper deck and three one deck higher.

The tremendous speed of the Nagatos and their powerful armament was not achieved at the expense of protection, although the 12-inch main belt was no more than equal to that of the previous generation of US and British dreadnoughts. By adopting the 'all or nothing' approach favoured by the US Navy, the Nagatos concentrated their armour where it mattered. The ends were unprotected and there was no upper belt while vertical protection was excellent: the lower deck was armoured and another armoured deck covered the secondary batteries, creating an armoured citadel.

In 1924 the fore funnel was swept aft at the top to divert smoke away from the foremast. From 1934 to 1936 both ships were reconstructed along the same lines as the Fuso and Ise classes, although the Nagatos did not receive new turbines. The distinctive heptapodal mast vanished under a massive

'pagoda' type bridge structure. The stern was extended, increasing length to 737 feet; anti-torpedo bulges increased their beam to 113 feet 6 inches; a triple bottom was provided; and their 21 mixed boilers were replaced by ten oil-fired boilers. *Nagato* made over 25 knots on trials after reconstruction, despite the addition of nearly 3000 tons of extra armour. Decks were now 7 inches thick over the vitals and the barbettes up to 22 inches.

The maximum elevation of the main armament was increased from 30 degrees to 43 degrees, increasing their maximum range from 20,800 yards to 30,480 yards. Two of the 5.5-inch guns were removed, the others were given increased elevation to thirty-five degrees. The 3-inch anti-aircraft guns were removed and four twin 5-inch anti-aircraft turrets and ten twin 25-mm mounts were added.

In December 1941 *Mutsu* and *Nagato* formed the first division of the 1st Battle Fleet. Like the rest of the battleship force, they played little role in a war dominated by aircraft carriers. On 8 June 1943 *Mutsu* was destroyed by an internal explosion in the Inland Sea.

Below: Nagato as she appeared from 1926–1934. The forefunnel was raked back to clear the foretop and bridge of smoke. The aircraft is a Heinkel HD25 developed specifically for the battleship by Ernst Heinkel.

Shipping an extra 98 25-mm anti-aircraft guns, *Nagato* served as part of the 2nd Carrier Division (the carriers *Hiyo*, *Junyo* and *Ryuho*),during the battle of the Philippine Sea in June 1944. When US divebombers swooped on her charges, the *Nagato* responded with every gun, even firing her 16-inch guns at full elevation! *Hiyo* was sunk, but the others survived. In October, *Nagato* accompanied both the giant Yamato class in the desperate attack at Leyte Gulf. Surviving innumerable air strikes, she engaged the US light carriers before Admiral Kurita ordered his

squadron to withdraw. *Nagato* escaped to Brunei and thence to Japan and was discovered intact at Yokosuka after the surrender.

Nagato was expended as part of the Bikini atoll tests, and her wreck has recently been declared open to divers.

Nagato class data:

Displacement, standard	33,800 tons
Displacement, full load	38,500 tons
Displacement, normal	33,800 tons
Length overall	708 feet (215.8 m)
Beam	95 feet (29 m)
Design draught	29 feet 9 in (9.1 m)
Complement	1,333

Class: *Mutsu, Nagato*
Completed 1920–21

Above: Mutsu in the fitting-out basin at Yokosuka Navy Yard in May 1936. The cause of the explosion that sank her remains unknown.

Armament:
8 × 16-in guns (4 × 2)
20 × 5.5-in guns
4 × 3-in guns
8 × 21-in torpedo tubes

Machinery:
4 Kampon turbines, 80,000 shp
4 shafts
26.7 (later 25) knots

Armour:
Belt	12 in
Decks	up to 3 in
Barbettes	12 in
Turrets	14 in
Casemates	1 in
Conning tower	12 in

Left: Kaga was completed as an aircraft carrier and served with Admiral Nagumo's First Carrier Division until her loss at Midway.

Tosa class

Provided for in the 1918 programme as the second pair of fast battleships in Japan's '8–8' plan, intended to achieve parity with the USA, the two ships of the Tosa class were improved Nagatos but with greater power for a designed 26 knots and an additional twin 16-inch turret. The secondary armament consisted of ten 5.5-inch guns on each beam located in casemates on the upper and forecastle decks. Armour protection was improved, the belt being sloped at 15 degrees to present incoming projectiles with a greater thickness of armour for them to penetrate. *Kaga* and *Tosa* were cancelled by the 1922 Washington Treaty. *Kaga* was converted into an aircraft carrier in 1923. Extensively reconstructed in the mid-1930s, she became one of the best-equipped aircraft carriers in the world, carrying 90 aircraft. She was sunk at Midway by US SBDs. The *Tosa* was expended as a target in 1925, the tests providing useful data for the armour protection installed on the Yamato class battleships.

Tosa class data:

Displacement, standard	39,930 tons
Length overall	768 feet (234.1 m)
Beam	100 feet (30.5 m)
Design draught	30 feet 9 in (11.4 m)
Complement	Not known

Class: *Kaga, Tosa*

Armament:
10 × 16-in guns (5 × 2)
20 × 5.5-in guns
4 × 3.1-in guns
8 × 24-in torpedo tubes

Machinery:
4 Brown-Curtis impulse-reaction turbines, 91,000 shp
12 Kampon boilers
4 shafts
26 knots

Armour:
Belt	11 in
Bulkheads	up to 11 in
Decks	up to 6.3 in
Barbettes	up to 11 in
Conning tower	up to 14 in

Amagi class

The first part of the battlecruiser force envisaged by the '8–8' Programme (eight battleships and eight battlecruisers), the four Amagi class were to have been the battlecruiser equivalents of the *Kagas*. Two were laid down in 1920 and two in 1921. Some 60 feet longer than Tosa and only 1 foot greater in beam, an additional 40,000 shp would propel the more streamlined hull at 30 knots. Unlike the Kagas, the Amagi class would have been flush-decked, with 'Q' turret one deck higher. At over 40,000 tons, they would have been impressive battlecruisers, although their 10-inch armour belt was inferior to the protection adopted by the later German battlecruisers in World War I.

The Washington Treaty led to the cancellation of the class in February 1922. However, it was decided to convert *Amagi*, by then about 40 per cent complete, into an aircraft carrier. Unfortunately, the hull was severely damaged in an earthquake the following year and it had to be scrapped. *Akagi* was completed as an aircraft carrier and was sunk at Midway by US SBDs.

Amagi class data:

Displacement, standard	41,217 tons
Displacement, full load	47,000 tons
Length overall	826 feet 9 in (251.8 m)
Beam	101 feet (30.8 m)
Design draught	31 feet (9.5 m)
Complement	1,600

Class: *Akagi, Amagi, Atago, Takao*

Armament:
10 × 16-in guns (5 × 2)
16 × 5.5-in guns
4 × 4.7-in guns
8 × 24-in torpedo tubes

Machinery:
4 Gijutsu turbines, 131,000 shp
4 shafts
30 knots

Armour:
Belt	10 in
Bulkheads	up to 11 in
Decks	up to 3.9 in
Barbettes	up to 11 in
Turrets	up to 11 in

Japan's '8–8' plan

In 1907 the Japanese government approved a plan to increase the navy's battleship force to two squadrons of eight ships. Such was the pace of technological progress, that it was assumed that a battleship would be in first line service for eight years; after that it could probably serve in the line of battle for the same period again, but would be out of date. New construction would have to build the fleet to this strength, and maintain it by replacing each capital ship after sixteen years. In 1909 Japan ordered the *Kongo* from Vickers, planning to build another three battlecruisers in Japan. Since the Dreadnought revolution rendered all Japan's pre-1907 battleships obsolete, to fulfil the 8–8 plan, the Japanese navy needed four more battlecruisers and eight new battleships. However, government approval was not forthcoming. *Fuso*, Japan's first proper dreadnought, was laid down in 1912, but navy demands for seven new dreadnoughts and another pair of battlecruisers were at first rejected. The government allowed a repeat *Fuso* and the two Ise class and by 1914 was finally prepared to put the 8–8 programme into action.

The USA's 1916 naval expansion programme stimulated Japanese naval building, America having been identified as Japan's most likely enemy immediately after the Russo-Japanese war. Four battleships and two battlecruisers were authorised by the Japanese government during 1916–17, and by 1919 the Japanese navy was becoming still more ambitious. The plan now was 24 battleships in three eight-ship squadrons. The Tosa and Amagi class 16– and 18-inch gun battleships would have formed the first line squadron.

Japan could not afford these grandiose plans in the 1920s, and the compromise at Washington gave her at least as favourable a ratio against the USA as she could ever have achieved by entering a full-scale building race. Massive lay-offs at Mitsubishi and Nagasaki followed, with the latter yard on the verge of bankruptcy by the end of the 1920s. Fortunately for the industry, if not the rest of the world, the war-hungry army officers who were then jockeying for power were supported by an equally strident 'fleet faction' which helped pull Japan out of the League of Nations in 1933 and initiated a new naval race.

Below: Amagi as she would have looked had she been completed as a battleship. With ten 16-in guns, she would have carried the heaviest broadside in the world.

Building the World's biggest battleships

The Japanese navy's war plan against the USA anticipated a succession of air attacks against the US fleet as the Americans steamed to defend the Philippines. The US fleet would then be defeated in a latter day Jutland. Although the Japanese battlefleet might still be outnumbered, its leading division would consist of the four largest battleships ever built, more powerful than any American warship, and able to engage targets beyond the horizon with their 18.1-inch guns.

To achieve this tactical surprise, no hint of the true dimensions of the Yamato class could be allowed to escape. Many navies had fed false information about new warships, some using the pages of *Jane's Fighting Ships* to do so. For instance, before World War I, the British Admiralty had told Jane's that its Invincible class were new armoured cruisers would be armed with 9.2-inch guns like the previous class. Germany retaliated with the *Blücher*, a fine armoured cruiser armed with twelve 8.2-inch guns – and hopelessly outclassed by the Invincibles which actually carried 12-inch guns. However, until the advent of the Yamatos, no navy had managed to conceal the construction of a whole class of battleships.

It was not possible to hide the fact that the Kure and Nagasaki yards were building something. While Kure could be sealed from the outside world, the yards at Nagasaki were visible from the city and the British and American consulates overlooked the slipway. The navy promptly built a storehouse to block

the consulates' view, and erected tall screens of hemp, some 75,000 square metres of it, all around the slipway. Allied intelligence knew the yards were busy, presumably on capital ships, but the unprecedented scale of these warships remained unknown.

Draconian security measures were enforced at both yards. The resident Chinese population at Nagasaki was subjected to successive pogroms to drive them out. The die-hards were simply rounded up and shipped to Shanghai. The Nagasaki design team was not spared either, an entire shift

of engineers were tortured by the secret police after one of the blueprints vanished. Few of them were ever mentally or physically fit enough to return to work after their treatment. A worker who bragged about the size of the warship they were building to his neighbours disappeared into the clutches of the secret police, never to return.

The dimensions of the battleships created new problems. A 430 ton, 1600 horsepower tug, the *Sakufu Maru* had to be specially made to manoeuvre the monstrous hulls once they were in the water. A purpose-built freighter, the *Kashino*, was needed to ferry the *Musashi's* armament from the naval arsenal at Kure to Nagasaki. *Yamato* was constructed in the dry dock at Kure, but the hull of the *Musashi* had to be launched down a slipway. Engineers studied the launch data of other large vessels like the 70,000 ton liner *Queen Mary* and were confident the hull would pass into the water, but there was a real danger it would achieve sufficient momentum to pass right across the harbour and ground on the opposite bank. Even the Germans had made a similar error with the *Gneisenau*, and she was

Above: Yamato, the world's largest battleship, was completed under such exceptional security arrangements that few details of her size and unprecendented armament leaked to the Allies.

half the size of a Yamato. On the day, a system of heavy chains provided enough friction, but the wave created by the hull hitting the water nevertheless flooded the shorefront houses.

Firing tests revealed the 18.1-inch guns to be accurate at extreme range, but the blast effects were phenomenal. Caged guinea pigs placed on deck by way of experiment disintegrated in the shock wave. No-one could afford to be in an exposed position topside if the main armament was fired: something that would assume critical importance when these battleships finally went into action.

The first American to see one of these monsters was probably the skipper of the submarine USS *Skate*, which torpedoed *Yamato* on one of her rare forays outside the Truk lagoon in early 1944. (The torpedo inflicted only minor damage). The remarkable specifications of the Yamato class was not known to the Allies until Japan's surrender.

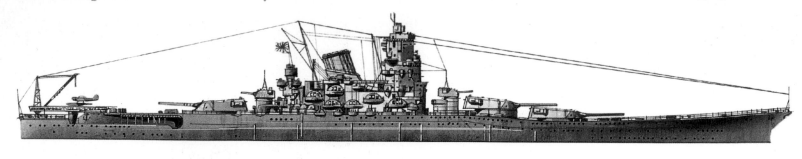

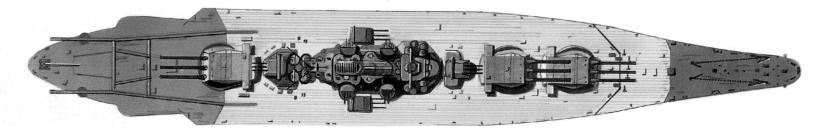

Yamato class

When Japan withdrew from the Second London Naval Conference in 1935, it was due to an unfulfilled demand for what was effectively non-limitation. In truth, she was already working on the design of a super-battleship, so big that any expected American 'reply' would be unable to transit the Panama Canal. At a time when Great Britain was trying to negotiate a reduction of battleship armament to a maximum of 14-inch calibre, the Japanese were developing a 460-mm (18.1-inch) gun. Four 69,000 ton battleships were planned around main batteries of three triple turrets. Each of the three triple 18.1-inch turrets weighed 2,774 tons. Their design was unique, but only six were completed, and all lost with *Yamato* and *Musashi*, so some details are uncertain. The guns fired shells weighing

3,240-lb, with a firing cycle lasting 30–45 seconds. Maximum range was 45,000 yards. Three 49 feet range finders were shipped, and remained more reliable than the fire control radar which was far inferior to those aboard US capital ships.

Yamato and *Musashi* were laid down in 1937. Their four-year building span was conducted under conditions of unprecedented secrecy. Even when completed, they remained an enigma to western intelligence. However, their bottle-shaped hull plan and main battery disposition was remarkably similar to the smaller American South Dakotas, under construction at the same time. The actual secondary armament of just six 6-inch reflected its relative lack of

importance but a full awareness of the menace of air attack was evident from the mass of light automatic weapons festooning the centre citadel.

To maximise protection, her vital machinery was concentrated in a space only slightly more than half her waterline. The armoured deck was designed to defeat a 2,200-lb armour-piercing bomb dropped from 10,000 feet. The main armour belt was angled at 20 degrees and built to withstand an 18-inch shell at 23,000 yards. An anti-torpedo bulkhead sloped down to the outer plates of the double bottom and extended fore and aft beneath the magazines.

Top: Yamato in her final guise, with her midships 6-in turrets removed in favour of extra light anti-aircraft guns.

Above: The bottle-shaped hull of the Yamatos was strangely similar to that of the US South Dakota class.

The third of class, *Shinano*, was completed as an aircraft carrier/transport following the disastrous losses at Midway in 1942. Emergency carrier construction then halted work on the fourth (unnamed) unit, only 30 per cent complete by the end of the war.

Despite being designed to resist air attack, both were overwhelmed by mass air strikes from American carriers. The *Musashi*, sunk during the Leyte Gulf actions, is estimated to have absorbed twenty torpedoes and seventeen bombs. The *Shinano* capsized following a salvo of six simultaneous torpedo hits from an American submarine; she had never entered service. *Yamato* was lost on a one-way suicide mission to attack the invasion beaches on Okinawa. By the time of her destruction, two of her triple 6-inch turrets had been landed in favour of twelve dual purpose 5-in guns and some 150 25-mm anti-aircraft guns.

Yamato class data:

Displacement, standard	68,010 tons
Displacement, full load	71,659 tons
Length overall	862 feet 9 in (263 m)
Beam	121 feet 1 in (36.9 m)
Design draught	34 feet 1 in (10.39 m)
Complement	2,500

Class: *Yamato, Musashi, Shinano*
plus one unnamed

Armament:
9 × 18.1-in guns
12 × 6.1-in guns
12 × 5-in dual purpose guns
24 × 25-mm guns
4 × 13.2-mm guns

Machinery:
4 Kampon geared turbines, 150,000 shp
4 shafts
27 knots

Armour:
Belt	16.1 in
Deck	up to 9.1 in
Barbettes	up to 21.5 in
Turrets	up to 25.6 in
Conning tower	up to 19.7 in
Torpedo bulkhead	up to 11.8 in

Above: Yamato on builder's trials during October 1941. She was commissioned two months later, just a week after Pearl Harbor, and soon became fleet flagship.

Left: One of the giants under air attack during their epic fight across the Sibuyan sea, 24 October 1944. Musashi was sunk before she could engage a single US warship.

Below: Yamato as built. The broad afterdeck allowed for boats to be stowed under cover along both sides. Five floatplanes could be carried in the hanger, transferred via a hatch to the quarterdeck catapult. Note the bulbous bow, the result of tank testing, which helped sustain 27 knots.

Battleship Designs B-64/65

Planned from 1939 as 'Super Type A (heavy) cruisers', the B-64 class ships, to which the hull numbers 795 and 796 were given under the 1942 programme, were essentially battlecruisers. Flush-decked, with an identical armament, funnel and bridge layout, they would have resembled Yamato class battleships. The design was redesignated B-65 in 1941–42 when the original main armament of nine 12.2-inch guns was altered to nine 14.2-inch to counter the American Alaska class battlecruisers (ironically built as an answer to non-existent Japanese 'pocket battleships'). Three aircraft were to have been carried, with a crane and catapult abaft the funnel. None were built as there was obviously no requirement for yet more powerful surface units in a war dominated by airpower. Also cancelled were two improved Yamato class battleships, allocated hull numbers 798 and 799. These monsters were to displace some 70,000 tons, and it was proposed that their main armament consist of six 20-inch guns.

B-64/65 class data:

Displacement, standard	31,495 tons
Displacement, full load	34,800 tons
Length overall	802 feet 6 in (244.6 m)
Beam	89 feet 3 in (27.2 m)
Design draught	28 feet 10 in (8.79 m)
Complement	unknown

Class: *B-64, B-65*

Armament:

(B-64):
- 9 × 12.2-in guns
- 16 × 3.9-in guns
- 8–12 × 25-mm guns
- 4–8 × 13.2-mm guns
- 8 × 24-in torpedo tubes

(B-65):
- 9 × 14.2-in guns
- then as B-64 but no torpedo tubes

Machinery:
- 4 Kampon geared turbines, 160,000 shp
- 4 shafts
- 33 knots

Armour:
Belt	up to 7.5 in
Deck	5 in

Below: The B-64 battleship design

1921 class fast battleships

Designed by Admiral Hiraga, these battleships were numbered 13, 14, 15 and 16, and were to be built by Yokosuka Dockyard, Kure Dockyard, Mitsubishi and Kawasaki, respectively. They would have been the last four of the eight battleships in the '8–8 Programme', and their designation as 'fast battleships' marked the end of the Japanese navy's brief enthusiasm for battlecruisers. Japanese battleships were already marginally faster than those of other powers, and the Nagato class were substantially faster – an advantage Japan managed to conceal until the late 1930s.

The design was similar to the Tosa class, also designed by Admiral Hiraga and were scheduled for completion in 1927. Their main armament was the 1922-pattern 18-inch gun, of which eight were to be shipped in two twin pairs of superfiring turrets. Secondary armament was the usual array of 5.5-inch guns in casemates along the upper deck. All four were cancelled under the terms of the Washington Treaty.

Battleship Design 1921 data:

Displacement, standard	47,500 tons
Displacement, full load	53,000 tons
Length overall	915 feet 4 in (279 m)
Beam	101 feet (30.8 m)
Design draught	32 feet (9.75 m)
Complement	Not known

Class: Never built, no names allocated.

Armament:
- 8 × 18-in guns (4 × 2)
- 16 × 5.5-in guns
- 4 × 4.7-in guns
- 8 × 24-in torpedo tubes

Machinery:
- 4 Gijutsu Honbu turbines, 150,000 shp
- 4 shafts
- 30 knots

Armour:
Belt	13 in
Deck	5 in
Barbettes	up to 11 in
Conning tower	up to 14 in

Battleships Designs 1930

Admiral Hiraga's design for a *Kongo* replacement, showed a compact superstructure with provision for aircraft catapults on 'B' and 'X' turrets and a casemated secondary armament. The unconventional disposition of the 6-inch guns in Fujimoto's design for a *Fuso* replacement was designed to save space in warships already noted for their intolerably Spartan standards of accommodation.

Battleship Design 1930 data:

Displacement, standard:	
(A)	35,000 tons
(B)	35,000 tons

Displacement, full load:	
(A)	39,200 tons
(B)	39,250 tons

Length overall:	
(A)	761 feet 2 in (232 m))
(B)	777 feet 6 in (237 m)

Beam:	
(A)	105 feet 8 in (32.2 m)
(B)	105 feet (32 m)

Design draught:	
(A)	29 feet 6 in (9 m)
(B)	28 feet 6 in (8.7 m)

Complement ... Not known

Armament:
- (A) 10 × 16-in
  - 16 × 6-in
  - 8 × 4.7-in AA
  - 2 × 24-in torpedo tubes
- (B) 9 × 16-in
  - 12 × 6-in
  - 8 × 4.7-in AA

Machinery:
- (A) 4 Kampon turbines
  - 10 boilers
  - 4 shafts
  - 80,000 shp
  - 26.3 knots
- (B) 4 Kampon turbines
  - 4 shafts
  - 73,000 shp
  - 25.9 knots

Armour:

not known

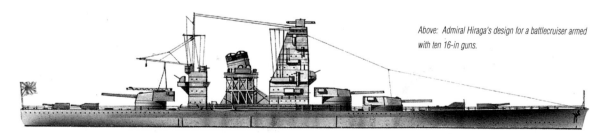

Above: Admiral Hiraga's design for a battlecruiser armed with ten 16-in guns.

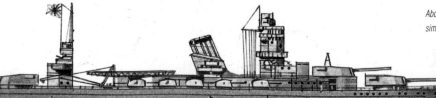

Above: With nine 16-in guns, Fujimoto's design has a similar profile to the Yamatos.

Giants at war

Unlike previous classes of Japanese battleships, the Yamatos did have air conditioning, which made conditions rather more bearable during the long months at Truk during 1943–44. The giants demanded vast quantities of fuel oil to operate at full speed; Japan's growing fuel shortage and the threat from US submarines combined to discourage anything more than dry training at anchor. *Musashi* revealed her sea-keeping qualities in a storm during her melancholy mission back to Japan, returning the ashes of fleet commander Yamamoto, but it was not until October 1944 that these unique warships fired in anger.

The core of the main Japanese surface group at Leyte Gulf (see p73), *Yamato* and *Musashi* crossed the Sibuyan sea on 24 October in company with *Nagato*. A second group, consisting of the battlecruisers *Kongo*, *Haruna* and six heavy cruisers accompanied them, steering for the San Bernadino strait and the American beachheads. Wave after wave of US aircraft attacked the Japanese, but the deck armour of the Yamatos seemed impervious to the dive-bombers. Even torpedoes had no apparent effect, *Musashi* suffering only a momentary loss of speed after her first hit. The use of the battleships' main armament against aircraft, firing incendiary shrapnel was spectacular, but not ultimately successful. The Yamatos' 18.1-inch shrapnel rounds contained 996 incendiary tubes with a combined lethal radius of 397 feet, but the blast damage of firing the guns at full elevation caused all sorts of minor damage and hampered the crews of the hundred or so 25-mm Hotchkiss type automatic weapons firing from around the superstructure.

Musashi was eventually slowed and fell behind, captain Iguchi ordering counter-flooding to check her developing list. Without the support of her consorts, *Musashi* was vulnerable, and the next wave of aircraft concentrated on her. Reduced to 12 knots at 14.30, she survived another four hours of aerial attack until her bows were all but submerged, the water washing past 'A' turret. A last minute attempt to beach her failed and she went down at 19.35 with half her crew still on board and captain Iguchi on his bridge where he had locked himself in after ordering the crew to abandon ship.

To his surprise, Admiral Kurita passed through the San Bernadino strait and emerged off Samar to engage US surface forces. The American carriers had been enticed away by the Japanese carrier fleet, leaving Rear-Admiral Clifton Sprague's escort carriers and accompanying light forces to face the mightiest battleships in the world. At 06.59 on 25 October, *Yamato* finally fired her 18.1-inch guns at an American warship. The escort carriers fled, conscious that their top speed of 17 knots was at least ten knots slower than the pursuing battlecruisers. Their destroyers laid smoke and delivered a torpedo attack that gained time and crippled one of the enemy cruisers. Rain squalls, smoke screens, and the aggressive destroyer tactics held up the Japanese onslaught. By 09.00, *Yamato* had fired 104 salvoes from her big guns, the carrier *Gambier Bay* had been sunk, but American airstrikes sank two Japanese cruisers. Uncertain exactly what he was facing, and unwilling to hazard his ships against more air attacks, Admiral Kurita withdrew.

Just as the defeat at Midway was concealed, the disaster of Leyte Gulf was hidden from the Japanese people as far as possible. Many survivors of the sunken warships, including crewmen from *Musashi* were expended as ground troops on the Philippines. Those brought back to Japan were held in isolation.

Yamato was among the surviving Japanese battleships assembled in Japanese home waters by the spring of 1945. The futility of the mission on which she was sacrificed testifies to the bankruptcy of Japanese strategy. On 1 April, US forces had landed on Okinawa, 400 miles from Japan. *Yamato* was despatched with only enough fuel to reach the island, there to run amok among the invasion force until her inevitable destruction. US Navy Task Force 58 launched 131 torpedo bombers, 75 dive-bombers and 180 fighters when *Yamato* was detected entering the East China Sea, 200 miles short of her target. Nine torpedo hits on the port side caused the battleship to capsize after two hours' fighting. The order was given to abandon ship, the captain lashed himself to the compass and Admiral Ito locked himself in his cabin on the bridge. Only 269 of the more than 3000 men on board were saved.

Left: One of the heavy cruisers accompanying the battleship force turns sharply as US divebombers attack. One survivor of this extraordinary action was the old battlecruiser Kongo.

Below: Yamato *fired 104 salvoes from her 18-in guns when the Japanese battleships engaged US light carriers off Samar. This picture was taken from USS* White Plains *during the action.*

Minor navies

Battleships of the minor navies

With all the world's main naval powers caught up in a race to build dreadnought battleships, the dreadnought type came to represent more than a warship. Powerful military units and engineering marvels, dreadnoughts were an expression of national pride. At around £2,000,000 each in 1914 prices, they could also be seen as an instance of conspicuous expenditure. It was not long before several of the world's minor naval powers ordered dreadnoughts of their own.

In 1905 Brazil's rapidly growing prosperity found expression in an ambitious naval building programme. This was intended to signal the country's emergence from the political turbulence of the 1890s, and dominate the navy of its regional rival Argentina. At the time, the Argentine navy consisted of four modern Italian-built protected cruisers, three older British-built cruisers and a pair of small coast defence battleships. While the warships were relatively modern, acquired during the 1890s while Argentina and Chile were close to war, Fred Jane noted in *Fighting Ships* that 'the

ships do very little service at sea, and the navy is practically a shore-trained institution'.

Chile, having used its small navy to good effect in the 1879 war with Peru, entered the 20th century with the best fleet in South America. Her force of seven protected cruisers and the coast defence battleship *Capitan Prat* were to be substantially reinforced by two 11,800 ton predreadnoughts, which would have trumped any other warships in South American waters. Ordered from Britain in 1901, they were sold to the Royal Navy after the resolution of the border dispute with Argentina in 1903.

The Brazilian building programme stimulated a dreadnought race in South America. Brazil ordered two dreadnoughts from Britain before *Dreadnought* herself had even commissioned. *Minas Gerais* and *São Paulo* were completed in 1910. Argentina, beset by economic difficulties retaliated that year, ordering two dreadnoughts from American yards. Chile ordered two from Britain, but the first was bought for the Royal Navy a few weeks after Britain declared war on Germany in

Above: The completion of Jaime I *was delayed by World War I since her guns and many other parts were being supplied from Britain. The España class were very compact dreadnoughts, mounting eight 12-in guns on a displacement of less than 16,000 tons.*

1914. Serving as HMS *Canada*, she was bought back in 1920 and survived until broken up in 1959.

The only other navies to operate dreadnoughts were Spain and Turkey. (Greece had two dreadnoughts building in Germany in 1914, but work stopped until 1918 and they were never delivered). The German *Goeben* sailed under Ottoman colours until 1918, Turkey retaining the Moltke class battlecruiser until 1961. The Spanish navy had been all but annihilated during the Spanish-American war and rebuilding was slow. However, three dreadnoughts were ordered in 1908 and all launched before World War I.

España class

Spain's 1908 Navy Law called for the building of a balanced, modern fleet to replace the obsolete survivors of the fleet so hopelessly out-matched in 1898. Three dreadnoughts were planned and built by an Anglo-Spanish consortium.

Displacing less than 16,000 tons at full load, the España class were the smallest dreadnoughts ever built. They were armed with eight 12-inch guns in four turrets, with the midships turrets echeloned. The British mountings, unlike contemporary German designs, allowed loading while trained at any angle and provided a faster rate of fire.

Armour protection was poor by dreadnought standards: a main belt only 8 inches thick, tapering to 3 inches at the bow and 4 inches aft. Anti-torpedo bulkheads were 1.5 inches thick. *España* logged 20.5 knots on trials, her Parsons turbines delivering 22,260 shp with forced draught. In service, actual maximum speed was a knot less.

España, *Alfonso XIII* and *Jaime I* were laid down at Ferrol and launched in 1912, 1913 and 1914 respectively. The Great War slowed construction to a crawl since much of the material was supposed to come from

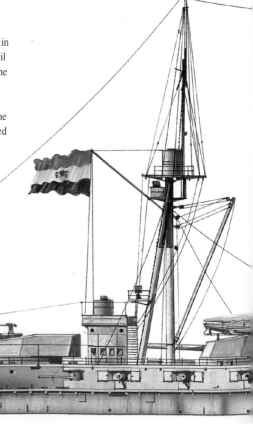

Britain. *España* and *Alfonso XIII* were completed 1914–15, but *Jaime I* did not go to sea until 1917 and only five of her guns had been delivered by mid-1919. A planned class of 21,000 ton dreadnoughts (Victoria Eugenia class) with eight 15-inch guns was abandoned as the World War ruled out further construction.

España was wrecked in 1923 after running on to a reef near Cape Tres Forcas, Morocco during heavy fog. Salvage proved impossible, although her 12-inch guns were retrieved for installation in coastal batteries.

Above: With her pair of tripod masts, the España's *profile is distinctly British.*

Right: In 1923 España *grounded on a reef while cruising off the Moroccan coast in dense fog. Beyond salvage, her armament was removed and the wreck left to break up.*

Alfonso XIII was re-named *España* in 1931. Lying at Ferrol when the Civil War broke out, she was captured by the Nationalists and sank off Cape Penas after striking a mine. *Jaime I* remained in government hands, but was damaged by air attack at Malaga in 1936. She was wrecked by an explosion while under repair at Cartagena in 1937 and so badly damaged that she was scrapped in 1939.

España class data:

Displacement, standard	15,452 tons
Displacement, full load	15,700 tons
Length overall	459 feet (140 m)
Beam	78 feet 9 in (24 m)
Design draught	25 feet 6 in (7.8 m)
Complement	854

Class: *España, Alfonso XIII, Jaime I*
Completed 1913–21

Armament:
Eight 12-in guns (4×2)
20 × 4-in guns

Machinery:
Steam turbines, 15,500 shp
4 shafts 19.5 knots

Armour:

Belt	8 in
Upper belt	6 in
Deck	1.5 in
Barbettes	10 in
Conning tower	10 in

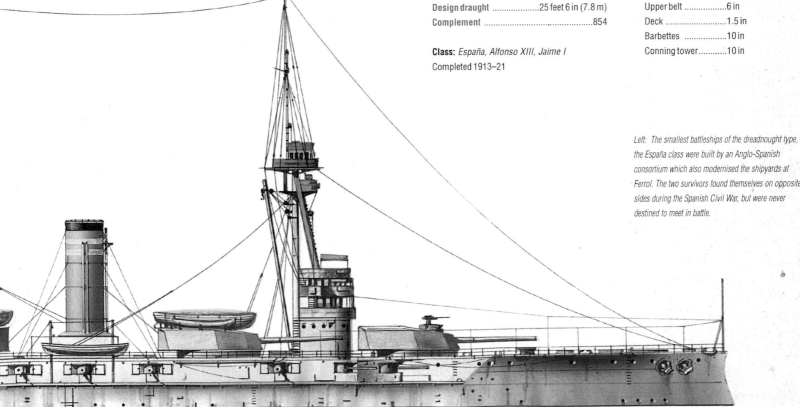

Left: The smallest battleships of the dreadnought type, the España class were built by an Anglo-Spanish consortium which also modernised the shipyards at Ferrol. The two survivors found themselves on opposite sides during the Spanish Civil War, but were never destined to meet in battle.

Rivadavia class

Argentina ordered two dreadnoughts in response to Brazil's naval programme. From an office in London, the Argentine navy invited European and American shipyards to submit designs; features from various designs were then combined and the ships ultimately ordered from America. British and German shipbuilders were equally outraged at what was regarded as very sharp practice indeed.

The Rivadavia class had widely spaced funnels not unlike the *Dante Alighieri*. The machinery was located amidships, with boiler rooms ahead and abaft. However, the main armament of twelve 12-inch guns was disposed in two superfiring turrets forward, two superfiring turrets aft and two echeloned turrets amidships. The echeloned turrets could fire over a 100 degree arc on the opposite beam.

The Rivadavias carried a powerful secondary armament of twelve 6-inch and sixteen 4-inch guns, the former carried on the upper deck and protected by 6-inch armour plate.

Armour protection was equal to the latest dreadnoughts of the major navies. The main armour belt was 12 inches thick, tapering to 5 inches at the bow and 4 inches at the stern. Additional protection was provided against underwater damage in the shape of a midships armoured deck over the double bottom.

Despite the twin provocations of U-boat attacks on her merchant shipping and biological weapons used against her livestock, Argentina did not declare war on Germany during World War I. Between the wars, Argentina discarded her fleet of 1890s warships and added modern cruisers and destroyers. *Rivadavia* and *Moreno* were comprehensively reconstructed in the USA, converted to oil-firing and their original British rangefinders replaced by modern fire control equipment. Eight 4-inch guns were landed in favour of 4-inch anti-aircraft guns. Both remained in service through World War II and were scrapped in 1956.

Rivadavia class data:

Displacement, standard	28,000 tons
Displacement, full load	30,000 tons
Length overall	594 feet 9 in (181.3 m)
Beam	98 feet 4 in (30 m)
Design draught	27 feet 8 in (8.5 m)
Complement	1050

Class: *Rivadavia, Moreno*
Completed 1914 and 1915

Armament:

12 × 12-in guns (6 × 2)
12 × 6-in guns
16 × 4-in guns
2 × 21-in torpedo tubes

Machinery:

Curtiss turbines, 39,000 shp
3 shafts
22.5 knots

Armour:

Belt	12 in
Upper belt	9 in
Deck	up to 3.5 in
Barbettes	up to 12 in
Casemates	up to 6 in
Conning tower	up to 12 n

Minas Gerais class

Built at Elswick and Barrow respectively, *Minas Gerais* and *São Paulo* were laid down in 1907 and completed in 1910. Their main armament of twelve 12-inch guns and speed of 21 knots, not to mention a range of 10,000 miles (at 10 knots) outclassed anything in South American waters. Thus, their acquisition catapulted Brazil to the top of the South American navy list and led to immediate retaliation by Argentina and Chile.

With her forefunnel between the bridge structure and the tripod mast, the long gap between the mast and the second funnel, and the shape of the funnels themselves, *Minas Gerais* was very obviously descended from the original *Dreadnought* design. However, her wing turrets were sited en echelon (although no cross deck fire was possible) and 'B' and 'X' turrets were superfiring.

Although *Dreadnought's* turbines had proved a great success, like the German navy, Brazil elected for reciprocating engines in her first dreadnoughts. As a result, she was slightly longer than *Dreadnought*, displaced over 19,000 tons at normal load and carried only a 9-inch armour belt. However, the belt extended all the way to the upper deck.

As the Argentine Rivadavias took shape, Brazil tried to trump them with a larger dreadnought, the *Rio de Janeiro*.

Ordered from Britain in 1911 and mounting the unprecedented armament of fourteen 12-inch guns, she was sold to Turkey after the economy faltered and a mutiny aboard *Minas Gerais* weakened political support for the navy. (See HMS *Agincourt*). A 15-inch gun super dreadnought, *Riachelo* was authorised in 1914, but overtaken by the outbreak of World War I and never actually ordered. Her coffee-based economy drastically affected by the U-Boat campaign, Brazil declared war on Germany in 1917. *Minas Gerais* and *São Paulo* sailed to the USA to refit for service in Europe, but the war ended before they could join the British and US battle squadrons in the UK. *Minas Gerais* was converted to oil-firing during the 1930s, but *São Paulo* had deteriorated so badly she was not worth modifying. She too suffered one of the mutinies that punctuated Brazilian naval history: raising the red flag in 1924 and firing a practice gun on her sistership.

Minas Gerais was scrapped in 1954. *São Paulo* foundered at sea while under tow to Italy for scrapping in 1951.

Below: Minas Gerais *in 1918 ready to join the British Grand Fleet*

Minas Gerais class data:

Displacement, standard	19,281 tons
Displacement, full load	21,200 tons
Length overall	543 feet (165.8 m)
Beam	83 feet (25.3 m)
Design draught	25 feet (7.6 m)
Complement	900

Class: *Minais Gerais, São Paulo*
Completed 1910

Armament:

12 × 12-in guns (6 × 2)
22 × 4.7-in guns
8 × 3-pdr guns

Machinery:

Triple expansion steam engines, 23,500 shp
2 shafts
21 knots

Armour:

Belt	9 in
Ends	4–6 in
Turrets	up to 12 in
Barbettes	up to 12 in
Casemates	up to 9 in
Conning tower	12 in

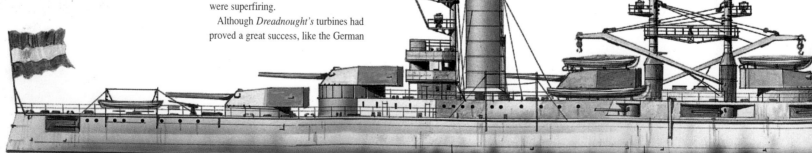

Above: Those minor navies that did not launch dreadnoughts continued to rely on 'coast defence ships' of which the Swedish Oscar II is typical. Completed in 1905 she displaced 4,300 tons and was armed with two 8.3-in guns in fore and aft turrets and eight 6-in guns in two pairs of turrets on either beam. If the armament and speed (18 knots) were on cruiser scales, she was rather better protected, with a 6-in belt and 2-in armoured deck.

Above Right: Turkey bought two obsolete predreadnoughts from Germany in 1910 and they saw limited action in the Balkan wars of 1912-13. However, it was the British-built cruiser Hamidiye, seen here, which proved more effective, raiding the Aegean and east Mediterranean to draw off the feared Greek armoured cruiser Averoff. Armed with two 6-in and eight 4.7-in guns, the 4000 ton Hamidiye survived World War I and was not decomissioned until the late 1940s.

Right: The Norwegian navy operated a number of coast defence ships ordered at the turn of the century from British yards. Here Harald Haarfagre and Tordenskjold are berthed at Oslofjord during the German invasion in 1940. Two other elderly coast defence battleships were sunk in action with modern German warships.

Right: Sverige was built in Sweden during World War I and is seen here after her 1932 refit which involved sweeping back her forefunnel. Armed with four 11-in guns in fore and aft turrets and six 6-in guns in beam turrets, the three Sverige class battleships displaced 7,000 tons and were capable of 22 knots.

Left: Built in the USA to a design acquired by devious means in Europe, the two Rivadavia class were Argentina's answer to Brazil's dreadnoughts. With twelve 12-in guns, a very powerful mixed secondary battery, and a 12-in main belt, they completely outclassed the Brazilian battleships, revealing just how rapidly battleship designs were evolving.

Russia

The Russian Navy in the 20th century

At the beginning of the 20th century, Russia was undergoing an industrial revolution that caused considerable alarm among her neighbours, Germany especially. Russia's capacity to manufacture everything from modern armour plate to heavy guns and railways was expanding rapidly. While the 1898 naval programme involved US and French yards building warships for the Russian fleet, subsequent ambitious construction programmes were all successfully undertaken within Russia.

In 1896 Russia occupied the Chinese Liaotung peninsula, building a naval base at its tip, Port Arthur. Russia had extracted a series of territorial concessions from Peking after the Chinese government failed to pay back war loans. Among these was the right to build the Trans-Siberian railway through Manchuria to the Russian port of Vladivostok. By 1904 the base at Port Arthur bristled with modern defences and seven modern battleships formed the core of a powerful squadron based there. In addition, the Russian navy maintained an equally strong squadron in the Baltic, while half-a-dozen mostly older battleships based at Sevastopol constituted the Black Sea fleet. The latter was about to be substantially reinforced by two more modern battleships of the Potemkin class.

Left: Petropavlovsk was the ill-fated flagship of Admiral Makarov's squadron, based at Port Arthur. She is seen here in the Imperial Russian navy's turn-of-the-century colour scheme: black hull, white upperworks, yellow funnels with black tops. By the time of her loss in 1904 she was painted grey all over.

Above: Orel was captured by the Japanese at the battle of Tshushima. Three of her sisterships were sunk in the same action.

If maintaining three separate fleets of relatively modern warships was a sign of Russia's growing economic strength, it was a traditional source of weakness. The Imperial navy had over 20 battleships, but they were several thousand miles apart. When, in 1904, Japan launched a surprise attack on the Pacific fleet at Port Arthur, Russia was unable to respond with the full strength of its forces. The Trans-Siberian railway was not completed, the newest battleships of the Baltic fleet had only just fitted out, and the torpedo attack on Port Arthur paralysed the Russian warships there while Japanese troopships unloaded in Korea.

The war that followed was an unmitigated disaster for the Russian navy, but the triumphal tone of Japanese accounts masks just how narrow the margin can be between victory and defeat. When the rival fleets engaged, Russian gunnery proved surprisingly accurate and crews fought their ships with tremendous courage.

The commander of the Russian Pacific fleet died in April when his flagship *Petropavlovsk* struck a mine as he led his ships against the Japanese. The loss of the dynamic Admiral Makarov was probably more serious than the loss of the battleship. Command devolved on Admiral

Vitgeft who led another sortie four months later. In two days' fighting off Round Island (also known as the Battle of the Yellow Sea) the Russians were defeated and driven back to Port Arthur. Vitgeft was an early casualty, killed when a 12-inch shell struck the conning tower of his flagship, *Tsarevitch*. She limped off to internment in China, while the rest of the squadron languished in the doomed port until Japanese army howitzers sank them at their moorings. The apathetic leadership of the fleet after Round Island was in dramatic contrast to the Japanese who maintained a vigorous blockade, even after losing two of their six battleships to Russian mines.

International treaties prevented the Russians from moving battleships from their Black Sea fleet through the Dardanelles, so the Baltic fleet was the only source of major units with which to rescue the situation in the Far East. Four of the five Borodino class battleships were made ready for a voyage around the world (*Slava* was not completed). Together with the modern French-built *Osliabia* and three obsolete battleships, the Baltic fleet was

Above: Russia's Pacific fleet was destroyed in its anchorage by Japanese heavy artillery at the end of 1904.

Below: Completed in 1897, the Sissoi Veliky was obsolete only seven years later when she was sunk at Tshushima.

Above: A notorious experiment of the Tsarist navy -- the circular coast defence battleship Admiral Popov, built to defend the mouth of the river Volga in the 1870s.

supported by a motley collection of cruisers and old ironclads. It set off on its remarkable cruise at the end of September 1904, through the North Sea (where it opened fire on British trawlers, identifying them as Japanese torpedo craft) and into the Atlantic. The fleet rounded the Cape of Good Hope, but when it reached Madagascar it learned that Port Arthur had fallen. The Russians set off again, meeting reinforcements off French Indochina, before steaming for the remaining Russian Pacific port, Vladivostok. The straits of Tsushima were the obvious place for the Japanese to intercept them, but the Russians had nearly passed through the Japanese cruiser patrols when they were finally located.

Weighed down by stores of extra coal to the point that their thickest armour was all but below the waterline, even the modern Borodinos were soon in trouble once the action began. Although Russian gunnery was accurate at first, the Russians were not rewarded with the sort of lucky hits that had so helped the Japanese the previous year. Instead, the steady gunnery of the Japanese fleet battered the Russians

to pieces. *Osliabia* hauled out of the line, sinking after several 12-inch hits opened her to the sea. The Borodinos died bravely: *Kniaz Suvorov* caught fire and circled out of control before being finished off with torpedoes; *Alexander III* went down with all but four of the 800 officers and men on board; *Borodino* suffered a massive explosion and rolled over, still firing from her secondary armament, leaving a single survivor. Only *Orel* remained afloat on the morning after: too badly damaged to fight, she struck her colours.

Tsushima was immediately recognised as the most decisive naval victory in modern times. The rest of

the Russian fleet, coast defence battleships and obsolete ironclads was annihilated. Nearly 5000 men were dead, another 6000 taken prisoner, and Russia was reduced to a minor naval power. The 1905–6 *Jane's Fighting Ships* makes telling reading: published as the results of Tsushima became known, ship after ship in the Russian navy section bears the legend 'sunk' or 'now Japanese'.

Repercussions were immediate. The 1905 revolution engulfed parts of the fleet, with the Black Sea battleship *Potemkin* mutinying. However, the foundations of the Tsarist state were stronger than perhaps even Tsar

Nicholas appreciated. The Baltic Works soon completed two new battleships before embarking on their first dreadnoughts. The speed of the Russian recovery was remarkable, with two Ganguts completed by the outbreak of World War I and two more ready by January 1915. Four Borodino class battlecruisers (12 × 14-inch guns, a 12-inch armour belt and a designed speed of 26 knots) were laid down in 1912. In the two years before 1914, Russian naval spending first matched and then surpassed that of Germany.

The battlecruisers were not completed before the Russian revolution halted all naval construction. Although three of the Ganguts were modernised and served after a fashion during World War II, inter-war plans for new battleships came to nothing. However, although President Kruschev ordered the scrapping of the surviving battleships in 1956, twenty years later the Leningrad yards began work on a class of four nuclear-powered and missile-armed battlecruisers that are still operational with the post-Soviet Russian navy today.

Retvisan

Built at Cramp's Yard, Philadelphia, USA, 1898–1901 for about £1,000,000, *Retvisan* was one of the seven battleships stationed at Port Arthur when the Russo-Japanese war began in 1904. Russia had seized the tip of the Liaotung peninsula, about 150 miles west of the China/Korea border, in 1896. The Russian naval base established there was a major cause of the ensuing war, and the main objective of Japanese army and navy operations.

Armour protection was reasonable, with a 9-inch main belt running the full length of the hull in two strakes. The lower strake stretched from 4-feet below the waterline to 3.5-feet above it; the upper strake connected the top edge of the lower strake with the main deck, and was 6-inch between the turrets. The main thickness of the belt was closed off by 7-inch bulkheads and beyond these the belt tapered to just 2-inch. The deck armour was 2-inch thick. Four 12-inch 40 cal. guns were located in two twin turrets before and abaft the superstructure, with eight 6-inch guns in a main-deck secondary battery and four more in upper-deck casemates.

Retvisan made nearly 18 knots on trials, with a foul bottom. On 12 hours trial she later managed a mean ihp of 16,121 for a speed of 18.8 knots.

The Japanese began the Russo-Japanese war with a surprise attack on the base at Port Arthur. *Retvisan* was one of the casualties, shipping some 2000 tons of water after a torpedo hit near the bow. She was repaired to take part in the battle of Round Island on 10–11 August 1904, suffering two 12-inch hits which temporarily disabled her. Once the Japanese army was able to bombard the ships in Port Arthur, *Retvisan* was soon sunk by 11-inch howitzer shells. Raised by the Japanese in 1905 and repaired at Sasebo between 1906 and 1908, she entered service with the Japanese Navy as the *Hizen*. She became a coast defence ship in 1922 and was sunk as a target in 1924.

Retvisan class data:

Displacement, standard	12,70 tons
Length overall	386 feet 8in (117.85 m)
Beam	72 feet 2 in (22 m)
Design draught	26 feet (7.92 m) max
Complement	738

Class: *Retvisan*

Armament:
Four 12-in guns (2 × 2)

12 × 6-in guns
20 × 11-pdr guns
24 × 2-pdr guns
8 × 1-pdr guns
6 × 15-in torpedo tubes

Machinery:
Triple expansion steam engines
2 shafts
18 knots

Armour:

Belt	up to 9 in
Belt ends	2 in
Turrets	up to 9 in
Casemates and battery	5 in
Conning tower	10 in

Borodino class

The Borodino class is notorious for losing four of its number in a single engagement: the annihilation of the Russian fleet at Tsushima in 1905. Built to form the core of the Baltic fleet, they were laid down in 1901 and completed quickly in 1904 to take part in the war with Japan.

Intended to be an improved version of the *Tsarevitch*, the Borodinos carried the same weight of armour (4000 tons) but slightly more widely – hence thinly – disposed. Anti-torpedo protection consisted of a 1.25-inch bulkhead joined to the deck by a slim flat. Upper and main deck armour was minimal.

Imperator Alexander III, *Kniaz Suvarov* and *Slava* were built by the Baltic Works and completed in 1903, 1904 and 1905 respectively; *Orel* was the work of Galernii Island and completed in 1904.

Slava was not completed in time to join Admiral Rozhdestvensky's ill-fated fleet, but he flew his flag in *Kniaz Suvarov*.

Borodino was destroyed by a magazine explosion at Tsushima; *Imperator Alexander III* foundered after being hit forward on the waterline by a large-calibre shell; *Kniaz Suvarov* was damaged by shellfire and then struck by an estimated five torpedoes, sinking her. *Orel* was badly damaged and surrendered to the Japanese, who repaired her and placed her in service as the *Iwami*. With her twin 6-inch turrets replaced by eight Japanese 6-inch guns in single mountings, she served until 1922 and was expended as a gunnery target two years later. *Slava* survived to take part in World War I but was badly damaged in the battle for Moon Island in October 1917. With 'A' turret broken down, and hit repeatedly by the German dreadnought *König*, she was unable to escape through the Moonsund channel as she drew too much water. The crew abandoned ship and the *Slava* was torpedoed by the destroyer *Turkmenets-Stavropolskii*.

Borodino class data:

Displacement, standard	13,516 tons
Length overall	397 feet (121 m)
Beam	76 feet 2 in (23.22 m)
Design draught	26 feet 2 in (7.97m) max
Complement	835

Class: *Borodino, Imperator Alexander III, Kniaz Suvarov, Orel, Slava*

Armament:

4 × 12-in guns (2 × 2)

12 × 6-in guns

20 × 11-pdr guns

20 × 3-pdr guns

4 × 15-in torpedo tubes

Machinery:

Triple expansion steam engines

2 shafts

18 knots

Armour:

Belt ....up to 7.5 in

Belt ends ....up to 5.75 in

Turrets ....up to 10 in

Secondary turrets ......6 in

Battery ....3 in

Conning tower...........8 in

Left: Slava was not completed in time to join her four sisterships in their epic voyage from the Baltic Sea to the straits of Tsushima. She served with the Baltic fleet during World War I.

Tsarevitch

Tsarevitch was built in France 1899–1904 as part of the Tsar's 1898 naval programme. With her pronounced tumblehome, she looked very obviously French-built. The secondary armament of twelve 6-inch guns were carried in six twin turrets, three on each beam: the forward and after turrets were located on the high forecastle deck, while the two centre turrets were sponsoned out from the inward sloping sides at the level of the upper deck.

The main armour belt ran the full length of the ship, stretching from 5-feet below the waterline to 7-feet above it. This belt had two strakes: the lower was 10-inch thick amidships and tapering to 7-inch at its lower edge; the upper was 8-inch thick. A lateral bulkhead was formed by a downward curve of the lower armoured deck from a point some 6.5-feet inboard of the waterline. Turning vertically down to join the ship's double bottom in the region of the bilge keel on each side, this 1.5-inch bulkhead was designed to save the ship from underwater attack. It had been tested by the French navy during the 1890s. The anti-torpedo bulkhead ran from just forward of 'A' turret to just aft of 'Y' turret, but when *Tsarevitch* was torpedoed on 9 February 1904 in Port Arthur, the hit was near the stern and the value of the system remained unproven.

In the Battle of the Round Island, on 10 August 1904, *Tsarevitch* was the flagship of Rear-Admiral Vitgeft. A 12-inch shell hit the fore mast, killing Vitgeft and leaving the Russian squadron in confusion. Later during the action another 12-inch shell hit the *Tsarevitch*, this time on the conning tower, jamming the helm. She escaped to Kaio

Chau, China, while the rest of the squadron was trapped in Port Arthur. Interned where she had made port, *Tsarevitch* was quickly repaired. Although her upperworks were much battered, her fighting efficiency had been little impaired by about a dozen heavy calibre shell hits.

During World War I *Tsarevitch* was part of the Baltic Fleet. Renamed *Grazhdanin* by the Provisional government, her movements largely dictated by sailors' committees, she sortied with the *Slava* to defend the Moonsund islands against German landings in October 1917. German sources testify to the accuracy of her long-range shooting, but it was an unequal struggle and *Grazhdanin* was obliged to withdraw after *Slava* was crippled. She was scrapped in 1922.

Tsarevitch class data:

Displacement, standard	..............12,915 tons
Length overall	...............388 feet 9 in (118.5 m)
Beam	..................................76 feet 1 in (23.2 m)
Design draught	.................26 feet (7.92 m) max
Complement	782

Class: *Tsarevitch*

Armament:

4 × 12-in guns (2 × 2)

12 × 6-in guns

20 × 11-pdr guns

20 × 3-pdr guns

4 × 15-in torpedo tubes (later removed)

Machinery:

Triple expansion steam engines

2 shafts

18.5 knots

Armour:

Belt ....up to 10 in

Belt ends ....up to 6.75 in

Main deck ....2.5 in

Lower deck ....1.5 in

Turrets ....10 in

Secondary turrets ......6 in

Conning tower............10 in

Below: With a pronounced tumblehome and the aft turret lower than the forward turret, the Borodino class had a distinctly French look. This is Slava, seen in 1907.

Gangut class

Russia's first dreadnoughts were laid down in June 1909. The contract had been won by Blohm & Voss, Hamburg, but Russian industrialists succeeded in forcing the government to give the orders to Russian yards. The German designs were modified by, among others, the British John Brown Yard, but the result bore the unmistakable influence of Vittorio Cuniberti's *Dante Alighieri*. The armament layout was 12 × 12-inch 52-cal guns in triple turrets on the centre line. The bow and stern turrets were sited near the ends, and these flush-decked ships were also fitted with ice-breaking bows of Russian design, making them wet when steaming at high speed or in a seaway. Unlike *Dante Alighieri*, secondary turrets were not fitted: the sixteen 4.7-inch guns were sited in casemates too low to be workable in bad weather, and directly beneath the muzzles of the main armament where they were vulnerable to blast damage.

The whole hull was protected, as a result of Russian conclusions from the Russo-Japanese war. The armour belt was 15 feet wide, with 5-feet below the waterline. A secondary internal belt 3–4-inch thick ran about 11-feet inboard above the armoured deck between the end barbettes. The space between the main belt and the internal belt was divided into watertight compartments. To achieve such comprehensive armour protection, the overall thickness was less than 9-inch: thinner than that of German battlecruisers.

The capital ships of the Baltic fleet took little part in World War I and fell into the hands of the Bolsheviks after the November revolution. On 18 August 1919 *Petropavlovsk* was torpedoed and sunk at Kronstadt by British torpedo boats *CMB31* and *CMB88*. Salvaged and repaired, she was renamed *Marat* and, with *Gangut* (now *Oktyabrskaya Revolutsiya*) and *Sevastopol* (now *Parizhskaya Kommuna*), formed the core of the Soviet fleet. *Poltava* (renamed *Mikhail Frunze*) was partly destroyed by fire in 1922 and eventually expended as a blockship at Kronstadt.

Marat was crippled by German Stukas at Kronstadt, 23 September 1941, but although partly submerged, served as a battery during the siege of Leningrad and eventually became the gunnery ship *Volkhov* until scrapped, 1952–53. *Parizhskaya Kommuna* was transferred to the Black Sea in the winter of 1929–30, suffering so badly from high seas in the North Atlantic that she had to be docked at Brest for repairs. Reverting to her original name in World War II, *Sevastopol* carried out coastal bombardment missions in the Black Sea until badly damaged in 1942; she was scrapped in 1956–57. *Oktyabrskaya Revolutsiya*, damaged by shore batteries and air attack in 1941–42, survived to bombard German troops from the Neva River in early 1944. She was scrapped in 1956–59.

Gangut class data:

Displacement, standard	23,000 tons
Displacement, full load	25,850 tons
Length overall	600 feet (182.88 m)
Beam	88 feet 3 in (26.9 m)
Design draught	27 feet 3 in (8.3 m) mean
Complement	1,125

Class: *Gangut, Petropavlovsk, Poltava, Sevastopol*

Left: After the Bolsheviks took control of the Russian fleet, Petropavlosk was sunk in Kronstadt harbour in a daring attack by British torpedo boats. She was raised and repaired, but sunk in 1941 by Junkers Ju-87 Stuka dive-bombers.

Armament:
12 × 12-in guns (4 × 3)
16 × 4.7-in guns (16 × 1)
4 × 3-pdr guns
4 × 18-in torpedo tubes

Machinery:
4 Parsons turbines
4 shafts
23 knots

Armour:

Belt	up to 8.9 in
Turrets	up to 8 in
Barbettes	8 in
Casemates	4.9 in
Deck	up to 1.5 in
Conning tower	10 in

Below: Oktyabrskaya Revolutsiya (previously Gangut) as she appeared on the eve of World War II. The fore funnel is raised and angled to keep the bridge clear of smoke and a floatplane is carried on No.3 turret.

Battleship Designs 1937–39

The Soviet navy requested three hybrid battleship-carrier designs from the American company Gibbs & Cox during the late 1930s. Up to 30 aircraft were to have been operated via catapults and a landing deck amidships. A design for a conventional battleship was also studied, but none of the plans were acted upon. Stalin already controlled the world's largest army and largest air force, and, since he was determined to prove that Communist industry could out-build that of the capitalist states, a grandiose scheme for 16 battleships was apparently under consideration when the navy was purged by party officials.

Battleship Design data:

Displacement, standard:

(A)	66,074 tons
(B)	71,850 tons
(C)	44,200 tons
(D)	45,000 tons

Displacement, full load:

(A)	72,000 tons
(B)	74,000 tons
(C)	55,200 tons
(D)	53,680 tons

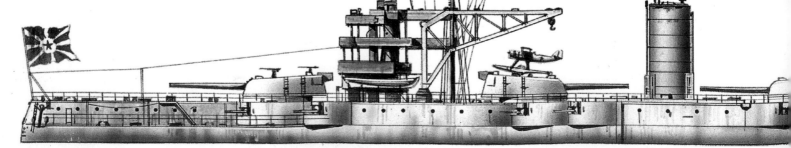

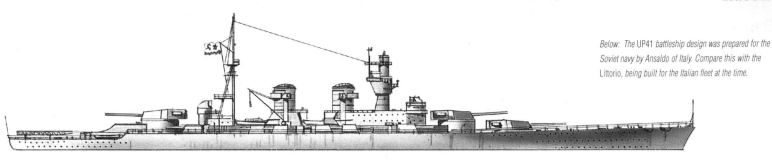

Below: The UP41 battleship design was prepared for the Soviet navy by Ansaldo of Italy. Compare this with the Littorio, being built for the Italian fleet at the time.

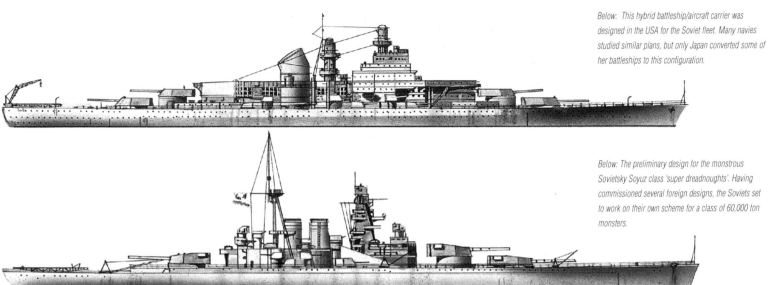

Below: This hybrid battleship/aircraft carrier was designed in the USA for the Soviet fleet. Many navies studied similar plans, but only Japan converted some of her battleships to this configuration.

Below: The preliminary design for the monstrous Sovietsky Soyuz class 'super dreadnoughts'. Having commissioned several foreign designs, the Soviets set to work on their own scheme for a class of 60,000 ton monsters.

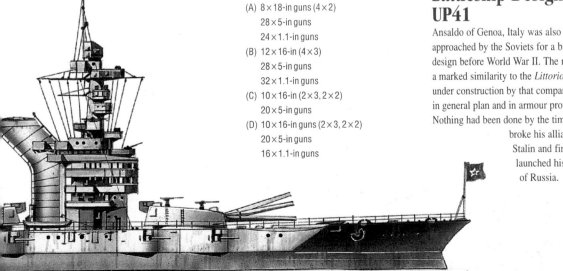

Length overall:
(A) ....1,000 feet (304.8 m)
(B) ....1005 feet (306.3 m)
(C) ....844 feet 10 in (257.5 m)
(D) ....903 feet 10 in (275.5 m)

Beam:
(A) ....126 feet (38.4 m)
(B) ....128 feet (39 m)
(C) ....129 feet 6 in (39.5 m)
(D) ....113 feet 6 in (34.6 m)

Design draught:
(A) ....34 feet 6 in (10.5 m)
(B) ....34 feet 6 in (10.5 m)
(C) ....33 feet 6 in (10.2 m)
(D) ....33 feet 6 in (10.2 m)

Complement ....Not known

Armament:
(A) 8 × 18-in guns (4 × 2)
    28 × 5-in guns
    24 × 1.1-in guns
(B) 12 × 16-in (4 × 3)
    28 × 5-in guns
    32 × 1.1-in guns
(C) 10 × 16-in (2 × 3, 2 × 2)
    20 × 5-in guns
(D) 10 × 16-in guns (2 × 3, 2 × 2)
    20 × 5-in guns
    16 × 1.1-in guns

Machinery:
Steam turbines
(A) 34 knots
(B) 31.9 knots
(C) 31.9 knots
(D) 31 knots

Armour:
not known

Battleship Design UP41

Ansaldo of Genoa, Italy was also approached by the Soviets for a battleship design before World War II. The result bore a marked similarity to the *Littorio* then under construction by that company, both in general plan and in armour protection. Nothing had been done by the time Hitler broke his alliance with Stalin and finally launched his invasion of Russia.

UP41 class data:

Displacement, standard ....42,000 tons
Displacement, full load.................50,000 tons
Length overall ....816 feet 7 in (248.9 m)
Beam ....116 feet 6 in (35.5 m)
Design draught ....29 feet 6 in (9 m)
Complement ....Not known

Armament:
9 × 16-in guns
12 × 7.1-in guns
24 × 3.9-in guns
48 × 45-mm guns
24 × 13.2-mm machine guns

Machinery:
4 steam turbines, 177,500 shp
4 shafts
32 knots

Armour:
Belt ....up to 13.2 in
Bulkheads ....up to 13.8 in
Upper deck ....2.2 in
Main deck ....2.6 in
Turrets ....up to 15.75 in
Barbettes ....13.8 in
Secondary turrets ......up to 7.1 in
Conning tower............up to 13.2 in

Below: It was long after World War II that the Soviet press finally carried artists' impressions of what the Sovietsky Soyuz class would have looked like had they been completed. Bearing a strange resemblance to the final classes of American battleships, these enormous battleships were almost as large as the famous Japanese Yamato class.

Sovietsky Soyuz

While warship designs were solicited from the USA, Germany and Italy – and cruisers actually ordered from their Nazi allies – the Soviets began work on a class of three very large and powerful battleships themselves. Ordered in January 1938, the *Sovietsky Soyuz* and her sisters were 65,000 ton behemoths armed with 16-inch guns and on a par with the giant battleships under consideration in Germany and actually building in Japan. Since Soviet construction was shrouded in mystery from the 1930s to the present day, no hint of their size escaped to the west before the German invasion in 1941. *Luftwaffe* reconnaissance flights identified the hull of a giant warship (*Sovietsky Soyuz*) on the slipway in Leningrad and, in August 1941 ground troops occupied Nikolayaev where the 889-feet hull of *Sovietskaya Ukraina* dominated the Marti Yard. *Sovietskaya Byelorussia* was never laid down, although material for her had been assembled in Leningrad and was used to build a floating battery during the siege.

With the German invaders deep inside Russia, further work on battleships not due for completion until the mid-1940s was obviously futile. The hulls were broken up on the slipways after the war.

Sovietsky Soyuz class data:

Displacement, standard ....59,150 tons
Displacement, full load.................65,150 tons
Length overall ....889 feet 1 in (271 m)
Beam ....127 feet 8 in (38.9 m)
Design draught ....33 feet 6 in (10.2 m)
Complement ....Not known

Class: *Sovietsky Soyuz, Sovietskaya Byelorussia, Sovietskaya Ukraina*

Armament:
9 × 16-in guns (3 × 3)
12 × 6-in guns (6 × 2)
8 × 3.9-in guns
32 × 37-mm guns
8 × 12.7-mm machine guns

Machinery:
2 steam turbines, 164,000 shp
4 shafts
28 knots

Armour:
Belt ....up to 16.75 in
Deck ....8.7 in
Torpedo bulkheads ....2.95 in
Turret faces ....19.7 in
Secondary turrets ......3.9 in
Conning tower............16.75 in

Kirov class

In July 1980 the Soviet navy commissioned the largest warship built since World War II (other than America's nuclear-powered aircraft carriers). Built at Leningrad, 1977–80, and taking the name of the Party boss and Soviet hero assassinated there on Stalin's orders, the *Kirov* was the first of four 22,000 ton missile cruisers.

The powerplant combines two nuclear reactors with oil-fired boilers to superheat the steam they deliver, boosting power output for high speed dashes.

The majority of the Kirovs' weapons are sited forward of the massive superstructure. Twenty SS-N-19 surface-to-surface missiles provide the main anti-ship capability. Launched from tubes sited below decks and angled at 45 degrees, they travel at Mach 2.5 to a maximum range of 250 nautical miles. Further towards the bow, and also below the deck are 12 eight-round rotary launchers for SA-N-6 surface-to-air missiles with a range of 50 nautical miles and capable of engaging multiple targets simultaneously, including sea-skimming missiles. Close-range defence against incoming missiles is also provided by 30-mm 'Gatling guns'. *Kirov* also carries SA-N-14 anti-submarine missiles which deliver an anti-submarine homing torpedo. *Frunze* does not, but is fitted with a more comprehensive anti-aircraft armament, including 16 SA-N-9 SAM launchers.

Up to three helicopters are stored in a below-deck hanger aft. The flight deck can handle only one at a time.

The Kamov Ka-25s are being replaced by Kamov Ka-27 helicopters, both served to detect submarines and to provide mid-course guidance for surface-to-surface missiles.

The third unit (*Kalinin*) was considerably improved, with superior fire control systems, surface-to-air missiles and anti-missile gun systems. With the collapse of the USSR, there was considerable doubt whether fourth unit of the class, *Yuri Andropov* would ever be built. The names were changed, with traditional Russian heroes replacing names from the communist pantheon: *Kirov* became *Admiral Ushakov*; *Frunze* is now *Admiral Lazarev*; *Kalinin* is *Admiral Nakhimov* and *Yuri Andropov* was re-named *Pyotr Velikiy* (Peter the Great).

The Russian navy was bedevilled by equipment shortages during the early 1990s and, desperately short of trained manpower, it was impossible to take these enormous

cruisers to sea since they demand nearly 700 men to operate. None of the Kirovs spent much time at sea between 1990 and 1995. However, the Russian navy resumed its submarine patrols right across the Atlantic in 1994–5 and the *Pyotr Velikiy* has now been completed. Whatever else happens to the Russian economy, the nucleus of a powerful fleet has been retained.

Kirov class data:

Displacement, standard	22,000 tons
Displacement, full load	24,300
Length overall	826.8 feet (252 m)
Beam	93.5 feet (28.5 m)
Design draught	29.5 feet (9.1 m)
Complement	692

Class: *Kirov, Frunze, Kalinin, Yuri Andropov*

Armament:
20 × SS-N-19 SSM launchers (no reloads)
12 × SA-N-6 SAM launchers (each with 8 missiles)
2 × SA-N-4 SAM (2 × twin launchers with 20 missiles)
2 × SA-N-9 SAM octuple launchers (not Admiral Ushakov)
2 × SS-N-14 ASW weapons (1 twin launcher with 16 missiles)
2 × SS-N-15 ASW weapons (not Admiral Ushakov)
2 × 3.9-in guns (Ushakov)
2 × 130-mm guns (not Ushakov)
6 × 30-mm guns (CIWS)
1 × RBU 6000 12-barrel ASW mortar (Ushakov and Lazarev)
1 × RBU 1200 10-barrel ASW mortar (Lazarev)
2 × RBU 1000 6-barrel ASW mortars
10 × 21-in torpedo tubes (2 × 5)

Machinery:
CONAS (2 nuclear reactors, plus oil-fired boilers for steam turbines)
c150,000 shp
30 knots

Above: Kalinin *(now Admiral Nakhimov) joined the Red Banner Northern Fleet just before the Communist system collapsed. The Russian fleet now includes four of these nuclear-powered battlecruisers.*

Left: Kirov *as commissioned in 1980. The gun turrets are for 30 mm anti-missile cannon, with the fearsome array of surface-to-surface missiles located below the forecastle deck.*

United Kingdom

The Royal Navy at the turn of the century

On 26 June 1897 Queen Victoria marked her Diamond Jubilee with a fleet review. The crowds that thronged the shores of Spithead that day went home well satisfied. They had witnessed the visible manifestation of the might that underpinned the Empire and commercial interests that spanned the globe. Although understandable, their confidence and enthusiasm was not, however, entirely justified. In effect, the Royal Navy was a metaphor for the ageing monarch herself. Virtually unchallenged for the better part of a century, it had become arthritic and complacent. The service's past success was greatly responsible for its current shortcomings - not least because only a few far-sighted people could even detect that there were shortcomings. A powerful sense of tradition had atrophied into powerful conservatism. In an age notable for rapid and continuous technological development, most senior officers remained blinkered by their formative years spent in sail, reluctant to acknowledge that strategy and tactics had

H. M. S. "Renown" (12 350 tons 1st Cl. Battleship).

Above: Armed with four 10-in guns, Renown was built at Pembroke dockyard 1893-5. Admiral Fisher's flagship on the North American station 1897-9, Renown carried the Prince and Princess of Wales to India in 1905.

been revolutionised by steam power. A strategic situation could now change so much more quickly, yet no detailed war plans existed. Nor yet was there a credible intelligence organisation to implement them.

Improvement in gun technology was not matched by improvements in gunnery, despite the potential of extra range and hitting power. Compulsory occasional gun practice was seen as detrimental to the high standard of paintwork and decks by which a ship was properly judged. Torpedoes, gyroscopes and engines were the province of engineers and technicians, qualified but not yet deemed fit to share a table with those of the seaman branch. As for submarines, surely no first-class navy could take them seriously.

Many of the greatest names in the Royal Navy's development, men who contributed immeasurably to the service's advancement, clashed personally or with the establishment. Churchill, Fisher, Beresford, Scott – all, at some time, were moved on.

Understandably, the fleet retained its best ships in home and Mediterranean waters. Policing the

Empire, therefore, were a variety of units, accumulated over years, which possessed little or no residual fighting value. In terms of new tonnage, the Royal Navy had received an enormous boost from the Naval Defence Act of 1889. The so-called Two Power Standard now required it to have a strength capable of defeating an alliance of the next two strongest maritime powers. Although the standard was first aimed at the French and Russians, it was already becoming more appropriate to include Germany, which was about to enact its own Navy Laws. Its emperor, Wilhelm II, entertained ideas of procuring a latter-day empire – 'Germany's place in the sun' – through the creation of a first division fleet. The newly opened Kiel Canal was a statement to the world that such a fleet would be neither incarcerated nor destroyed in its own base (like the Danish fleet at Copenhagen). A well-disposed United Kingdom at first saw no threat but the Kruger telegram betrayed a new mood for political interference by the Germans. Their naval estimates, hitherto fairly static, increased suddenly by 50 per cent, the seven battleships authorised going far to offset the eight 'Royal Sovereigns' funded by the Naval Defence Act. Britain's self-appointed role of

Above: The senior officers of the Edwardian navy had first gone to sea aboard ironclads like the Agincourt, launched in 1861. The late 19th century was an era of unprecedented technological change.

Below: Queen was typical of the pre-dreadnought battleships built by the Royal Navy in the early 20th century. Armed with four 12-in guns, she was capable of 19 knots.

Above: Victorious was one of the nine Majestic class battleships, the most numerous class of battleships ever built. She served in the Royal Navy's China Squadron and Mediterranean Fleet.

Below: Another Majestic class battleship, Prince George, with her forward guns trained to port. The secondary armament of 6-in guns was mounted along the main and upper decks.

supreme naval power was being challenged directly, and friction was inevitable. That the Kaiser did not intend to fudge the issue was apparent also by his appointment, in this same June of 1897, of von Bülow as Foreign Minister and Tirpitz as Minister of Marine, the one charged with putting Germany on the map, the other with constructing the means to keep it there. The Jubilee Review was not, therefore, only a celebration – it was a show of strength, a flick of the cape to show the sword beneath.

For the 1987 Spithead review, the Royal Navy was able to concentrate more battleships than any other navy in the World. It was British policy to have a stronger fleet than the second and third largest navies added together.

Duncan class

The so-called 'Naval Scare' of 1893 triggered the nine-ship Majestic programme. This set the standard for a first-class battleship design which, for a decade, was to change remarkably little. A main battery of four 12-inch guns, in twinned turrets, and a secondary armament of twelve 6-inch weapons in casemates, were shipped on a standard displacement that varied between 13,000 and 15,000 tons. This figure varied depending on whether the priority was increased speed or improved protection. In the days of triple-expansion machinery, the Majestics' 12,000 ihp and 17 knots were not easily improved upon, but developments in armour quality were continuing apace, permitting thinner and lighter protection.

This was a period of rapid construction. Nine Majestics, laid down in 1893–5, were followed by six Canopus (1896–8), eight Formidable/Londons (1898–1901) and six Duncans (1899–1900). The overlapping chronology was a function of careful, almost cautious, evolution. To achieve a new high of 19 knots in the Duncans, the hull was finer and longer than that of the preceding Londons, but was capped at 1,000 tons less in displacement. As the scale of armament remained unchanged, protection inevitably suffered.

Engagement at perhaps only 3,000 yards was expected in this era. Most armour was, therefore, expended in a thick belt (7 inches of Krupp Cemented in the case of the Duncans), backed by 10 feet (about 3 metres) of coal bunkers. The upper edge of the belt supported a 2-inch main deck while, one level below, a one-inch deck curved downward to link with the belt's lower edge. The upper protective deck was intended to detonate any projectile penetrating the unarmoured side, while the lower blocked the penetration to the machinery spaces of splinters and debris. Any projectile penetrating the main belt would have lost so much energy that it would be deflected upward by the glacis of the splinter deck. The system was never to be seriously tested in action.

Duncan class data:

Displacement, standard	13,640 tons
Displacement, full load	15,100 tons
Length overall	432 feet (131.7 m)
Beam	75.7 feet (23.0 m)
Design draught	25.7 feet (7.8 m)
Complement	720

HMS Africa: the penultimate British pre-dreadnoughts, the Edward VII class formed part of the Grand Fleet in 1914. By the time of Jutland, they were based at Sheerness with the Dreadnought.

Class:

Albemarle, Cornwallis, Duncan, Exmouth, Montagu, Russell. All completed 1903–4.

Armament:

Four 12-in guns (2 × 2)
Twelve 6-in guns (12 × 1)
Ten 12-pounders (10 × 1)
Four 18-inch torpedo tubes

Machinery:

Triple expansion steam engines 18,000 ihp (13,400 kW)
Two shafts 19 knots

Armour:

Belt	up to 7 in
Bulkheads	up to 11 in
Decks	up to 2 in
Turrets	up to 10 in
Barbettes	up to 11 in

Below: Most pre-dreadnoughts carried their secondary armament so low they could not be operated in heavy seas or while manoueuvering. Here, Dominion's 6-in guns are mostly awash.

King Edward VII class

This group of eight was the final evocation of the design that had originated with the Majestics. Adverse criticism was already being made of the Duncans, when it was learned that the American Virginia class and the Italian Benedetto Brin would, on a similar displacement, mount 8-inch guns, in addition to the customary mix of 12– and 6-inch. Although, in retrospect, there was little justification for a third major calibre, the Admiralty could not be seen to have been left behind. Going one better, it rejected the proposed 7.5-inch in favour of 9.2s.

On a displacement limited to 16,000 tons similar machinery was fitted, but a half-knot decrease in speed had to be accepted as part-price for adding four 9.2s. Even with a larger hull, further sacrifice was necessary. Adequate stability required that the turrets be set lower, resulting in a lower freeboard and a reputation for wetness. Protection, pared on the Duncans, reverted to London standards. A retrograde step, however, was to site the 6-inch tertiary guns in an armoured box battery rather than in separate, but heavier, casemates, which were designed to contain an explosion at the gun as well as to protect the gun itself. They were set so low that they were theoretically awash with just a 14 degree roll.

Known as very handy ships, their manoeuvrability resulted from a lack of longitudinal stability. Their attempts to steer in a straight line as a squadron were legendary and they well earned their label of the 'Wobbly Eight'.

King Edward VII, on allowing the lead ship to bear his name, stipulated that she always serve as a flagship. On the first occasion that she did not, she was sunk.

King Edward VII class data:

Displacement, standard.................15,630 tons
Displacement, full load ....17,000 tons
Length overall ....453.8 feet (138.3 m)
Beam..78 feet (23.8 m)
Design draught.......................25.6 feet (7.8 m)
Complement...777

Class: *Africa, Britannia, Commonwealth, Dominion, Hibernia, Hindustan, New Zealand, King Edward VII.* All completed 1905–7

Armament:
Four 12-in guns (2 × 2)
Four 9.2-in guns (4 × 1)
Ten 6-in guns (10 × 1)
Four 18-in torpedo tubes

Machinery:
Triple expansion steam engines 18,000 ihp
   (13,400 kW)
Two shafts 18.5 knots

Armour:
Belt ....up to 9 in
Bulkheads ....up to 12 in
Decks ....up to 2.5 in
Turrets ....up to 12 in
Barbettes ....up to 12 in

Lord Nelson class

Only two Lord Nelsons were constructed as the Royal Navy had just acquired the two small Swiftsures, building for Chile. Laid down in 1905 and not completed until 1908 they were, in any case, overtaken by events. Increasingly, it was felt that the outcome of future battles would be decided at longer ranges, in which case, secondary and tertiary armament was superfluous because it would never come into action, and protection should be on a scale to defeat the larger projectiles that were anticipated. First drafts of the Lord Nelson design are believed to have included a homogeneous 12-inch battery but its time had not yet quite come. Instead, the tertiary 6-inch guns of the preceding class were replaced by further 9.2s. Both these and the 12-inch mountings were supplied with new 45-calibre barrels that increased muzzle velocity, range and penetration.

An odd limitation was put on the design by a Board insistence that they be able to use dry docks closed to previous classes. They were, therefore, both shorter and narrower but, with their improved and heavier protection, they were deeper. They had full midship sections that contributed towards their being steady rollers and good gun platforms. The restricted beam was detrimental in that, while the belt was continued from a waterline 12-inches by an 8-inch extension to the upper deck, the trunks of the 9.2 turrets were set within the coal bunkers, placing the magazines very close to the sides of the ship. They were the last British battleships to have reciprocating engines.

Lord Nelson class data:

Displacement, standard................16,090 tons
Displacement, full load ....17,820 tons
Length overall ....443.5 feet (135.2 m)
Beam....................................79.5 feet (24.2 m)
Design draught.....................26.1 feet (8.0 m)
Complement..809

Class: *Agamemnon, Lord Nelson.*
Completed 1908

Armament:
Four 12-in guns (2 × 2)
Ten 9.2-in guns (4 × 2) and (2 × 1)
Five 18-in torpedo tubes

Machinery:
Triple expansion steam engines 16,750 ihp
   (12,500 kW)
Two shafts 18 knots

Armour:
Belt ....up to 12 in
Bulkheads ....up to 8 in
Decks ....up to 4 in
Turrets ....up to 12 in
Barbettes ....up to 12 in

Below: Agamemnon *spent much of World War I in the Mediterranean, taking part in the Dardanelles operations. In 1916 she managed to bring down a German zeppelin off Salonika. Her secondary armament of 10 9.2-in guns was the heaviest carried by any predreadnought.*

Dreadnought

As with most successful concepts, that of the Dreadnoughts did not lack putative parents. Its genesis lay almost certainly with the transition of the torpedo from capricious novelty to serious threat, causing naval thinkers to promote engagements from greater ranges. In 1903, the Italian designer Cuniberti outlined his conception of an 'ideal' future British battleship – 17,000 tons, twelve 12-inch guns, 12-inch belt and 24 knots. While an ambitious package on the planned displacement, it was based on his belief in the Nelsonian principle of annihilation.

Influenced by William S. Sims, the Americans too had come to accept the argument for a homogeneous big-gun armament. Large calibres were essential to engage from beyond torpedo range. The quickest way to get on target was to fire in close-grouped salvoes, with visual spotting to correct for 'overs' and 'unders'. Such a method was unworkable with mixed calibres. Once persuaded (but not without reservations), Congress authorised the two Michigans in March 1905.

Fisher meanwhile claimed that the idea had occurred to him as early as 1900. As a newly-appointed First Sea Lord, he formed and chaired an expert committee, which deliberated in early 1905. Reports from the Far East indicated that the Japanese had successfully engaged the Russians at about 10,000 yards, while the Japanese flagship had sustained a hit at over 14,000 yards. Clearly a 12-inch armament was essential. Probably by virtue of his knowledge of the newly introduced steam turbine (about to go into service in the light cruiser *Amethyst*), the Chairman coupled this armament with a requirement for a

Right: The launch of HMS Dreadnought *at Portsmouth Dockyard on 10 February 1906. With a uniform armament of 12-in guns and powered by steam turbines, she rendered every other battleship obsolete.*

21-knot speed. Aware of developments abroad, the committee concluded quickly; design was rushed and the keel laid in October 1905.

An apostle of pursuit and destruction, Fisher demanded maximum end-on fire. American-style superimposed turrets were rejected on grounds of likely mutual damage and vulnerability through close grouping. The *Dreadnought's* two wing turrets could, theoretically, supplement the axial mountings to give a six-gun end-on fire. Only a degree or two deviation, however, would reduce this to four.

While her steam turbines saved about 1,000 tons compared with reciprocating machinery of similar power, the ship had indifferent protection. There was insufficient margin to incorporate longitudinal bulkheads to protect the lower parts of the turret trunks, of which those of the wing mountings were a bare 5 metres from the ship's side.

Patches of 2– and 4-inch armour were thus worked in. Unlike the Lord Nelsons' spaces above the main deck were unprotected.

To speed construction, the 12-inch mountings were appropriated from the still-completing Lord Nelsons. Only quick-firing 12-pounders were fitted in addition, so the ship lacked the 'bristling' appearance given by 6-inch casemates. Although commencing trials just a year and a day after being laid down, she was not finally complete until December 1906. For such a revolutionary ship, her life was short, ended by the mass scrappings of the early 1920s.

Dreadnought data:

Displacement, standard	18,110 tons
Displacement, full load	21,850 tons
Length overall	527 feet (160.6 m)
Beam	82 feet (25.0 m)
Design draught	26.5 feet (8.1 m)
Complement	773

Armament:
Ten 12-in guns (5 × 2)
27 × 12-pounders (27 × 1)
Five 18-in torpedo tubes

Machinery:
Steam turbines 23,000 shp (17,160 kW)
Four shafts 21 knots

Armour:

Belt	up to 11 in
Bulkheads	up to 8 in
Decks	up to 4 in
Turrets	up to 11 in
Barbettes	up to 11 in

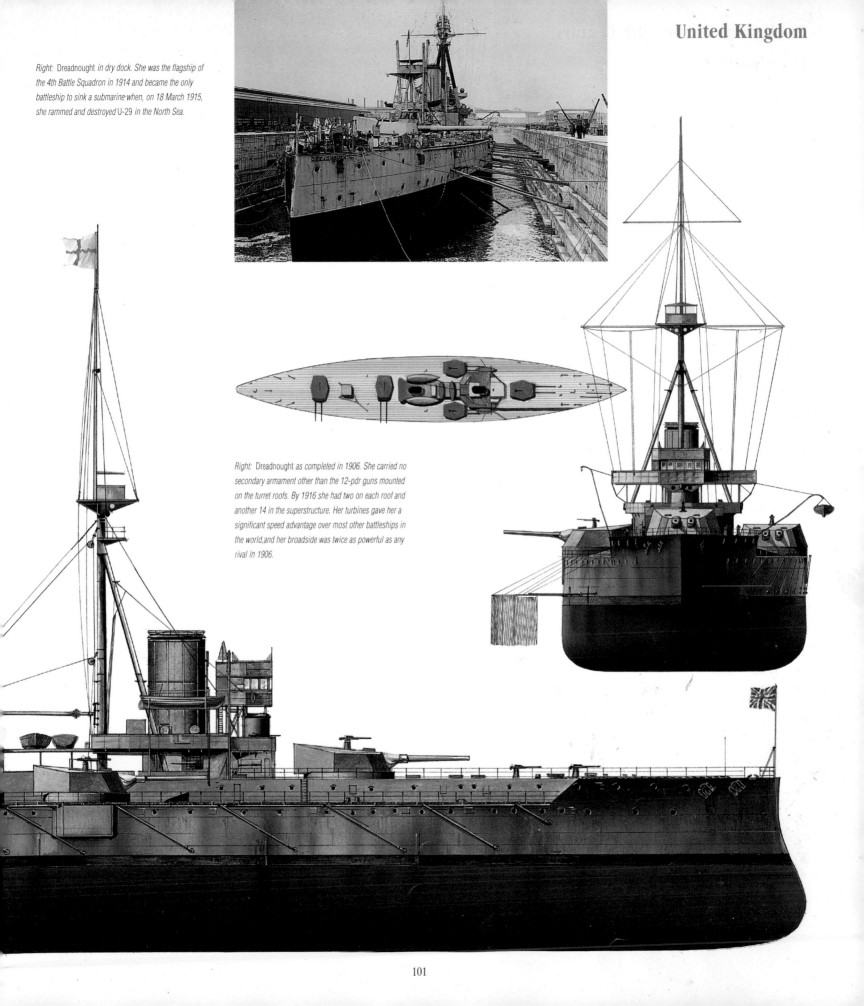

Right: Dreadnought *in dry dock. She was the flagship of the 4th Battle Squadron in 1914 and became the only battleship to sink a submarine when, on 18 March 1915, she rammed and destroyed U-29 in the North Sea.*

Right: Dreadnought *as completed in 1906. She carried no secondary armament other than the 12-pdr guns mounted on the turret roofs. By 1916 she had two on each roof and another 14 in the superstructure. Her turbines gave her a significant speed advantage over most other battleships in the world,and her broadside was twice as powerful as any rival in 1906.*

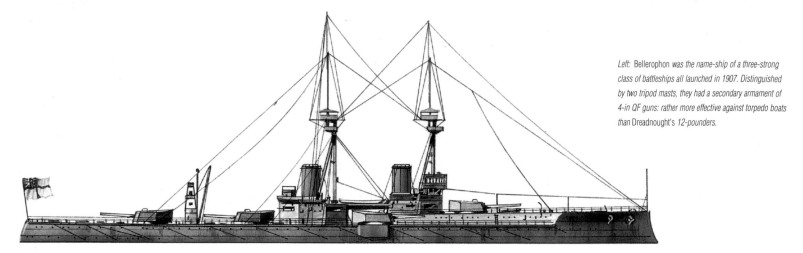

Left: Bellerophon was the name-ship of a three-strong class of battleships all launched in 1907. Distinguished by two tripod masts, they had a secondary armament of 4-in QF guns: rather more effective against torpedo boats than Dreadnought's 12-pounders.

Bellerophon

With the completion of the *Dreadnought*, the British Admiralty had, effectively, brought about the obsolescence of its own battle fleet. Fully expecting a powerful reaction from foreign maritime powers, the British proposed to lay down a quartette of 'Dreadnoughts' in each of the 1906 and 1907 construction programmes but, exercising caution, the powers abroad waited to see how effective the British prototype was in service. Inevitably, this resulted in political pressure to slow the programme and the navy was fortunate in getting three in each year.

The lead ship of the first group, *Bellerophon*, was laid down virtually on the day of Dreadnought's final completion, also at Portsmouth Dockyard. On the same length there was a fractional increase in beam. Greater draught was accepted in order to allow for improvements to address her predecessor's obvious deficiencies. With a similar main battery she received a continuous longitudinal bulkhead, extending down to the tank tops and running outboard of the magazines, to protect against torpedo strikes. An inch was pared off the main belt to enable a general thickening of protective decks.

Dreadnought's 12-pounders had been derided as useless to deter destroyer attack. The 4-inch was thus specified. Eight of these were mounted on turret roofs. Obviously unworkable if the main battery was firing, they were later casemated high in the superstructure. With spotting now essential to fire control, the *Dreadnought's* control top had been sited badly, with smoke and heat from the forward funnel often rendering it uninhabitable. The Bellerophons thus introduced a pair of lofty tripods, one forward of each funnel,

that soon became a feature of British construction.

Bellerophon data:

Displacement, standard	18,800 tons
Displacement, full load	21,100 tons
Length overall	526 feet (160.3 m)
Beam	82.5 feet (25.1 m)
Design draught	27.2 feet (8.3 m)
Complement	733

Class: *Bellerophon, Superb, Temeraire.* All completed 1909

Armament:
Ten 12-in guns (5×2)
Sixteen 4-in guns (16×1)
Three 18-in torpedo tubes

Machinery:
Steam turbines 23,000 shp (17,160 kW)
Four shafts 20.5 knots

Armour:
Belt	up to 10 in
Decks	up to 8 in
Turrets	up to 11 in
Barbettes	up to 9 in

St. Vincent

Justification for the commencement of the three St Vincents of the 1907 programme appears rather limited, but the Royal Navy had powerful parliamentary allies, among them M.P.s whose constituencies were dependent upon naval construction and maintenance. Pre-dating significant French, German and American classes, the St. Vincents can be said to have accelerated naval rivalry.

Coming so quickly after the *Bellerophon*, they included only slight improvements. The only visible one was the increase in the barrel length of the main battery, from 45 to 50 calibres. Greater muzzle velocity and penetration were bought, however, at the expense of reduced accuracy, as the long tubes 'whipped' on firing, causing greater salvo dispersion at long ranges.

Lord Armstrong (who made guns as well as ships) was for the virtual abandonment of armour in favour of greater speed and overwhelming offensive power. Sir William White, soured by relinquishing his Directorship of Naval Construction, was 'anti-Dreadnought' and campaigned for a 6-inch secondary armament. The unsatisfactory 4-inch were persisted with, but armour was rearranged, being noticeably reduced at bow and stern but with the addition of powerful transverse bulkheads forward, to protect against end-on hits from a fleeing enemy.

St Vincent class data:

Displacement, standard	19,550 tons
Displacement, full load	23,050 tons
Length overall	536 feet (163.4 m)
Beam	84 feet (25.6 m)
Design draught	26.8 feet (8.2 m)
Complement	760

Class: *Collingwood, St Vincent, Vanguard.* All completed 1910

Armament:
Ten 12-in guns (5×2)
Twenty 4-in guns (20×1)
Three 18-in torpedo tubes

Machinery:
Steam turbines 24,500 shp (18,300 kW)
Four shafts 21 knots

Armour:
Belt	up to 10 in
Bulkheads	up to 8 in
Decks	up to 3 in
Turrets	up to 11 in
Barbettes	up to 9 in

Below: Hercules as completed in August 1911. She was one of several dreadnoughts added to the building programme at the insistence of the Navy League, whose slogan 'we want eight, and we won't wait' helped accelerate the Anglo-German arms race.

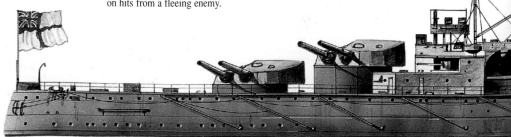

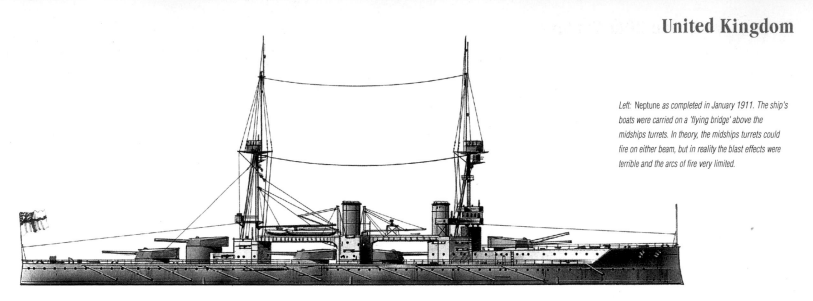

Left: Neptune *as completed in January 1911. The ship's boats were carried on a 'flying bridge' above the midships turrets. In theory, the midships turrets could fire on either beam, but in reality the blast effects were terrible and the arcs of fire very limited.*

Neptune/Colossus class

The British 1908 programme provided for only two capital ships, the battleship *Neptune* and the *Indefatigable*, the first improved Invincible class battle cruiser. With seven Dreadnoughts already commissioned or under construction, the Government (but not the Admiralty) felt able to trim building rate and expenditure. Such altruism was, however, wasted as construction abroad was already being accelerated.

Spurred by the American Delaware class's ability to mount a ten-gun broadside, *Neptune's* layout was significantly revised. The wing turrets amidships were sited en echelon so that, for broadsides, one would need to fire across the ship. This resulted in the superstructure being split into three 'islands', bridged by unsightly spar decks to carry the many boats. Staggering these turrets demanded greater length and, to avoid an undue increase in overall length, the after mountings were superimposed. The arrangement was not satisfactory. Blast effects prevented the superimposed

turret firing over Y-turret. Neither wing turret could be fired within five degrees of the axis. Broadside fire had been purchased at the expense of end-on fire, a reversion to earlier practice.

Neptune's protective system was very much a repeat of the St Vincent's. The two Colossus-class half-sisters of the following year's programme increased the thickness along the main belt and around the barbettes. As a result they were weight-sensitive, needing to revert to patches of armour over the magazines, last seen in the prototype *Dreadnought* For the first time, the extreme ends were 'soft', devoid of

vertical armour. A further reversion was that to a single mast. This saved weight but, being placed abaft the forward funnel, smoke again badly affected fire control. A further design complication was the substitution of the much larger 21-inch torpedo for the earlier 18-inch.

Neptune/Colossus class data:

Neptune:

Displacement, standard	19,680 tons
Displacement, full load	22,700 tons
Length overall	546 feet (166.4 m)
Beam	85 feet (25.9 m)
Design draught	26.3 feet (8.0 m)
Complement	757

Class: *Neptune, Colossus, Hercules.*
All completed 1911.

Armament:
Ten 12-in guns (5 × 2)
Sixteen 4-in guns (16 × 1)
3 × 18-in torpedo tubes

Machinery:
Steam turbines 25,000 shp
Four shafts 21 knots

Armour:

Belt	up to 10 in
Bulkheads	up to 8 in
Deck	up to 3 in
Turrets	up to 11 in
Barbettes	up to 9 in

Colossus and Hercules:

Displacement, standard	19,680 tons
Displacement, full load	22,700 tons
Length overall	546 feet (166.4 m)
Beam	85 feet (25.9 m)
Design draught	26.8 feet (8.2 m)
Complement	757

Armament:
Ten 12-in guns (5 × 2)
Sixteen 4-in guns (16 × 1)
3 × 21-in torpedo tubes

Machinery:
Steam turbines 25,000 shp
Four shafts 21 knots

Armour:

Belt	up to 11 in
Bulkheads	up to 10 in
Deck	up to 4 in
Turrets	up to 11 in
Barbettes	up to 11 in

Left: The foredeck of Inflexible showing the two 12-pdr guns on top of 'A' turret. Built at Clydebank, Inflexible fought at the Falklands, the Dardanelles and Jutland.

Invincible class

Armoured cruisers could be much of a size as battleships but sacrificed some proportion of armament and protection in favour of extra speed. As late as 1904–5 the Japanese could use them directly against the Russian battle lines. This war indicated, however, that future actions might be fought at longer ranges. The three armoured cruisers of the British 1905 programme thus adopted the Dreadnought all-big-gun principle. Compared with the orthodox Minotaurs that preceded them, they were lengthened by about 12 metres to accommodate the 31 boilers required for 25 knots speed, i.e. an improvement of two knots.

Officially 'armoured cruisers', but soon dubbed 'battle cruisers', the Invincibles were intended for reconnaissance in force and, in superseding the armoured cruiser, became also its natural foe. Their broadside of 6800 lb (3091 kg) almost quadrupled that of the mixed 9.2 and 7.5-inch battery of

the Minotaurs. Following Fisher's dictum that speed equalled protection, however, their armour was on a similar scale. The belt was very shallow and, in view of the longer engagement ranges anticipated, horizontal protection was meagre. The design featured a very long forecastle. This not only gave the freeboard necessary for hard driving but also gave extra height for the waist turrets. These were arranged en echelon but had very restricted broadside arcs.

Their bold concept rendered armoured cruisers, including the 35 in the Royal Navy, obsolete. They were, like armoured cruisers, supposed to decline action when circumstances were unfavourable. That their captains did not was, ultimately, to prove their downfall. Used within their design limitations they have to be judged successful. For so revolutionary a concept they were also surprisingly cheap, working one hundred pounds per ton displacement.

Invincible class data:

Displacement, standard ....17,420 tons
Displacement, full load ....20,135 tons
Length overall ....567 feet (172.8 m)
Beam.....................................78.5 feet (23.9 m)
Design draught ....26.8 feet (8.0 m)
Complement 784

Class: Indomitable, Inflexible, Invincible.
All completed 1908

Armament:
Eight 12-in guns (4 × 2)
Twelve 4-in guns (12 × 1)
Five 18-in torpedo tubes

Machinery:
Steam turbines 41,000 shp (30,600 kW)
Four shafts 25 knots

Armour:
Belt ....up to 6 in
Bulkheads ....up to 7 in
Decks ....up to 2.5 in
Turrets ....up to 7 in
Barbettes ....up to 7 in

Below: Indomitable in the camouflage scheme she wore in the Mediterranean during early 1915 when taking part in the Dardanelles operations. She bombarded the Turkish forts in February and March but was disabled by a mine on 19 March and sent to Malta for repairs.

The action off Heligoland on 28 August 1914 was intended by the Royal Navy to assert an early ascendancy. Submarine reconnaissance had detected a high level of routine activity by German light units. A powerful group of Harwich Force destroyers and light cruisers was thus planned to make a sweep, forcing enemy units onto a submarine trap. In case of a foray by the High Seas Fleet, Admiral Beatty was in distant support with five battle cruisers.

Enemy forces proved to be widely scattered and, in conditions of poor visibility, the action degenerated into an uncoordinated brawl. Initially surprised, the Germans reacted quickly, their light cruisers pressing the British hard. Realising the situation, Beatty braved unknown minefields and elbowed his way in. His intervention resulted in a severe blow to the morale of the enemy, who lost three light cruisers and a destroyer. Heligoland proved little about battle cruisers but much about leadership. The Falklands was different.

Graf von Spee's China-based East Asiatic squadron broke for home at the outbreak of war. Three months later, on 1 November 1914, and having crossed the Pacific, it defeated a scratch British squadron at Coronel,

Battles of the Heligoland Bight and the Falklands

off the Chilean coast. The Admiralty reasoned that von Spee would double the Cape and raid the Falklands for bunkers before running the length of the Atlantic. Fisher despatched a cruiser squadron headed by two Invincibles.

The Germans duly arrived off the islands on 8 December. Surprise was absolute. Conditions were calm and visibility excellent. Von Spee's only hope lay in flight but, long out of dock, his ships were relentlessly run down. The two German armoured cruisers *Scharnhorst* and *Gneisenau* had been reduced

to only 445 main battery rounds apiece by the Coronel action and the British kept to long 12-inch range. Manoeuvring to avoid their own copious funnel smoke, the battlecruisers expended 1200 rounds over four hours, completing the task with minimum risk.

The battle cruiser concept was proven. Their speed had enabled them to cover 7,000 miles quickly and to remain beyond a dangerous range when the action was joined. Overwhelming firepower did the rest.

Admiral Sir Jackie Fisher

Probably the Royal Navy's greatest reformer and innovator, 'Jackie' Fisher gained prominence as captain of the *Inflexible* at Alexandria in 1882. Achieving flag rank and a seat on the Board of Admiralty in the 1890s, he imposed change on an inefficient and reluctant navy. As First Sea Lord (1904–10) his concern at the rise of the German fleet, and developments in the United States and Japan, saw him rush the *Dreadnought* through conception and construction. He championed the early development of destroyers and submarines, and the introduction of water-tube boilers and oil fuel. Officer training and the lot of the ordinary matelot were also reformed. Inefficient, over-age tonnage was scrapped ruthlessly.

He resigned following the celebrated feud with Beresford, but was recalled by Churchill in 1914. Argument over the Dardanelles fiasco caused a second resignation. He died in 1920 at the age of 79 as Admiral of the Fleet, Baron Fisher of Kilverstone.

Top left: An aerial view of Inflexible *shows how little room there was for the midships turrets to fire on the opposite beam.*

Centre: Inflexible *opens fire on the German cruisers at the Falklands, 8 December 1914. Picture taken from the maintop of* Invincible.

Above: Three surviving 'I' class battlecruisers at the surrender of the German fleet in 1918. The 'Invincibles' proved the validity of their design at the Falklands, destroying the German cruisers from outside the range of the enemy's 8.2-in guns. It was not the fault of the designers that these powerful cruisers found themselves at Jutland fighting warships with twice their weight of armour protection.

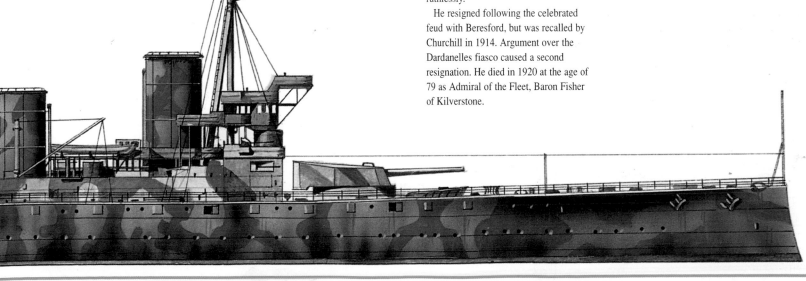

Iron Duke class

The four Orions were quickly followed by a lengthened and marginally improved quartette of King George Vs. So rapid now was the pace of battleship construction that the latter group and the four Iron Dukes that followed were all laid down in the space of seventeen months in 1911–12.

The major improvement in the Iron Dukes was the upgrading of the secondary armament from the earlier 4-inch to 6-inch. The primary function of these weapons was the deterrence of attack by flotillas of enemy torpedo craft and, somewhat tardily, the increase in calibre recognised the fact that foreign destroyers had increased in size and striking power, so that the 4-inch no longer had sufficient lethality or range. The 6-inch were grouped in casemates, mostly at upper deck level from the bridge forward. The disposition introduced the characteristic faceted bows to British battleships. Three-inch anti-aircraft guns were carried permanently for the first time.

Despite a further jump in size and displacement, the extra weight of secondary armament prevented any real improvement to protection. Where the King George Vs had not reintroduced longitudinal torpedo bulkheads, they did provide limited vertical protection below the level of the main belt and running continuously from Q-turret amidships to Y-turret. This covered the engine room but left the boiler spaces without any below-the-belt protection. This arrangement was repeated in the Iron Dukes, but appeared questionable as the protected machinery space could not

Right: Jellicoe's former flagship Iron Duke *bombards Bolshevik positions at Kaffa Bay in 1919. She spent 1919–20 in the Black sea, supporting the White Russians against the communist forces before being transferred to the Mediterranean fleet.*

function without the unprotected boilers. As it happened, *Marlborough* was thoroughly tested by a torpedo hit at Jutland. The 500 mm weapon (launched by the German cruiser *Wiesbaden*) hit the starboard side, ahead of the forward boiler space. Good damage control kept the resulting list to no more than eight degrees, the ship maintaining her place in the line.

Iron Duke class data:

Displacement, standard	25,800 tons
Displacement, full load	30,400 tons

Length overall	622.8 feet (189.8 m)
Beam	90 feet (27.4 m)
Design draught	28.5 feet (8.7 m)
Complement	950

Class *Benbow, Emperor of India, Iron Duke, Marlborough.* All completed 1914

Armament:
Ten 13.5-in guns (5×2)
Twelve 6-in guns (12×1)
Two 3-in guns (2×1)
Four 21-in torpedo tubes

Machinery:
Steam turbines 29,000 shp (21630 kW)
Four shafts 21 knots

Armour:

Belt	up to 12 in
Bulkheads	up to 8 in
Decks	up to 2.5 in
Turrets	up to 11 in
Barbettes	up to 10 in

Below: Iron Duke *seen in 1917 with a Sopwith Camel positioned on a flying-off platform mounted on 'B' and 'Q' turrets. The aircraft were used to drive off German zeppelins, flying back to England to land afterwards.*

Orion class

Attempts by the United Kingdom to slow its rate of Dreadnought construction were brought to the ground during 1908, when Austria annexed Bosnia and Herzegovina. This was with explicit German support. Though alarmed, the British Government still needed to be cajoled into action by a threat of resignation from the First Lord, supported by alarming figures (subsequently proved incorrect) regarding German construction plans. The result was a 1909 programme that funded no less than eight capital ships.

The first fruits of the accelerated programme were the two Neptune half-sisters but these were trumped before they were even in the water by the laying-down of the four Orions. These adopted a 13.5-inch main battery, a calibre last used only twenty years previously in the seven successful Royal Sovereigns, and re-adopted because of a German hike to 30.5 cm (12-inch) guns in the five Kaisers. Where the latter copied the Neptune's unsatisfactory turret disposition, the Orions went for the more logical American-style all-centreline layout, but without the eccentricities.

The turrets were heavy and the elevated weight of the superimposed mountings, together with upgraded side protection, demanded increased size for stability. Although length could be increased, beam was still limited by dry-dock dimensions. The class thus had finer lines and a roll problem. Continuing difficulties with weight distribution is evident from the adherence to the unsatisfactory single tripod mast and the repeated lack of longitudinal torpedo bulkheads.

A ten-gun broadside from an Orion weighed at least 12,500 lb (5682 kg), against the 8,500 lb (3864 kg) of a Neptune. Barrel length and muzzle velocity were, however, less, requiring an increase in elevation to achieve a satisfactory range.

Orion class data:

Displacement, standard	22,200 tons
Displacement, full load	25,850 tons
Length overall	581 feet (177.1 m)
Beam	88.5 feet (27.0 m)
Design draught	26.8 feet (8.2 m)
Complement	752

Right. The four Orion class carried new 13.5-in guns that gave them a substantially heavier broadside than contemporary German battleships.

Class: *Conqueror, Monarch, Orion, Thunderer*
All completed 1912

Armament:
Ten 13.5-in guns (5 × 2)
Sixteen 4-in guns (16 × 1)
Three 21-in torpedo tubes

Machinery:
Steam turbines 27,000 shp (20150 kW)
Four shafts 20.5 knots

Armour:

Belt	up to 12 in
Bulkheads	up to 10 in
Decks	up to 4 in
Turrets	up to 11 in
Barbettes	up to 10 in

Fire control

In days of sail, range to target could be measured by two simultaneously taken sextant angles, using own ship as a baseline. Long-base optical range finders began to appear in the 1890s for the same purpose. Own ship movement greatly affected firing accuracy. Captain (later Admiral Sir) Percy Scott, using extemporised techniques, demonstrated conclusively that, with regular practice, gunlayers could continuously adjust in elevation and training, quickly enough to allow for ship movement.

To hit a target at long range required prediction. In 1902, the 'Dumaresq' mixed known data (own speed and course, enemy bearing) with two estimates (enemy course and speed) to produce the useful output of rates of change in enemy range and bearing. This enabled the guns to aim at where the enemy would be at the end of time of flight, and not where he was at the time of the last observed fall of shot. This device was incorporated by Dreyer into a Fire Control Table, where its data was mixed mechanically with Pollen's separate range and bearing plots, updated continuously by observation. Each refined the accuracy of the other, aided by input from the 'spotters'. It was then a short step to director firing, introduced officially in 1913, where identical data was passed to each gun. When each had indicated it was ready, all were fired simultaneously by a single key.

Above: The Orions could bring all guns to bear on either beam.

Lion class

The three Indefatigable-class battle cruisers that succeeded the Invincibles were slightly improved with a layout that allowed a genuine eight-gun broadside. Design shortcomings were repeated. Insufficient protection was marginally redistributed, but remained insufficient. Total flooding of any of the large machinery spaces would

Right and below:
Battlecruiser equivalents of the Orion class battleships, the Lions were handsome indeed, but they purchased their impressive 27 knots at the expense of protection. Beatty's flagship at Dogger Bank and Jutland, Lion narrowly survived hits on her turrets that could easily have destroyed her. Queen Mary was hit by five shells from Derfflinger at Jutland and sank in a massive explosion.

probably have caused the loss of the ship. Critics had already pointed out, on the other hand, that they would at some time be used as a fast battle squadron in a fleet action, where their speed would probably be little utilised but their poor protection would inevitably be exposed.

Against this background were conceived the Lions, of the 1909 and 1910

Programmes. As with the then-building Orions, they were to carry the new 13.5-inch gun, but the greatest impact was made by a requirement for a 27-knot speed. To give this 2-knot margin over the contemporary German Moltkes, a total of 42 boilers needed to be accommodated in a considerably enlarged hull. Some 120 feet (36.6 m) longer than the Orion, they were imposing ships, engendering pride in both Service and public alike.

Unfortunately, an even larger area of hull needed to be protected, again resulting in inadequate thickness of armour. Adoption of a Q-turret, instead of a more logical superimposed mounting in 'X'-position, had the advantage of splitting the vast boiler spaces into two less vulnerable groups. It also lessened the considerable concentrated masses sited toward the extremities of a weak hull girder. It squandered protection, however, as it required larger areas to protect two separate barbettes (Q & Y) than two closely-grouped (A & B).

Turret, barbette and belt alike were limited to a maximum of 9-inch plate, insufficient to resist a standard German

11-inch projectile. Barbette protection tapered to a mere 3 inches once below the upper belt level. Except at extreme bow and stern, horizontal armour amounted to a near non-existent one inch. A comparatively small plunging projectile could thus, quite simply, penetrate the deck inboard of the belt and strike a lower barbette at its thinnest point. For such a concept the 'zone of immunity' is limited. An armoured cruiser, such as an 8.2-inch gunned Scharnhorst could be tackled at a range short enough to guarantee flat trajectories (where the belt would be effective) or, conversely, at beyond 8.2 range altogether. However, against an 11-inch gunned opponent, the only option was to use superior speed to remain beyond 11-inch range. It was the tragedy of the battle cruiser that the realities of war denied them the luxury of deciding their range.

At Jutland the *Queen Mary* was destroyed by an 11- or 12-inch round penetrating a forward turret or barbette. Her sister, *Lion*, had Q-turret wrecked by a 12-inch hit, the ship being saved only by rapid flooding of the magazine below.

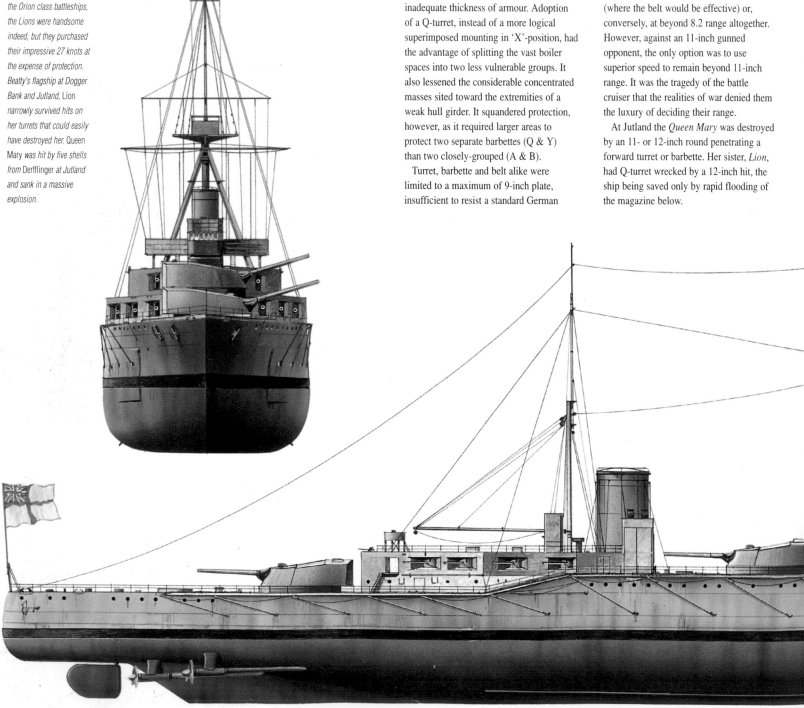

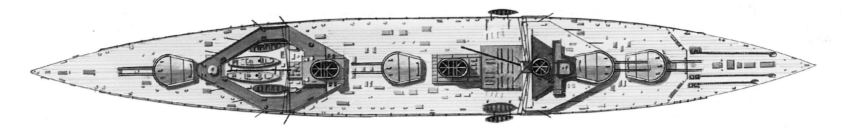

Lion class data:

Displacement, standard	26,250 tons
Displacement, full load	29,700 tons
Length overall	700 feet (213.4 m)
Beam	88.5 feet (27.0 m)
Design draught	27.6 feet (8.4 m)
Complement	995

Class: *Lion, Princess Royal, Queen Mary.*
Completed 1912-13

Armament:
Eight 13.5-in guns (4×2)
Sixteen 4-in guns (16×1)
Two 21-in torpedo tubes

Machinery:
Steam turbines 70,000 shp (52,200 kW)
Four shafts 26.5 knots

Armour:

Belt	up to 9 in
Bulkheads	up to 4 in
Decks	up to 2.5 in
Turrets	up to 9 in
Barbettes	up to 9 in

Above: The 42 boilers required to provide 70,000 shp occupied a great deal of space. Retaining a midships turret meant splitting the magazine and handling rooms, creating a vulnerable and inadequately armoured area.

Right: Princess Royal *leads two 'I' class battlecruisers into the Solent in the summer of 1914. The Royal Navy was fully mobilised for exercises when the murder of Archduke Franz Ferdinand brought Europe to the brink of war.*

Agincourt

The last of the Royal Navy's 12-inch gunned battleships was by far the most individual. At a time when the United Kingdom built much of the world's warship tonnage, the Admiralty looked upon foreign account hulls as a useful buffer in times of tension, an asset to be appropriated by purchase.

In the autumn of 1911 the British shipbuilder Armstrong laid down a battleship for Brazil. This country's neighbour, Argentina, had recently contracted in the United States for the two Rivadavias. These would have the respectable armament of twelve 12-inch guns but, not to be outdone, Brazil trumped this by specifying twelve 14-inch, not a calibre familiar to the British. A change in political office soon had the design altered to a slightly smaller ship, armed with 12-inch guns and, thus, compatible with the earlier British-built pair of Minas Geraes. No less than fourteen guns were called for, necessitating seven twin turrets (triples were still being used only abroad). The result was a splendidly long-hulled, belligerent-looking ship with forward superimposed turrets, of which 'A' mounting was on the same level as the amidships, centreline 'P' and 'Q' turrets, which were also on the long forecastle deck. Right aft, was a three-turret grouping with a superimposed centre mounting, an arrangement unique until re-adopted by Japanese heavy cruisers of the late 1920s.

Nearly the length of a Lion, she shared the problem of protection. Again barbette armour was thinned drastically once behind the belt, vulnerable to plunging fire that the 1.5-inch upper deck could never withstand. She was launched as the *Rio de Janeiro* but, probably because the 13.5-inch gun had now been introduced, the Brazilians put her up for sale. Still fitting out, she was acquired by Turkey and re-named *Sultan Osman* I. As such she was taken over by the Royal Navy and named *Agincourt*.

Later removal of the unsightly after tripod resulted in a truly magnificent looking ship.

Awe-inspiring in action, she came through Jutland without damage. She lacked director control but still hit the Markgraf and Kaiser, the latter twice.

Agincourt data:

Displacement, standard	27,500 tons
Displacement, full load	30,250 tons
Length overall	671.5 feet (204.7 m)
Beam	89 feet (27.1 m)
Design draught	27 feet (8.2 m)
Complement	1120

Completed 1914

Armament:
Fourteen 12-in guns (7 × 2)
Twenty 6-in guns (20 × 1)
Ten 3-in guns (10 × 1)
Three 21-in torpedo tubes

Machinery:
Steam turbines 34,000 shp (25,350 kW)
Four shafts 22 knots

Armour:
Belt	up to 9 in
Bulkheads	up to 6 in
Decks	up to 2.5 in
Turrets	up to 12 in
Barbettes	up to 9 in

Ships appropriated by the United Kingdom

In 1911 Turkey placed an order in the UK for two capital ships. Embroiled in a Balkan war, however, the Turks were obliged first to delay construction, then to cancel one unit. The remaining battleship, *Reshadieh*, was approaching completion in 1914 when the Brazilian *Rio de Janeiro* unexpectedly came on the market. The Turks bought the latter too, partly by public subscription after a government propaganda campaign. Inevitably, the Greeks were unhappy about the distortion that these acquisitions would cause to the balance in the Aegean, threatening countermeasures.

The latter issue was resolved in August 1914 by Churchill subsuming both ships into the Royal Navy as the *Erin* and *Agincourt*. Turkish outrage was met by a British offer to pay for the ships' use for the duration of the war, but the Ottomans were not to be placated.

Churchill's move was, in any case, astute as the Turks and Germans had just signed a Treaty of Alliance, the Turks actually offering their new allies the services of their new acquisition. Their loss was partly made good by the Germans, whose *Mittelmeerdivision*, comprising the battle cruiser *Goeben* and light cruiser *Breslau*, were quickly chased by the Allies into the neutral sanctuary of Turkish waters. There followed the farce of the German ships being 'sold' to Turkey (while retaining their German crews and their commander, Rear Admiral Souchon, eventually becoming a Turkish vice-admiral with certain rights of command).

The *Goeben* was a considerable loss to the High Seas Fleet and proved to be of little use in the Black Sea. While the Royal Navy was required to devote capital units to watching against her escape, these were already involved in the Dardanelles operation. On balance the British were the main beneficiaries.

The ship gained, renamed *Erin*, was a useful 23,000-tonner, armed with ten 13.5s.

Effectively a diminutive of the Iron Dukes, she actually mounted four more 6-inch guns in her secondary battery and was only a half-knot slower. Inevitably, this resulted in a marginally lower standard of protection. She was regarded as a very successful compromise, due mainly to her designers being able to increase her beam to beyond that imposed on British battleships.

Chile, as usual in competition with Argentina and Brazil, ordered a pair of

Below: Agincourt, as completed in 1914 when the Royal Navy seized her from Turkey. The butt of much humour in the Navy, she fired full 14-gun broadsides at Jutland, the sight appearing to onlookers like a battleship exploding!

Right: Agincourt leads the 4th Battle Squadron in 1915. The cumbersome 'flying bridge' structure has been removed.

27,400-ton battleships from the United Kingdom in 1911. Only one, the *Almirante Latorre*, was advanced quickly, the other (*Almirante Cochrane*) having to wait for a slip to be vacated by Brazil's *Rio de Janeiro*. Nearing completion, the *Latorre* was taken over by the Royal Navy, as

HMS *Canada*, for the duration of hostilities. A stretched Iron Duke, she was a useful acquisition, with ten 14-inch and sixteen 6-inch. With no political problems apparent, she was refitted and returned to Chilean ownership early in 1920. Modernised, she survived until 1959.

The Cochrane, meanwhile, was far from complete in August 1914, even losing her designated gun mountings for use in monitors. Her construction suspended, she was purchased outright by the Admiralty in 1917 and converted into the aircraft carrier *Eagle*.

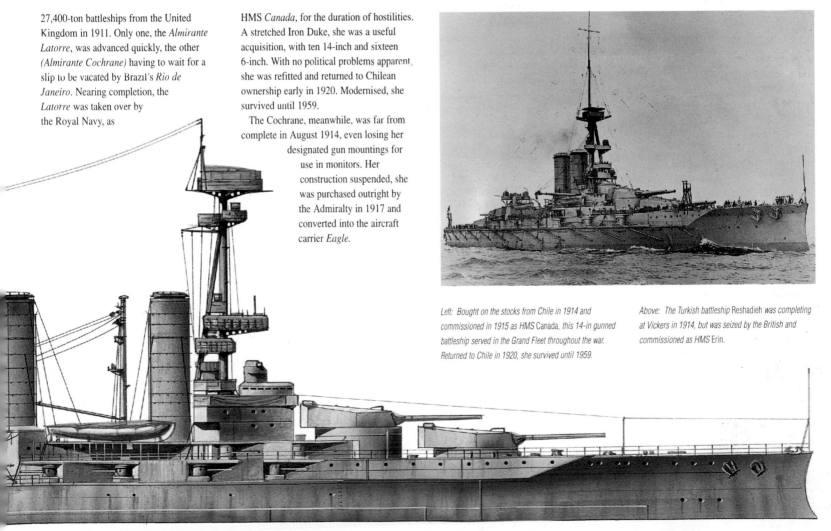

Left: Bought on the stocks from Chile in 1914 and commissioned in 1915 as HMS Canada, this 14-in gunned battleship served in the Grand Fleet throughout the war. Returned to Chile in 1920, she survived until 1959.

Above: The Turkish battleship Reshadieh was completing at Vickers in 1914, but was seized by the British and commissioned as HMS Erin.

Tiger

With her symmetrical trio of funnels, the one-off *Tiger* was unmistakable in appearance. While graceful, however, she lacked much of the 'presence' of the preceding Lions. Originally intended to be a fourth unit of this class, she was completed to a modified design, due to the influence of the Japanese battle cruiser *Kongo*, newly delivered by Vickers. This yard had improved somewhat on the deficiencies of the Lions and these improvements were incorporated into a delayed *Tiger*.

The closer-spaced funnels betrayed a continuous series of boiler spaces, five in all. Engineering development meant that three fewer boilers than were installed in the Lions produced over 20 per cent more power. With her increased beam and greater displacement, this translated into only one extra knot in speed. A great conservatism reigned in boilers, the Germans using the more compact but more technically demanding small-bore boiler tubes, resulting in far more compact units.

Externally, the abolition of after superstructure enabled the 'Q' mounting to fire dead astern, its distance forward of 'X' turret obviating overpressure effects on the latter. Protection was on a similar scale as the Lions but better distributed, aided by the disposition of the casemated 6-inch secondary armament.

The ship received no less than fifteen 11-inch hits at Jutland, her survival illustrating the great element of chance in battle. 'X'-turret barbette was struck at the awkward junction of 9- and 3-inch armour, the projectile only partially detonating. Simultaneously, a shell hit the roof of 'Q' turret at a shallow angle. Exploding external to the structure, it blew a large hole but did not destroy the guns. In addition, 'A' turret barbette was struck by an 11-inch projectile that had penetrated the unarmoured ship's side. Fortunately, it impacted at a structurally stiff point - just a half-metre lower, the 8-inch plate was thinned to just 4-inch.

Tiger data:

Displacement, standard	28,450 tons
Displacement, full load	35,150 tons
Length overall	704 feet (214.6 m)
Beam	90.5 feet (27.6 m)
Design draught	28.5 feet (8.7 m)
Complement	1120

Completed 1914

Armament:
Eight 13.5-in guns (4 × 2)
Twelve 6-in guns (12 × 1)
Two 3-in guns (2 × 1)
Four 21-in torpedo tubes

Machinery:
Steam turbines 85,000 shp (63,400 kW)
Four shafts 28 knots

Armour:

Belt	up to 9 in
Bulkheads	up to 5 in
Decks	up to 3 in
Turrets	up to 9 in
Barbettes	up to 9 in

Below: Developed from the Lion class, Tiger's more sensible turret arrangement was not only more efficient, but gave her a very graceful profile. A very lucky ship, she survived 15 hits by heavy shells at Jutland. Most caused only minor damage, but one unexploded shell came to rest on the floor of a gun turret.

Shortly after 07.00 on 24 January 1915 Beatty, with five battle cruisers, surprised a powerful German force near the Dogger Bank. Good intelligence work had indicated an enemy sweep which, in fact, comprised three battle cruisers of Hipper's group, supported by the armoured cruiser *Blücher*.

First contact was made by supporting light forces, and Hipper, uncertain of the opposition, turned onto a precautionary SE course. It was over an hour before he became aware that the ships overhauling him were, in fact, also battle cruisers. *Blücher* could manage only 23 knots at the tail of the line.

A little after 09.00 Beatty's *Lion*, in the van, could range the *Blücher* at the then great distance of 20,000 yards (18,300 m). Within a half-hour all of Hipper's ships could be reached and Beatty ordered his units to engage their opposite numbers. With five ships to four, this signal was clearly ambiguous and resulted in the *Moltke* being undisturbed. She opened a deliberate fire on the *Lion*, which ship, hit heavily also by the *Seydlitz* and *Derfflinger*, received sixteen heavy-calibre projectiles. Her power failing, she slowed and fell out of line.

A false submarine sighting at this juncture caused the four remaining British ships to turn eight points together, losing ground and fouling the range. The hapless Beatty, two miles astern, made a flag signal to order his second-in-command, Moore, to maintain a hot pursuit. This, too, was ambiguously worded and Moore read it as an instruction to finish off the sorely tried *Blücher*, which he did, as Hipper escaped with his three survivors, *Seydlitz* badly damaged. An incandescent Beatty finally

succeeded in reaching the scene, having transferred to a destroyer, but it was too late, further pursuit being out of the question. The lost victory featured the failings that would dog the Grand Fleet throughout the war - poor signal procedures, an exaggerated fear of submarines, and a lack of initiative in subordinate commanders. As Fisher raged afterwards: '... in war the first principle is to disobey orders! Any fool can obey orders!'

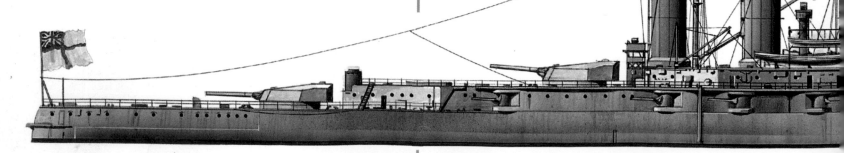

The Battle of Dogger Bank

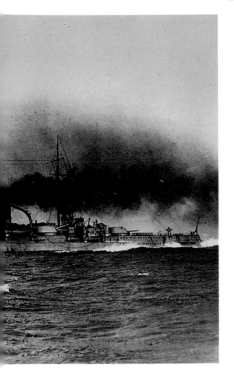

Above: The unfortunate German armoured cruiser Blücher was armed with 8.2-in guns and too slow to escape the British battlecruisers at Dogger Bank.

Left: Tiger fired off a lot of ammunition at Dogger Bank, but her gunnery was completely ineffective. Mistaking her consorts' shell splashes for her own, she continued to fire about 3,000 yards 'over' the German line throughout the battle.

Admiral Sir David Beatty

From Irish fox-hunting gentry, David Beatty was handsome, controversial and courageous. His valour in the Sudan and at the Boxer Rebellion saw him created Captain at only 29. In August 1914 he was serving Churchill as naval secretary, but was immediately given command of the Grand Fleet's battle crüisers. He led them in the *Lion*, with great dash but taking appalling risks. In August 1914 he rescued the Harwich Force at the Heligoland Bight but, five months later, was let down by his second-in command at the Dogger Bank losing a marvellous opportunity to cripple the German battlecruiser squadron. Jutland brought out the best and worst in Beatty. In taking on Hipper without waiting for his dedicated support, his squadron suffered grievous loss but its leader pressed on both to sight the advancing High Seas Fleet and to prevent Hipper detecting Jellicoe's approach.

Beatty succeeded Jellicoe soon after but the Grand Fleet never had the chance of a second Jutland. As Admiral of the Fleet Earl Beatty, he served as First Sea Lord from 1919 until 1927, when he retired. He died in 1936 aged 65.

Above: Admiral Sir David Beatty's dashing style of leadership made him a popular hero and the only choice to succeed the ailing Jellicoe in command of the Grand Fleet. His pugnacious handling of the battlecruisers off Heligoland involved great risks, but achieved a valuable early victory. At Jutland, his sangfroid under fire passed into legend. 'There seems to be something wrong with our bloody ships today,' he observed as another of his squadron exploded astern of Lion.

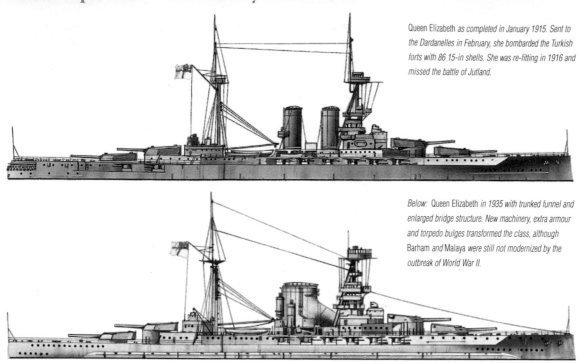

Below: Queen Elizabeth in 1935 with trunked funnel and enlarged bridge structure. New machinery, extra armour and torpedo bulges transformed the class, although Barham and Malaya were still not modernized by the outbreak of World War II.

Queen Elizabeth class

With the 'QEs' the designers achieved a near-perfect balance between speed, protection and armament. Their arrival was timely and, by virtue of surviving the wholesale scrapping following the Washington Treaty, their life was long. Through their service in both World Wars they were also excellent value for money.

All were laid down in 1912–13. The American New York and Texas, laid down in 1911, had already adopted the 14-inch gun, followed closely by the Japanese Harunas. As this had already surpassed the 13.5s of the Iron Dukes, the new First Lord, Churchill, succeeded in pushing through the development of a 15-inch weapon. This turned out to be one of the most successful and reliable guns yet produced, but the associated weight meant that only eight barrels could be carried on a reasonably sized hull in place of earlier battleships' ten or more. Lack of a 'Q' mounting, however, freed valuable space amidships for a more

compact arrangement of machinery, which improved on the Iron Dukes' output by over 150 per cent, giving them an invaluable 2.5 knot edge.

Protection included a thickened (13-inch) belt from 'A' to 'Y' barbettes, thinned fore and aft of these positions and leaving extreme ends 'soft'. Compared with the preceding class, the main deck armour (immediately above the main belt) was quite drastically reduced, from eight to six inches. A 2-inch longitudinal bulkhead gave some protection from torpedo attack over the complete span of machinery spaces and magazines. It was accepted, however, that being the world's first exclusively oil-fired battleship, this fuel was stowed both in-and-outboard of the torpedo bulkhead. In earlier classes, these spaces were filled with coal, a material that had a measure of absorption of large explosions. Oil, being liquid, was effectively incompressible and without voids, so that a shock wave would travel

through it, virtually without attenuation. Anti-torpedo bulges were fitted during the twenties.

The nameship, the first completed, used the Dardanelles to effect a most impressive calibration of her

main armament, with aircraft-spotted indirect fire. The remaining four were at Jutland and, in supporting Beatty's battle cruisers, all but the *Valiant* suffered, and survived, significant damage.

As the Royal Navy's primary battleships, the Queen Elizabeths were much modified between the wars. *Malaya* and *Barham* were least changed, gaining an imposing trunked funnel in place of the earlier pair, cranes and hangar space for four aircraft and a considerable 4-inch and 2-pounder anti-aircraft armament. With treaty prohibitions against new construction, their three sisters were greatly rebuilt. All had completely remodelled superstructure. *Warspite* retained some of her original 6-inch secondary guns but the others gained the far more useful high-angle 4.5-inch in twin mountings. The main armament was re-engineered to give a maximum of 30 (rather than 20) degrees elevation. As protection was also improved, displacement inevitably increased, despite being offset by a completely new set of modern and lighter machinery.

Barham was sunk in 1941 by a salvo of three torpedoes, and only the shallow waters of Alexandria harbour saved the *Queen Elizabeth* and *Valiant* when they were 'Tarantoed' by the Italians soon afterward.

Queen Elizabeth data:

N.B. Data is for *Queen Elizabeth* only. As rebuilt there were considerable differences between units

As built:

Displacement, standard................26,250 tons
Displacement, full load ....33,000 tons
Length overall...............645.8 feet (196.8 m)
Beam...................................90.5 feet (27.6 m)
Design draught ....30.2 feet (9.2 m)
Complement 938

Class: *Barham, Malaya, Queen Elizabeth, Valiant, Warspite*
Cancelled: *Agincourt*

Armament:
Eight 15-in guns (4×2
Sixteen 6-in guns (16×1)
Two 3-in guns (2×1)
Four 21-in torpedo tubes
Four aircraft

Machinery:
Steam turbines 75,000 shp (55950 kW)
Four shafts 24 knots

Armour:
Belt ....up to 13 in
Bulkheads ....up to 6 in
Decks ....up to 3 in
Turrets ....up to 13 in
Barbettes ....up to 10 in

As modernised:
Displacement, standard................32,450 tons
Displacement, full load ....36,000 tons
Length overall ....645.8 feet (196.8 m)

Beam...................................104 feet (31.7 m)
Design draught ....30.2 feet (9.2 m)
Complement 1190

Class: *Queen Elizabeth, Valiant, Warspite* only

Armament:
Eight 15-in guns (4×2
Twenty 4.5 guns (10×2)
32×40 mm guns
Four 21-in torpedo tubes
Four aircraft
Aircraft removed 1943

Machinery:
Steam turbines 80,000 shp (59700 kW)
Four shafts 24 knots

Armour:
Belt ....up to 13 in
Bulkheads ....up to 6 in
Decks ....up to 4 in
Turrets ....up to 13 in
Barbettes ....up to 10 in

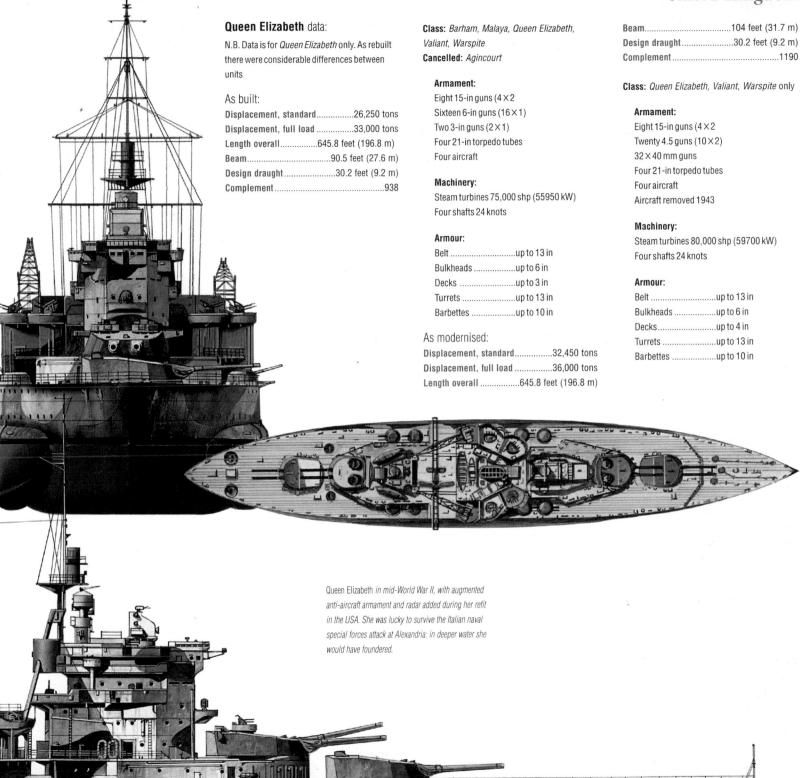

Queen Elizabeth *in mid-World War II, with augmented anti-aircraft armament and radar added during her refit in the USA. She was lucky to survive the Italian naval special forces attack at Alexandria: in deeper water she would have foundered.*

The Battle of Jutland

Left: Moltke was one of the few German battlecruisers to escape serious damage at Jutland. She scored many hits on HMS Tiger, survived the 'battlecruiser charge' against the Grand Fleet and slipped past the British squadrons to reach safety by dawn.

Right: Admiral Sir John Jellicoe was never really forgiven for failing to achieve a Trafalgar style victory at Jutland. His own caution and a crippling lack of initiative throughout the fleet enabled the Germans to escape the disaster they had courted.

Directed by the Kaiser to take no unjustifiable risks with his fleet, Vice-Admiral Scheer decided to make a large-scale demonstration towards the Skaggerak. The British Grand Fleet would, inevitably, be lured to sea, only to fall foul of a carefully placed submarine trap. Days of poor weather delayed the operation so that, by 31 May 1916 when the High Seas Fleet actually sailed, the submarines were scattered and near the end of their endurance. British radio intelligence of Scheer's impending movement caused Admiral Jellicoe to sail promptly. Missing the U-boats, the Grand Fleet was, by the early afternoon, converging almost at right angles on the Germans. At 14.28, the light cruiser *Galatea* signalled 'Enemy in sight', as she brushed with enemy light forces investigating a stationary merchantman.

Vice-Admiral Beatty, with six battle cruisers, responded immediately without waiting for the supporting 5th Battle Squadron of four fast Queen Elizabeths. His opposite number, Vice-Admiral Hipper, with five battle cruisers, was heading for the same spot. Sighting Beatty at 15.40, Hipper recalled his light forces and turned about onto a SE course to lure the British on to Scheer's Battle Fleet.

Running parallel courses at a range of some 13,000 yards (11,900 metres) the battle cruisers engaged in a fierce gunnery duel. At 16.05, apparently being hit by two complete salvoes, the *Indefatigable* disintegrated in a magazine explosion. At this point, providentially, the 15-inch guns of the 5th B.S. found the range at 19,000 yards (17,400 metres). Heartened, Beatty closed Hipper to head off his 'escape'. In doing so, the *Queen Mary* was heavily hit amidships. At 16.26, she too blew up.

Hipper, under heavy pressure, headed away covered by his light forces, but suddenly the situation was transformed. Beatty's light cruisers, scouting ahead, came into view of Scheer's battle line, advancing northward. The range was a bare 12,000 yards (11,000 metres) and closing fast. Beatty's duty was clear. Reversing the situation, he turned about at 16.40, hoping to lure both Hipper and Scheer onto the yet-unsuspected Jellicoe. He was covered by the 5th B.S. whose 15-inch guns still had Hipper's range. Under heavy fire, the latter bore off north-eastward, only to run into three further battle cruisers. These were Hood's 3rd B.C.S., attached to Jellicoe. Their fire, and that of Beatty, forced Hipper back. Jellicoe remained unobserved.

Jellicoe himself was in a quandary. He was receiving only scraps of information. His fleet was still in cruising formation, six parallel columns, each of four battleships. He needed to deploy into a battle line but the order would depend upon the direction of Scheer's approach. Beatty provided the vital visual link at 18.14. With the High Seas Fleet only seven miles distant, the Grand Fleet began, correctly, to deploy on the port wing column. To cover this critical manoeuvre, the battle cruisers continued to engage Hipper fiercely. The cost of keeping the enemy back was the loss of Hood's *Invincible* to yet another catastrophic explosion.

Below: British dreadnoughts in line ahead. At Jutland, Jellicoe deployed 24 battleships across the head of the German line, exposing the leading ships to a crushing fire. The Germans reversed course and escaped, covered by their destroyers.

The Grand Fleet was still deploying when Scheer's column came into view. Its 'T' crossed, the van of the High Seas Fleet came in for a torrent of fire from the British line. Under intolerable pressure, Scheer ordered a 16-point (i.e. 180-degree) 'battle turn'. Covered by smoke from light units, the Germans melted into the patchy visibility. Firing petered out at 18.42.

Jellicoe was heading generally southward with Scheer on a parallel course a safe ten miles further west. At 18.55 the latter made the inexplicable decision to charge again at the British centre. At 19.10 he was, again, predictably battered and, to cover a second battle turn, he flung Hipper's sorely tried squadron on its famous 'death ride' at the Grand Fleet. His destroyers also made a torpedo attack and Jellicoe felt obliged to fall off by two points. This was a critical decision for there was now a bare hour of daylight remaining.

Tactically already defeated, Scheer had to steer southward for safety. Jellicoe anticipated this and, as the last of the light died, at 20.40 the two lines were on gradually converging courses, only seven miles apart. Jellicoe did not want to sacrifice his numerical advantage in the lottery of a night melee, and again bore away on a course best calculated to renew the battle at first light. Throughout the night, supporting squadrons and flotillas encountered each other in fierce and bloody clashes but Jellicoe, still poorly served for intelligence, steamed on. Scheer, aware of his intentions, was able to ease up and cut across the Grand Fleet's wake. By 03.00, a little before sunrise, the British C in C knew that the battle had ended. Scheer was 30 miles to the east, the Horns Reef swept

channel clear before him. With the High Seas Fleet beyond reach the British turned for home.

The great opportunity, 'Der Tag', had come and gone. For all the gallantry and sacrifice there was to be no Trafalgar. Indisputably, Scheer had won the material victory, sinking 155,000 tons against a loss of 61,000, but it was all to no effect. The balance sheet was barely affected. The North Sea was still barred by the Grand Fleet. The Germans turned to the U-boat to win the maritime war.

Below: Minutes after entering action, Admiral Hood's flagship Invincible *exploded. Only three men survived from her crew of 1031. Her opening salvoes inflicted mortal damage on the German battlecruiser* Lutzow, *but a hit from* Derfflinger *penetrated 'Q' turret and detonated her magazine.*

Left: Hercules fires a salvo from one of her wing turrets. British fear of a night action helped the Germans to escape at Jutland. Only after World War I did the Royal Navy devote serious attention to night-fighting.

Below: Struck by an early salvo from von der Tann, *HMS* Indefatigable *suffered a magazine explosion which broke her back.*

Bottom: Seas breaking over the forecastle of one of the Queen Elizabeth class 'fast battleships'. Capable of 25 knots, they supported Beatty's battlecruisers in the opening phase of the battle.

Courageous class

This extraordinary trio defies classification, and are here included only by virtue of their unusual size and armament, and an original official categorisation as battle cruisers, which they were not. To understand their function requires an understanding of Admiral Fisher's Baltic plan. This, conceived well before World War I, and before the doctrines of amphibious warfare had ever been considered, envisaged correctly the need of bombardment prior to, and during, the assault phase. Expendable predreadnoughts, even if used with the flair and imagination that was totally lacking at the Dardanelles, would probably have been unable to penetrate the Baltic. Thus the *Courageous* and her sisters were expected to manoeuvre in the shallow waters for which they were designed (as at Mobile Bay, it would have had to be a case of 'Damn the torpedoes', i.e. mines), delivering heavy salvoes on the terror-stricken defenders. In practice, four 15-inch

Above: The deck plan of Courageous *in 1918. Flying-off platforms are fitted to both turrets and a Sopwith 1½ Strutter is mounted atop 'A' turret.*

Below: Courageous *as she appeared on the eve of World War II, converted to an aircraft carrier. She was an early casualty, sunk by U-29 in September 1939 with the loss of nearly half the 1200 men aboard.*

guns were barely enough for accurate salvo firing, while of the hapless third unit, Furious, saddled with a planned two 18-inch guns, the less said the better.

To attain the required 32 knots, even as the first major British warships to adopt the more compact small-tube boilers, required a hull of enormous length. This had a long and fine forward entry and after run, but was devoid of protection save for a thin splinter deck at Middle Deck level. Resistance was increased by virtue of the addition of anti-torpedo bulges. These served to increase displacement somewhat, but the belt (stretching from the forward to the after barbette) was still of only 3-inch plate, extended forward some distance as 2-inch plate to cover the zone that would have caused rapid instability if flooded.

Fortunately, the ships were not complete at the time of Jutland. The two 15-inch units were involved in a crass, indecisive action in November 1917, but it was obvious that they had little role beyond that originally intended for them. All three were successfully converted to aircraft carriers after the war.

Courageous class data:

Courageous/Glorious:
Displacement, standard ....19,300 tons

Displacement, full load ....22,700 tons	
Length overall ....786 feet(239.6 m)	
Beam.......................................81 feet (24.7 m)	
Design draught ....23.4 feet (7.1 m)	
Complement 835	

Completed 1917

Armament:
Four 15-in guns (2 × 2)
Eighteen 4-in guns (6 × 3)
Two 3-in guns (2 × 1)
Two (later 12) 21-in torpedo tubes

Machinery:
Steam turbines 90,000 shp (67,150 kW)
Four shafts 32 knots

Armour:
Belt ....up to 3 in
Bulkheads ....up to 3 in
Decks ....up to 1.8 in
Turrets ....up to 13 in
Barbettes ....up to 7 in

Furious:

Displacement, standard...............19,100 tons	
Displacement, full load ....22,900 tons	
Length overall ....786.5 feet (239.8 m)	
Beam......................................88 feet (26.8 m)	
Design draught ....21.9 feet (6.8 m)	
Complement 835	

Completed 1917

Armament:
Two 18-in guns (2 × 1)
Eleven 5.5-in (11 × 1)
Two 3-in guns (2 × 1)
Six (later 18) 21-in torpedo tubes

Machinery:
Steam turbines 94,000 shp (70,100 kW)
Four shafts 31.5 knots

Armour:
Belt ....up to 3 in
Bulkheads ....up to 3 in
Decks........................up to 1.8 in
Turrets ....up to 13 in
Barbettes ....up to 7 in

Fisher's Baltic plan

In retrospect, it is hard to understand how the European War was allowed to degenerate into muddy stalemate when many fertile minds at the British Admiralty advocated amphibious warfare on a grand scale. As early as 1909, Fisher could declare, 'Were the British Army to seize and entrench that strip (i.e. the Baltic coast of Pomerania), a million Germans would find occupation; but to dispatch British troops to the front in a Continental war would be an act of suicidal idiocy'.

Churchill was an ardent enthusiast for the seizure of islands (this continued into World War II with Pantellaria and Leros), and the North German islands of Borkum and Heligoland were favourite potential targets. How any garrison was subsequently to be maintained seems to have been glossed over. Fisher's dream was to put 'a million' Russian soldiers ashore, barely eighty miles from Berlin, to end the war at a stroke. His power was such that he succeeded in getting approval for a varied armada of 612 warships ranging from the shallow-draught Courageous trio to the world's first true beach landing craft.

Details of the plan (if they ever fully existed) are sketchy. Seizure of a North Sea island or a landing on the coast of Holstein would have occupied the Germans' attention sure enough. The army would then probably have had to seize neutral Danish islands controlling the Baltic exits. Mining and a powerful naval force would have closed the east end of the Kiel Canal to prevent an enemy riposte. The operation would have relieved pressure on the Russian front but, as it happened, Turkey was chosen instead. Fisher's plan collapsed as his fleet 'was diverted and perverted to the damned Dardanelles'.

The 18-inch gun

Until the Yamatos of World War II, Fisher's *Furious* had the distinction of mounting the world's largest naval guns. With only two 18-inch instead of her sisters' four 15-inch, however, it is most unlikely that she would ever have hit a moving target, while trials with the after mounting strained her fragile hull. She was, by stages, converted into an aircraft carrier, releasing three barrels (one was a spare) for alternative service.

The Dover Patrol had a requirement for long-range bombardment, so three of the existing 12-inch monitors were earmarked for conversion. Only the *Lord Clive* and *General Wolfe* were, in fact, modified. The huge 40-calibre weapons were mounted pointing permanently to starboard from an unarmoured gunhouse. Trained primarily by turning the ship, the gun could be elevated to a surprising 45 degrees firing a 3,320-pound (1507 kg) projectile out to 40,000 yards (36,570 metres).

Top: Furious as planned, with two turrets each mounting a single 18-in gun. Middle: Furious at the end of World War I, with flight deck forward and landing deck aft. Above: Furious as camouflaged while serving in the Mediterranean in 1942

Below : Known as the 'Outrageous' throughout the Grand Fleet, the Courageous and her bizarre sisterships were really enormous light cruisers. Their battleship armament was ineffective: four guns are not enough for adequate spotting. In a cruiser clash during 1917 Courageous and Glorious fired nearly 400 rounds of 15-in shell but achieved no hits.

Renown class

An example of how 'lessons' from battle experience can be wrongly interpreted, the two Renowns owed their existence to the Battle of the Falklands in December 1914. The consummate ease with which Sturdee's battle cruisers had used superior speed and firepower to destroy von Spee's armoured cruisers impressed Fisher, who promptly ordered two more. Eight Revenges had been authorised, five under the 1913 programme and three in 1914. The latter group were 'put on hold', as it was not felt possible to complete them within the six months that it was thought the war would last. Materials had, however, been assembled and after an extremely rapid re-design, two of the last group were built as Renown-class battle cruisers. Propelled by Fisher's still-urgent Baltic ambitions, the two would have been finished in about 18 months, but the intervention of Jutland during their fitting out caused a further 500 tons of protection to be worked in.

The requirement for a 32-knot speed re-created earlier problems. An immensely long hull was necessary to accommodate six boiler rooms and two machinery spaces. Only three 15-inch turrets could be supplied for each, but even the lack of a fourth did not release sufficient weight margin to provide an adequate level of protection. Their lack of vertical belt protection was offset somewhat by partly internal anti-torpedo bulges, designed as an integral part of the ship's structure.

Both ships underwent comprehensive refits between the wars. The *Renown*, less well protected, gained an eventual 'Queen Elizabeth' style modernisation receiving greatly improved horizontal protection, a modern AA armament, new machinery and improved elevation for her main battery. Her final speed was lowered. She served with distinction as a unit of the Gibraltar-based Force 'H' during the critical periods of the Mediterranean war before service with the Eastern Fleet.

Renown class data (data for Renown):

As built:

Displacement, standard	27,950 tons
Displacement, full load	32,730 tons
Length overall	794 feet (242 m)
Beam	90 feet (27.4 m)
Design draught	26.7 feet (8.1 m)
Complement	970

Class: *Renown, Repulse*

Armament:
Six 15-in guns (3×2)
Seventeen 4-in (5×3)+(2×1)
Two 3-in guns (2×1)
Two 21-in torpedo tubes

Machinery:
Steam turbines 130,000 shp (89,500 kW)
Four shafts 32 knots

Armour:
Belt	up to 6 in
Bulkheads	up to 4 in
Decks	up to 3 in
Turrets	up to 11 in
Barbettes	up to 7 in

After final modernisation:

Displacement, standard	32,000 tons
Displacement, full load	37,400 tons
Length overall	794 feet (242 m)
Beam	90 feet (27.4 m)
Design draught	30.2 feet (9.2 m)
Complement	1200

Armament:
Six 15-in guns (3×2)
Twenty 4.5-in guns (10×2)
Twenty-four 40-mm
Four aircraft (until 1943)

Machinery:
Steam turbines 130,000 shp (97,000 kW)
Four shafts 29 knots

Top: Lightly-armoured but exceptionally fast, the two Renown class battlecruisers were already obsolete when they joined the Grand Fleet a few months after Jutland.

Above: Repulse received additional armour in 1918, but was still very lightly protected by battleship standards. Handled with great skill by her captain, she survived the Japanese air attack longer than her more modern consort Prince of Wales.

Armour:
Belt	up to 9 in
Bulkheads	up to 4 in
Decks	up to 3 in
Turrets	up to 11 in
Barbettes	up to 7 in

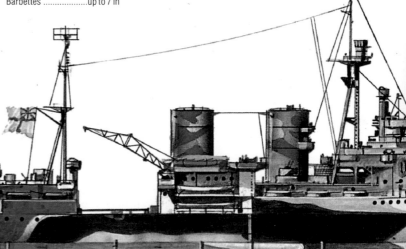

Force 'Z': The loss of the *Prince of Wales* and *Repulse*

With France defeated and the Soviet Union preoccupied, Japan showed interest in a southward expansion. In October 1941, the Admiralty was pressured to mount a show of strength to deter any move toward the Malayan peninsula.

The *Prince of Wales* duly rendezvoused with the *Repulse* at Colombo before proceeding to Singapore, where they arrived on 2 December. Their designated carrier, *Indomitable*, was unavailable following grounding damage. During the night of 7/8 December, Japanese landings were reported at the northern end of the peninsula, some 350 miles from Singapore. The newly promoted Flag Officer, Admiral Sir Tom Phillips, was inexperienced in fleet work but was confident that he could defeat the landings by attacking the transports offshore. His stated prerequisites were surprise and air cover. On the evening of the 8th, the two capital ships and four destroyers, code-named Force 'Z', sailed.

Early on the 9th, Phillips learned that shore-based air support would not be available. Now depending upon surprise, he aimed to hit the landing zone at first light on the 10th. He was favoured by thick weather but, although following a devious route, he was unaware that his position, course and speed had already been reported by the Japanese submarine *I-65*.

With clearing skies that evening, Force Z's presence was confirmed by cruiser-based float planes. Phillips, his surprise gone, debated briefly with his senior officers and decided to abandon the operation. At 20.15 he made course for Singapore. Just after midnight came a report of a further landing at Kuantan. It was strategically imperative that such a Japanese move be nipped in the bud, so Force Z detoured. The report was false but, at 02.10 on the 10th, its presence was again reported,

this time by the *I-58*. Suspicious, Phillips dallied off Kuantan, where he sighted a further enemy aircraft. It was now 10.15 but nemesis had already been aloft for over four hours. Flying from bases near Saigon were 85 strike aircraft, 34 with bombs, the remainder with torpedoes. Initially overshooting, the force, divided into several wings, located Force Z on its return leg.

The flagship sighted the enemy shortly after 11.00. By 11.15 the *Repulse* had been bombed, suffering one hit. Half an hour later the flagship was skilfully attacked by sixteen torpedo aircraft, eight from either flank. In evading one threat, she ran foul of the other. Her port-outer shaft was hit. Detached from its 'A'-bracket, it flailed, opening up the after end. With steering also damaged, and losing power, the *Prince of*

Wales began to settle. Proceeding slowly and unable to evade, she took four more torpedoes, all on the starboard side, at about 12.20.

The *Repulse*, still relatively untouched and manoeuvring at 25 knots, was then attacked by no less than twenty torpedo bombers, again split between either side. Evasion was impossible. Five hits were too much for the ageing ship, which rolled over and quickly disappeared.

Even with her modern sub-division, the flagship was now in a poor state, flooding progressively. A final assault scored a valedictory hit with a 500 kg bomb, which added fire to her problems and caused evacuation of her machinery space. The destroyer *Express* was signalled alongside and, abandoned in an orderly manner, she went down at 13.20. Admiral Phillips and

Above: Prince of Wales *flew the flag of the controversial Admiral Tom Phillips whose contempt for airpower was widely known. She was the first battleship to be sunk by aircraft while at sea and able to manoeuvre and defend herself.*

her commanding officer, Captain Leach, went with her.

At Pearl Harbor, three days previously, the battleships had been stationary and slow to respond. Here, however, were two fast, manoeuvrable ships, battle-experienced and not surprised. Mass air attack was of obvious effectiveness and was to become the pattern for the Pacific war. It signalled the demotion of the big-gun capital ship to the position of an auxiliary to the aircraft carrier.

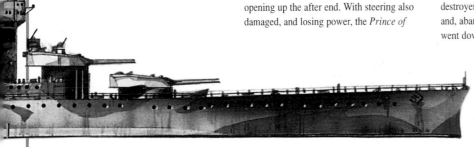

Left: Extensively re-constructed from 1937-9, Renown engaged Scharnhorst *and* Gneisenau *off Norway in 1940, driving them off in the teeth of a gale. She later served with 'Force H' in the Mediterranean, escorting the carrier* Ark Royal.

British inter-war reconstructions

Revenge, or 'R' class

Although having a similar main battery and a superior protective arrangement to the Queen Elizabeths, the Rs were always the poor relations. The reason was lack of speed. Following the bold all-oil-firing policy of the QEs, the government had misgivings regarding guaranteed supply of the fuel in wartime. As a result, the Rs were designed with most of their eighteen boilers coal-fired. This policy was countermanded, but too late, by a newly appointed Fisher. From the outset, the fewer boilers could be served by a single funnel, whose parallel sides differed from the huge, trunked casing common to the QEs after their first updates.

Earlier battleships were designed with great reserves of stability. This quality is linked to a large metacentric height (GM) and has the drawback of lively rolling. To improve the steadiness of the Rs as gun platforms, a 1– to 2-inch protective deck was worked in at maindeck level, connected by a 2-inch glacis plate to the lower edge of the belt. At a stroke, this lowered the GM, improved the overhead protection of the boiler room and raised by one level what was effectively the freeboard deck. It was somewhat ironic, therefore, that the class was the first to be fitted with anti-torpedo

Above: Royal Oak *fought at Jutland but was not substantially altered between the wars. Stationed at Scapa Flow, she was torpedoed and sunk with heavy loss of life when Prien's* U-47 *penetrated the anchorage defences on 14 October 1939.*

bulges from the outset, increasing their beam by 14 feet (4.3 metres) and giving them (particularly the *Resolution*, or 'Rolling Reso') a reputation for heavy rolling. The bulging did nothing for their form, their speed dropping by a further half knot.

Considering the treaty ban on new construction between the wars, it is somewhat surprising that so little was spent in improving the Rs. To the end they retained their casemated 6-inch secondary armament and little-changed tophamper They proved useful in second-line duties such as covering convoys and in fire support. The only war loss was the *Royal*

Oak, whose bulging proved of little use against two/three torpedoes exploding beneath the bottom plating.

Revenge class data:

Displacement, standard	28,000 tons
Displacement, full load	31,200 tons
Length overall	624.3 feet (190.3 m)
Beam (over full bulges)	102.5 feet (31.2 m)
Design draught	29.3 feet (8.9 m)
Complement	940

Class: *Ramillies, Resolution, Revenge, Royal Oak, Royal Sovereign.* Completed 1916-17

Armament:
Eight 15-in guns (4×2)
Fourteen (later twelve) 6-in guns (14/12×1)
Two 3-in (later eight 4-in (4×2)) guns (2×1)
Four 21-in torpedo tubes (later removed)

Machinery:
Steam turbines 40,000 shp (29,850 kW)
Four shafts 21 knots

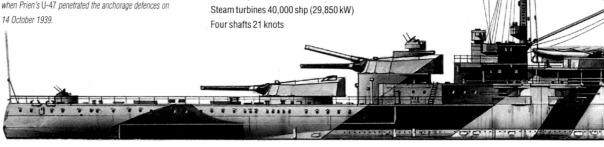

Armour:

Belt	up to 13 in
Bulkheads	up to 6 in
Decks	up to 2.5 in
Turrets	up to 13 in
Barbettes	up to 10 in

Long accustomed to pre-eminence, the Royal Navy was sadly reduced by international treaty. Agreement reached in Washington in February 1922 limited the strength in capital ships to twenty, with a long moratorium on new construction. Before this agreement's expiry, the London

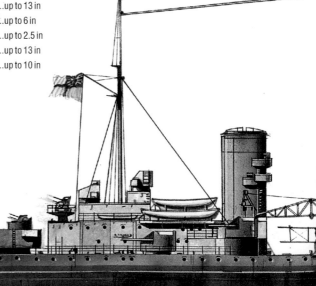

Naval Treaty of 1930 required disposal of the four Iron Dukes and the *Tiger*. For the fifteen remaining hulls, replacement keels could not be laid within seventeen years of the date of completion of the ship being replaced. In 1919 the British Government introduced the notorious 'Ten-Year Rule'. Defence expenditure was to be based on the assumption that there would be involvement in no major war for a decade. The Rule was to be renewed annually from 1928, a piece of legislative folly ironically championed by the then Chancellor of the Exchequer, Winston Churchill.

With 'making do' the order of the day, the Admiralty first modified the Queen Elizabeths in line with war experience. Between 1924 and 1930 they were stemmed in sequence to receive anti-torpedo bulges and a huge trunked, funnel casing in place of the earlier two, to reduce smoke nuisance to the remodelled superstructure. Dedicated anti-aircraft (AA) armament made its appearance, later units receiving the new eight-barrelled, two-pounder 'pompoms'.

Hard on the heels of the last of these modifications (*Barham* in 1933), *Malaya* and *Warspite* were put in hand for further work. *Malaya's* was restricted to the addition of full facilities for four aircraft, together with extra AA armament. *Warspite*, followed by *Valiant* and *Queen Elizabeth*, was virtually rebuilt. By replacing the full outfit of boilers and machinery with modern plant, there was sufficient weight saved to

further augment AA defences and, notably, horizontal protection, attesting to renewed interest in the effects of bombing. A tower bridge structure and smaller funnel did nothing for their appearance.

As the Washington Treaty provided for the signatories' converting, to carriers, two hulls which would otherwise be scrapped, the *Glorious* and *Courageous* were also allocated for rebuilding. The *Furious* gained a through flight deck, with hangar stowage for 33 aircraft, and no island, by 1925. Her sisters, with the now conventional starboard-side island superstructure, emerged as carriers a couple of years later.

Churchill's aborted 1939 Baltic plan ('Catherine') called for the conversion of two R-class battleships. Removal of 'B' and 'X' turrets would allow for considerable additions in horizontal protection. 'Super bulges', capable of being flooded or evacuated, would have increased their beam to about 140 feet (42.7 metres) giving comprehensive protection and a means of reducing draught when required.

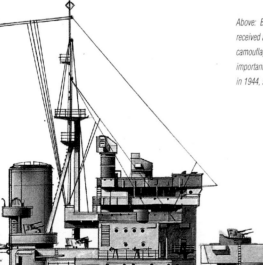

Above: Built at Portsmouth 1914–16 Royal Sovereign received anti-torpedo bulges 1927–8. She wore this camouflage scheme in 1942. Used mainly to escort important convoys, Royal Sovereign was leased to Russia in 1944, serving in the Northern Fleet as the Arkangelsk.

Top: Royal Sovereign follows Revenge and Resolution. The 'R' class and the Queen Elizabeths formed the core of the post-1918 fleet. New classes of 16-in gunned battleships were scuppered by the Washington treaties and the effective bankruptcy of the nation.

Below: What might have been. In July 1939 Vickers Armstrong began work on the first of a new class of heavily-armoured, fast battleships armed with nine 16-in guns. This is how the Lion would probably have appeared if completed. Work was halted after the outbreak of war and never resumed.

Hood

The German 1914 construction programme included the first of four Mackensen-class battle cruisers, known to be of over 30,000 tons standard displacement and capable of better than 30 knots. While their main armament was limited to a calibre of 35.56 cm (14 inches) the British Admiralty decided to trump these with the new 15-inch mountings already being produced for the Queen Elizabeths. Unlike the Renowns, the planned new ships were to have a four-turret battery and a speed of 32 knots. This demanded a truly immense hull, fine to realise the speed, long to accommodate four large boiler rooms and three machinery spaces. The considerable spread of the concentrated masses of turrets and barbettes caused high stresses in the hull, whose design had, from the outset, to incorporate plating in a manner that added strength to the main girder. That said, the protection was to be similar to that of the *Tiger*.

Few yards could construct an 860-foot hull and the first-of-class had to await a slip coming free following the great surge of early war programmes. Just three months before her laying-down came Jutland, and a total reappraisal of battle cruisers and their role. Their now proven inability to meet their peers in a gunnery dual obliged a reworking of the new ship's design into something more closely akin to a fast battleship (for its era, ultra-fast). The

Right: Hood *was the first British capital ship of the twentieth century to feature a clipper bow: earlier designs still harked back to the rams of the late nineteenth century.*

chosen name, *Hood* (the third of the name), was officially to honour a family that had produced many of the Royal Navy's senior officers, but was particularly appropriate in commemorating the most recent, who had died with virtually all his crew aboard the *Invincible* at Jutland.

An extra 5,000 tons of protection was worked in including a shallow, 12-inch main belt that was also continued further forward and aft. Unusually, it was flared along its length in order to increase the obliquity of the path of incoming projectiles, decreasing their chances of penetration. Bulged from the outset, the *Hood's* protection was well faired to minimise any increase in resistance. The bulges were backed by oil bunkers, themselves outboard of a torpedo bulkhead. Between bulge and bunker was an expansion space and 1.5-inch plating that transferred the weight of the belt to the double bottom structure. There was little amiss with her anti-torpedo arrangements,

Below: The sheer size - 860 ft in length - and symmetrical layout of the Hood *combined to make her the most distinctive warship of her era. Serving all around the World between the wars, her planned modernization was interrupted by the start of World War II.*

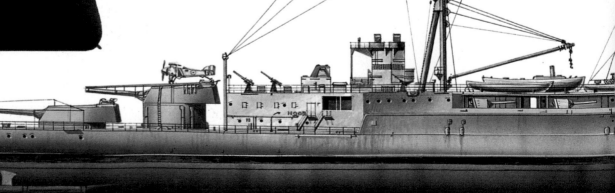

and she had also three protective decks, totalling up to 5 inches. The result was a very wet ship, floating about three feet deeper than originally conceived. By then, the German Mackensens had been halted and so too were the *Hood's* three sisters.

Casemated secondary armaments had, by now, been abandoned. *Hood* adopted the unusual 5.5-inch calibre gun (whose 82-pound shell allowed a faster rate of fire than the 100-pound 6-inch in these days of hand working) mounted at a useable height above the waterline.

It had been planned to modernise her in 1939 à la *Renown*. New machinery and the removal of the 600-ton conning tower would have gone a long way to improving her horizontal protection. Unfortunately, because of endless flagship commitments in the troubled late thirties, the work was never carried out and, on 24 May 1941, she fell victim to the same plunging fire that had devastated her three predecessors at Jutland.

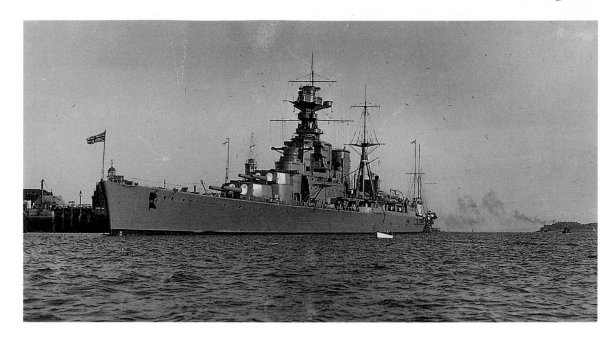

Above: Hood was the lead ship of a class of four battlecruisers, but her sisters were cancelled in 1917 when it was discovered that the Germans had ceased building battleships.

Hood data:

Displacement, standard	42,450 tons
Displacement, full load	48,350 tons
Length overall	860 feet (262.1 m)
Beam	104 feet (31.7 m)
Design draught	31.5 feet (9.6 m)
Complement	1480

Class: *Hood*
Completed 1920
(Planned: *Anson, Howe, Rodney*)

Armament:
Eight 15-in guns (4×2)
Twelve 5.5-in guns (12×1)
Four 4-in guns (4×1) later fourteen 4-in (7×2)
Six 21-in torpedo tubes

Machinery:
Steam turbines 144,000 shp (107,500 kW)
Four shafts 32 knots

Armour:
Belt up to 12 in
Bulkheads up to 5 in
Decks up to 3 in
Turrets up to 15 in
Barbettes up to 12 in

Right: The sheer and flare of Hood's hull helped her seakeeping as well as her appearance. It was also supposed to prevent enemy shells striking her armour square on.

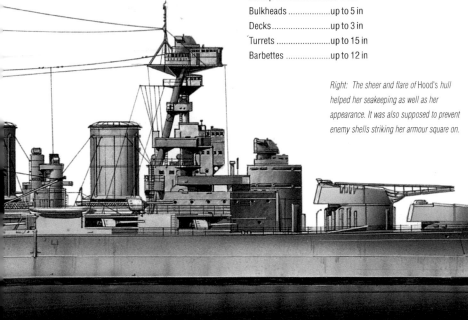

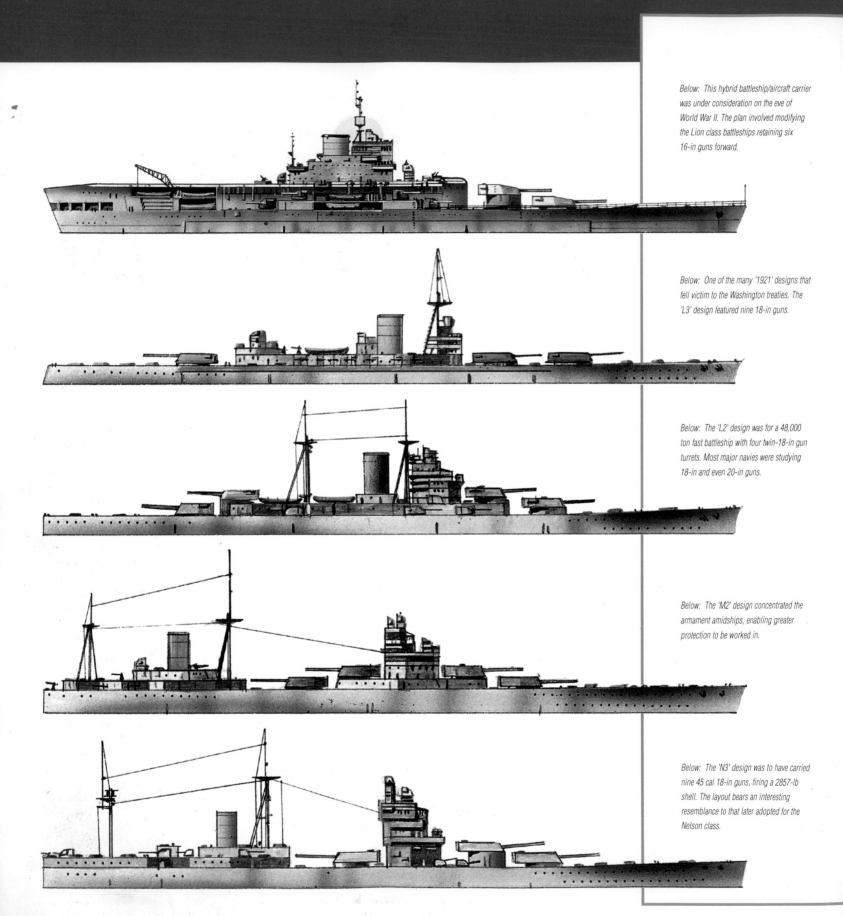

Below: This hybrid battleship/aircraft carrier was under consideration on the eve of World War II. The plan involved modifying the Lion class battleships retaining six 16-in guns forward.

Below: One of the many '1921' designs that fell victim to the Washington treaties. The 'L3' design featured nine 18-in guns.

Below: The 'L2' design was for a 48,000 ton fast battleship with four twin-18-in gun turrets. Most major navies were studying 18-in and even 20-in guns.

Below: The 'M2' design concentrated the armament amidships, enabling greater protection to be worked in.

Below: The 'N3' design was to have carried nine 45 cal 18-in guns, firing a 2857-lb shell. The layout bears an interesting resemblance to that later adopted for the Nelson class.

The Washington treaties and the Royal Navy

Above: New Zealand *served in the Grand Fleet and had the reputation of a 'lucky' ship. Here she arrives home in 1919, carrying Admiral Jellicoe on his tour of the Dominions. Listed for disposal under the treaties, she was broken up in 1922.*

Above: With the 'R' class and the Queen Elizabeths, the Royal Navy had ten battleships armed with 15-in guns by 1918. Japan and the USA had already developed 16-in guns for their latest battleships.

With the cessation of hostilities came the unpalatable fact that both the Japanese and the Americans were engaged in programmes to produce battleships and battle cruisers with 16-inch guns. To maintain naval supremacy, the United Kingdom had to respond. The result was a planned quartette of 48,000-ton battle cruisers, mounting nine 16-inch guns apiece. To reduce the area of heavy armour, the guns were tripled - a new departure for the Royal Navy - and close-grouped around the bridge structure. At the cost of a 40-degree blind arc astern, the arrangement allowed for 12/14-inch belt protection. Sloped at 18 degrees to the vertical, this took the idea of obliquity (pioneered on the *Hood*) one stage further. To withstand the overpressures from the adjacent heavy guns, the bridge became a tower-like structure.

Heavier armour

As was customary, the side protection was integral with anti-torpedo bulges. The extra displacement allowed for patches of protective deck up to 7 and 9 inches in thickness. Secondary armament was sixteen 6-inch, all grouped in twin turrets. These were disposed in two groups, one aft, one about the base of the bridge. Each group was separately controlled. Slightly shorter and beamier than the *Hood*, their designed output was an increased 160,000 shp (119,000 kW) which would, however, have given a knot or two less. Ordered from four separate yards on Trafalgar Day in 1921, it was believed they would perpetuate the 'I' names of previous battle cruisers, but all were almost immediately suspended and

cancelled, mere bargaining chips at the table in Washington.

From July 1915 a powerful American lobby mounted a strengthening campaign for a fleet 'second to none'. The United Kingdom (whose navy they would have to outbuild to achieve this) emerged three years later from a war that had left her weakened and weary, with huge demands on available budgets. Reluctantly, she was responding to ambitious American and Japanese building programmes with one of her own. By the end of 1920, however, the British Admiralty privately conceded that earlier adherence to a Two-Power Standard was no longer financially supportable. Parity with the other most powerful fleet was the best that could be expected. The long era of unchallenged British maritime dominance was nearing its end.

The Washington Conference of 1921/2 nonetheless caused severe shocks to the naval system. Where the British had expected to negotiate some agreements on capital ships' sizes and gun calibres, they were met with a series of major American proposals. Among these were that capital ship tonnage would be regarded as the measure of naval strength; that existing strength in capital ships should determine the relative future strengths for the signatories; that all capital ship building

programmes (approved or projected) should be abandoned; that there should be a ten-year building moratorium and that capital ship strength should be reduced by scrapping older tonnage.

Both the Americans and Japanese were in stronger positions than the British, being able to abandon their current grandiose construction programmes (totalling 840,000 tons in the American case) while retaining modern tonnage that had seen little or no war service. In contrast, Britain could barter only the four *Hood* 'follow-ons' and would need to scrap completed tonnage; what was left would already have been well worn by four years' arduous war service. By the end of the ten-year construction 'holiday' the Royal Navy would thus be obsolescent in comparison with a numerically equivalent American navy.

Scrapping battleships

The British agreed finally to a total of 580,450 capital ship tons. This involved the demolition of 22 Dreadnoughts, i.e. every one predating the King George Vs. Individual hulls could not be replaced until they were twenty years old, but the United Kingdom was permitted to construct two new units (which became the *Nelson* and *Rodney*), on whose completion the four oldest units would be scrapped. Total

tonnage at this juncture, 525,000 tons, would then be on a par with that of the United States.

Individual new-construction displacement (less fuel and reserve feed water) was not to exceed 35,000 tons, the minimum considered by the British to permit a design with balanced speed, protection and armament. A maximum gun calibre of 16-inch was agreed, reflecting the current programmes of the Americans and Japanese.

An unforeseen result of the agreements was that the signatories, in general, built up to ceiling dimensions rather than observing them as limits. This was particularly true of cruisers (10,000 tons and 8-inch guns), at the design of which the Japanese proved particularly adept. In the absence of American and British capital ships and carriers in the Western Pacific early in 1942, cruisers were to be the main arbiters of sea power.

A further result of the Washington Conference had been a non-renewal of the Anglo-Japanese alliance of 1902. The United States had long been concerned at the alliance's combined naval strength in the event of a war over trade or expansionism. This abrogation, together with the tight limitations imposed on her fleet by the conference, were contributing causes to Japan's alienation.

Nelson class

The two Nelsons were permitted by the terms of the Washington agreements because the Royal Navy would, otherwise, have had no 16-inch gunned ships to match those of the United States and Japan. They were thus the first battleships to be designed to the newly imposed 35,000-ton limit. This, and the hard-won lessons of the late war, resulted in a revolutionary layout.

Adoption of triple turrets meant that the ships could carry one barrel more than their foreign peers, while only three turrets needed to be accommodated. The arrangement was, of course, derived directly from that of the aborted 1921 battle cruisers, and enabled a maximum thickness of armour to be spread over the smallest area. As always, there was a penalty. 'C' turret was sited between the superimposed 'B' position and the front of the tower bridge structure. Firing arcs were limited, there was no astern fire from the main battery, and any firing at bearings abaft the beam caused great problems for personnel and the bridge structure itself. Secondary armament comprised six twin 6-inch, cruiser-type turrets, all aft. Such of these as would bear provided astern fire.

The thick belt was very limited in area to allow for a greatly improved scale of horizontal protection. It was situated within the ship, about 4 feet from the outer plating. This allowed the hull to be better faired, the shell plating also acting to disturb incoming projectiles before they struck the vertical armour. There were no bulges. Freeboard was high for good seakeeping, with the upper deck flushed clear through over the full length of the ship.

Fighting power and protection were bought at the expense of speed. The low power had an advantage in being absorbed on only two propellers but 23 knots proved generally insufficient for the needs of war.

Nelson class data:

Displacement, standard................33,950 tons
Displacement, full load ....38,000 tons
Length overall ....710 feet (216.4 m)
Beam....................................106 feet (32.3 m)
Design draught.........................30 feet (9.1 m)
Complement..............1320 (peace) 1640 (war)

Class: *Nelson, Rodney.* Completed 1927

Armament:
Nine 16-in guns (3 × 3)
Twelve 6-in guns (6 × 2)
Six 4.7-in/Eight 4-in AA guns
Eight (later 48) 2-pounder pompoms
   (1 × 8)/(6 × 8)
Sixteen 40-mm (later)
Two 24.5-in torpedo tubes

Machinery:
Steam turbines 45,000 shp (33,570 kW)
Two shafts 23 knots

Armour:
Belt ....up to 14 in
Bulkheads ....up to 14 in
Decks ....up to 6.25 in
Turrets ....up to 16 in
Barbettes ....up to 15 in

The challenge of harnessing the potential of aviation to the requirements of the Fleet triggered a positive flowering of imagination in the Royal Navy of World War I. By the close of hostilities, scout/spotter planes were being deployed from capital ships, float planes from converted cross-channel packets. The world's first bomber strike had been mounted against a defended target on German soil. Destroyers towed sleds at high speed to launch wheeled

Aviation and the battleship

Left: Nelson arrives in the East Indies in 1945. Her armament of nine 16-in guns was still one of the most powerful afloat, but she was hopelessly slow by US and Japanese standards.

Right: A Sopwith Camel is launched from HMS Inflexible in 1917. Having pioneered aviation at sea during World War I, the Royal Navy fell behind the US and Japanese navies during the 1930s.

fighters against reconnaissance Zeppelins. A squadron of the first purpose-designed torpedo bomber had joined the first through-deck carrier. Exploring every avenue in offensive, defensive and support roles, the Royal Navy was undisputed world leader in the field.

On 1 April 1918 the Royal Naval Air Service (RNAS) was assimilated into the newly formed Royal Air Force (RAF), generating debilitating inter-service wrangling that laid the foundation for the disappointing performance of the Fleet Air Arm in World War II. The Americans did not repeat this mistake, retaining aviation as an integral part of the fleet, and seeing it gain in stature at an inverse rate to British decline. In 1929, for instance, when the Royal Navy could field a total of only 150

carrier aircraft, the Americans had 250 participating in their annual manouevres.

During the twenties the Americans and Japanese both benefited from the large carrier conversions permitted under the Washington agreements. Each had a pair of ships with individual capacities of eighty and more aircraft, enabling them to explore the possibilities of large-scale air strikes. The Royal Navy, with its narrow-gutted Courageous conversions, could put only 34 aircraft aboard. The possibilities thus offered aligned nicely with postwar policy-makers who still ached from the squandered opportunities of Jutland. If aviation meant better tactical intelligence, it would be the means by which a decisive gun action could be brought about. Matapan and the pursuit of the *Bismarck* would be instances.

Much debate concerned the defence of the battleship against aircraft. It was assumed,

correctly, that it could not carry its own fighter defence, but moves to put aboard spotter/reconnaissance aircraft, and their paraphernalia, caused friction with those who wished to mount barrage-defence weapons, such as the eight-barrelled pompoms, a weight-consuming solution to the defeat of air attack.

With the Americans investigating the effects of heavy bombs on horizontal armour, the Admiralty took the view that the air-dropped torpedo was the more serious threat. Within the strict weight limitations imposed by treaty, it would thus be better to improve bulges and to install torpedo bulkheads rather than to upgrade armoured decks. In the event, this instinct was probably the more correct, as even when heavily damaged by bombing or plunging shellfire, a hull usually needed to be finished off by torpedo.

This policy was rather reversed when the British began to build fleet carriers. Their protected decks allowed them to absorb a degree more punishment than their American counterparts. This was at the cost of effectiveness, however, their design still limiting them to two-thirds the number of aircraft.

The interactive nature of ship design is obvious, there being no 'ideal'. The real villain was insufficient funding to provide a balanced force of capital ships and carriers, whose alliance would have been to mutual benefit.

Below: Rodney as she appeared in 1942, a year after playing a vital role in sinking the Bismarck. Her armour was fitted on the 'all or nothing' principle: concentrated on the belt, turrets, magazines and machinery spaces.

Right: The Admiralty insisted that the quadruple 'A' turret should be able to fire at low elevation. The inevitable consequence was that the class proved very wet forward.

Seeking capital ships that could be afforded, the British proposed a unit displacement no greater than 25,000 tons, with guns not exceeding 12-inch calibre. The Americans, with an eye to Pacific warfare, were not prepared to relax the existing 35,000-ton limit. They would probably accept 14-inch guns if the other signatories followed suit. In the event, the Japanese would not ratify the agreement and the Americans exercised their option for a 16-inch maximum.

The ratification on gun calibre was not due until 1 April 1937. The British, however, were not able to wait that long. With the French, Italians and Germans all building fast battleships, the Admiralty had to act to avoid being out-classed. As a result, 35,000 tons and 14-inch guns were its major design parameters. Drafts showed that three quadruple mountings could be accommodated, the larger number of barrels somewhat offsetting their smaller calibre. Full-scale tests, however, showed that planned protection was insufficient. Two guns were, therefore, sacrificed from the superimposed 'B' mounting to provide for an extra margin of protection. As the ships were considerably longer to accommodate machinery for over 29 knots, the layout reverted to a more conventional two forward turret, one aft arrangement.

Despite the increase in the area thus to be protected, the great saving in armament weight actually allowed a higher percentage of the displacement to be devoted to armour. The main belt reverted to a straightforward vertical arrangement, mounted externally. In place of bulges was a system of longitudinal bulkheads, separating alternate oil tanks and void spaces.

They were the first British battleships to have a dual-purpose secondary armament, but the 5.25-inch calibre was really too slow for AA work and too light against surface targets. All were designed to carry four aircraft, space-consuming anachronisms that were landed once sufficient carrier support could be guaranteed.

All were laid down in 1937. Still to be launched at the outbreak of war, they were given the benefit of extra protection as limitations were scrapped. This, particularly in conjunction with their low forward sheer, made them very wet.

King George V class data:

Displacement, standard	38,000 tons
Displacement, full load	44,800 tons
Length overall	745 feet (227.1 m)
Beam	103 feet (31.4 m)
Design draught	36.8 feet (11.2 m)
Complement	1650

King George V class

As the Nelsons were products of the Washington agreements, so were the King George Vs, the last class of British battleship to be completed, the result of the London Naval Conferences of 1930 and 1935. At the former, both the Americans and the British agreed not to exercise their rights to lay down replacement tonnage before 1936, but allowed the French and Italians to go ahead with their, quite legitimate, quotas.

By 1933, the Germans had initated another arms race, but, at this point, were less of a threat to the Admiralty than the Royal Air Force. Fighting its corner at a time of tight budgets, the RAF succeeded in convincing a cash-strapped Treasury that the bomber had made the capital ship totally obsolete. With the time of expiry of agreed construction 'holidays' approaching, the signatories decided on a further conference in London in 1935. This was set against a very different world order. Japan, now the dominant Far Eastern power, and involved in a military campaign in China, was no longer to be curtailed as at Washington. A rearming Germany had tabled its plans for a fleet, 'by 1942', which would include six battleships and two carriers.

Class: *Anson, Duke of York, Howe, King George V, Prince of Wales.* Completed 1940–42.

Armament:
Ten 14-in guns (2×4) + (1×2)
Sixteen 5.25-in guns (8×2)
64 × 2-pounder pompoms (8×8)
Ten 40-mm

Machinery:
Steam turbines 125,000 shp
 (93,250 kW) max.
Four shafts 29 knots

Armour:
Belt ....up to 15 in
Bulkheads ....up to 15 in
Decks ....up to 6 in
Turrets ....up to 16 in
Barbettes ....up to 16 in

Right: King George V *seen in 1940, still uncamouflaged and with a URP (Unguided Rocket Projectile) launcher atop 'B' turret. Her sistership* Prince of Wales *was hurried to sea, with workmen still on board when the Bismarck sortied in May 1941.*

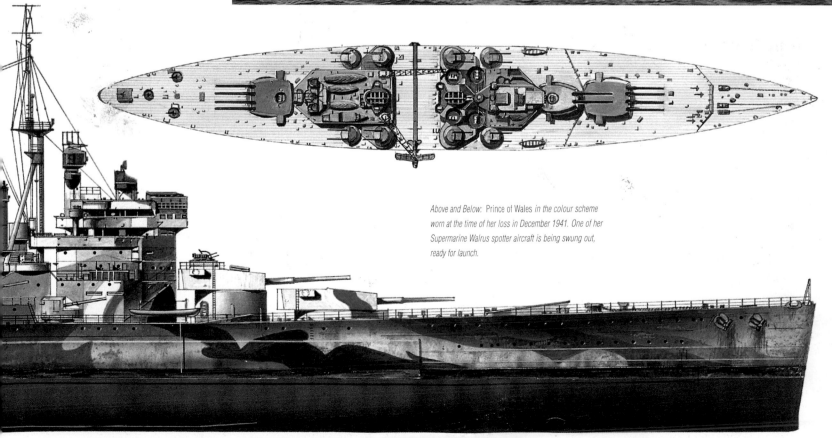

Above and Below: Prince of Wales *in the colour scheme worn at the time of her loss in December 1941. One of her Supermarine Walrus spotter aircraft is being swung out, ready for launch.*

British battleships in the Mediterranean 1940–43

With the fall of France and the entry into the war of an unplacated Italy, the Royal Navy in the Mediterranean at once lost a powerful ally and gained an equally powerful opponent. North Africa and the Western Desert then became a crucial theatre, the British committed to preventing an Axis military campaign from overrunning the Suez Canal and thrusting onward to the oil-rich Gulf and, perhaps, India.

The Axis' weakness lay in its armies' dependence upon the vital north-south convoy route. The British, in turn, relied on Malta as a base for effective interdiction of these convoys but, in doing so, depended on an east-west convoy route of their own, as Malta was suffering from a prewar defensive neglect and a large population with no natural resources.

The Royal Navy's main bases were, therefore, at Gibraltar (where Admiral Somerville's Force H was based) and at Alexandria (Admiral Cunningham's Mediterranean Fleet). Their opponents, in the two Cavours and the two Dorias, had thoroughly modernised battleships whose 320 mm (12.6-inch) guns could outrange the 15-inch on those of the British ships yet unmodernised. They also had a useful three-knot speed advantage. In addition there were the two new 15-inch Littorios, with two more fitting out.

There was never any prospect of an old-fashioned line action as the Italians were under strict high-level instruction not to engage a superior force. In addition, they rarely cruised speculatively owing to a chronic shortage of fuel oil. Somerville, in the Western basin, enjoyed the more modern ships, such as the *Renown* and the carrier *Ark Royal*, and was augmented as required by Home Fleet units. On occasion the *Nelson*, *Rodney*, *Prince of Wales* and *Malaya* made an appearance to fight convoys through from the United Kingdom to Malta. In July 1940, with *Hood* in company, Force H had the distasteful task of putting out of action an intransigent French force at Mers-el-Kebir (Oran).

East-west convoys had to be fought through against not only the Italian surface fleet but also against a *Luftwaffe* that dominated the air from bases on both north and south shores. Such operations involved

complex diversionary moves, which used the combined resources of Somerville and Cunningham to confuse or block any enemy move.

Off Calabria (Punta Stilo) in July 1940, the first brush between opposing capital ships saw the only modernised British unit, *Warspite*, hit the enemy flagship at 23,000 yards (21,000 metres). The Italians retired immediately, setting the trend for future engagements.

In March 1941 the *Vittorio Veneto* was torpedoed by an aircraft from the carrier *Formidable* but, even in a damaged condition, it could still out-distance Cunningham's every effort to intercept. The resulting battle of Matapan cost the Italians three heavy cruisers, and showed that the Royal Navy had assimilated the lessons of Jutland in seeking and fighting a night action. The escape of the Italian flagship, however, emphasised the material

shortcomings of the British ships. Despite these, their presence shortly afterwards in deep cover of the evacuations from Greece and Crete was sufficient to guarantee no interference from the Italians.

The *Barham*, having survived an Admiralty demand that she be used to block Tripoli harbour, fell victim to a U-boat's torpedoes in November 1941. In the following month the Italians neatly avenged Taranto by using frogmen to place explosive charges under the *Queen Elizabeth* and *Valiant* at Alexandria, putting them both on the bottom in shallow water.

Valiant returned in time to engage in bombardment details during the campaign in Italy. At Salerno, in September 1943, she was accompanied by the *Warspite*, which was hit squarely by one of the new German gliderbombs. This drilled through her horizontal protection with ease, passing through a boiler room and the double

bottom before exploding. The battleship's war was light years from that of World War I. Danger of damage by heavy projectile had almost disappeared, replaced by gliderbombs, hand-placed mines and the ever-present submarine torpedo.

Top: British light cruisers make smoke as they manoeuvre to protect a convoy from an Italian battlesquadron. Italy's six modern or modernized battleships posed a major threat to Malta's lifeline.

Right: The Queen Elizabeth class had a fifth unit named after, and paid for, by the States of Malaya. Malaya provided part of the heavy cover for several Malta convoys.

Left: After her reconstruction, Renown certainly looked more imposing, but the long lines of scuttles betray the lack of an armoured belt. Note the improved anti-aircraft armament: in the Mediterranean, aircraft proved the most serious danger.

Below: Duke of York in heavy seas. The most modern battleships had to be retained in the UK to deal with another Atlantic sortie by the remaining German battleships. Duke of York sank the Scharnhorst in 1943 on 26 December.

Mers-el-Kebir July 1940

With the collapse of France in June 1940, the British were gravely concerned that the French fleet might fall into German hands. Despite repeated assurances from the French that this would be resisted, the danger was obviously from German perfidy. Some units responded to British blandishments to join the Royal Navy or to intern themselves in British-controlled ports. Many, including Admiral Gensoul's powerful force based at Mers-el-Kebir, in Algeria, did not. This squadron consisted of the fast battleships *Dunkerque* and *Strasbourg*, the older battleships *Bretagne* and *Provence*, a seaplane carrier and six 'super-destroyers'.

In accordance with the War Cabinet's instruction to use 'whatever force may be necessary', Admiral Somerville arrived off the base on 3 July, his Force H including for the occasion the *Hood*, *Valiant*, *Resolution* and *Ark Royal*. The ultimatum presented to Gensoul gave him four options: join the British, be interned at a British-controlled

port, demilitarise in the French West Indies, or be sunk.

Ten hours of negotiation between the British emissaries and the French resulted only in deadlock, as Somerville, waiting outside, grew increasingly apprehensive of the submarine danger to his ships. Finally, on direct order from London, he opened fire at 17.54 from 15,000 yards (13,700 metres). The French, still Mediterranean-moored, stern-on to the mole, were little able to reply to the thirty-six 15-inch salvoes that fell among them in little over ten minutes. The *Dunkerque* was crippled by a group of three projectiles, the *Bretagne* blazed uncontrollably and capsized. The *Provence*, also heavily hit, had to be quickly beached. Only the *Strasbourg* escaped, through a gap made in the boom defence. She was pursued only half-heartedly and arrived at Toulon. Nearly 1,300 French seamen died in this, the most controversial of British actions. It had, however, achieved its aims and indicated British resolve to 'go it alone' against Nazi Germany.

Top: Resolution *took part in the bombardment of the French squadron at Mers-el-Kebir.*

Above: Ark Royal's *aircraft failed to stop the battlecruiser* Strasbourg *escaping to Toulon.*

Hunting the *Bismarck*

Above: Viewed from the cruiser Prinz Eugen, *the* Bismarck *fires a salvo at HMS* Hood. *Trying to close the range rapidly,* Hood *could only reply with her forward turrets, but was destroyed by a magazine explosion just as she brought her full armament to bear.*

When the *Hood* and the *Prince of Wales* sighted the Bismarck, at 05.35 on 24 May 1941, the range was about 38,000 metres. Admiral Holland sought to close the range as quickly as possible, making an end-on approach, which allowed only his forward main battery guns to bear. He was well aware that the inadequate horizontal protection of the *Hood* would be pierced easily by a 380 mm projectile plunging from long range. He needed to get inside this critical range, yet not so close that enemy projectiles would have sufficient terminal energy to penetrate *Hood*'s thick vertical belt. While all capital ships have a theoretical 'zone of immunity', it is likely that, in the *Hood*'s case, her deficiencies vis-à-vis a modern opponent were such that this zone did not exist, i.e. her belt could be penetrated at ranges at which her horizontal protection was still suspect.

There was a further problem in end-on approach. A falling salvo was usually very much more accurate in deflection than in range, normally resulting in a line, rather than a group, of splashes. Thus, where the small end-on silhouette was of little real advantage, the whole length of the ship was vulnerable to the straggling line of a falling salvo.

The range at the point of the critical interchange of fire had dropped to about 18,000 metres, at which the shells would

still have a high velocity but a falling angle of only about 14 degrees. The cause of the fatal explosion that destroyed the ship remains open to conjecture but the projectile is likely to have penetrated the upper belt, which was thinner than that on the waterline. Eyewitness accounts agree on one or more hits near the mainmast, followed by a comparatively slow and silent, catastrophic deflagration, suggesting the origin was a magazine of propellant rather than projectiles.

By the morning of the 27th, the *Bismarck* had been torpedoed three times by British carrier aircraft. An 18-inch aircraft torpedo carried a much smaller warhead than a 21-inch weapon, but one had detonated among the rudders and steering gear, severely weakening the whole stern section. Unable to steer, the German was meandering slowly into a full gale. She was, by now, totally surrounded by British heavy units, the battleship *Rodney* and *King George V* closing to finish the job.

At 08.47 the *Rodney* opened fire at 23,000 metres, followed almost immediately by the

Above: Admiral Tovey exhibited a caution worthy of Jellicoe in the hunt for the elusive German battleship, but thanks to a hit from an aerial torpedo, the Bismarck was intercepted by Rodney and King George V outside the range of German aircraft based in France.

Below: Rodney's 16-in broadsides devastated the Bismarck, reducing it to a wreck in less than 30 minutes. Her opening salvoes destroyed the Bismarck's central fire director, forcing the guns to go to local control.

Above: Prince of Wales experienced terrible problems with her new 14-in guns in the first action with Bismarck. Safety systems caused repeated stoppages, and she was forced to break off the fight.

Below Bismarck seen from her consort in Norway on the eve of their Atlantic raid. The dazzle pattern stripes and false bow wave were toned down before she sailed. Luckily for the British, the Tirpitz was not yet operational and could not join her sister ship.

flagship, a mile away to starboard. Their wallowing target was fairly fine on the starboard bow and still dangerous. Both British units had adequate vertical protection and the tactics were to press in to a very short range. Again the 14-inch armament of the King George V class proved liable to drop-out under concentrated use but, with variable numbers of guns firing, she closed eventually to a mere 4,000 metres. The 16-year-old battery of the Rodney was of simpler and more robust design, experiencing little problem. Her nine-gun broadsides did spectacular damage to an opponent that was rapidly reduced to a wreck, the British ships pounding her from either bow. In all, the Rodney loosed 380 rounds of 16-inch and the King George V about 340 of 14-inch. The number of hits probably ran to hundreds, but the Bismarck would neither blow up nor sink. Three torpedoes from the cruiser Dorsetshire performed the coup de grâce by admitting water to the hull. Hundreds of survivors made it into the water, but reports of U-boats in the area forced the British to leave them to their fate.

Defeating the convoy raiders

By the time that a convoy system had been initiated in World War I, the menace posed by the surface raider had all but passed. World War II was fought to a very different pattern, with regular convoy cycles in the North Atlantic, to North Russia and through the Mediterranean, being long threatened in various degrees by heavy surface units.

Badly under-strength in U-boats, the Germans repeated their initial use of regular and auxiliary warships to harass merchant shipping. Auxiliary raiders were skilfully disguised armed merchantmen, which confined their attentions almost exclusively to independents. Against escorted convoys, battleships, the so-called 'pocket battleships' and heavy cruisers were employed. Deployed from ports in occupied Europe, they posed a potential menace even when not at sea.

It took a while for the British to realise that, as with U-boats, there was little to be gained in 'hunting them down'. Far better to view the convoy as the bait to bring the predator to the hunter. Capital ships thus had a significant role to play in the convoy system. They were, of course, not always available, but after the gallant sacrifice of Armed Merchant Cruisers such as the *Jervis*

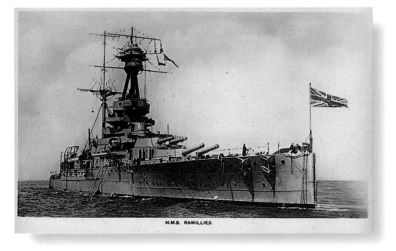

H.M.S. RAMILLIES.

Bay in futile defence, the system was tightened up with a battleship accompanying a major convoy instead of following up an incident.

In February 1941, for instance, the *Scharnhorst* and *Gneisenau* sighted the east-bound Halifax convoy HX106 but were deterred from attacking by the presence of the *Ramillies*. A few days later they easily destroyed five ships from a just-dispersed convoy, then headed for the Central Atlantic. On 8 March they discovered a

Freetown-UK convoy, SL67, but again broke off on seeing it accompanied by the *Malaya*. Such incidents were typical and, while the old battleships were denied by their fleet opponents the satisfaction of a gun duel, the value of their presence far outweighed the risk of exposing them to submarine attack.

In the Mediterranean campaign, until the end of 1942, the problem was one of battling a convoy through, usually to Malta, in the face of submarines, enemy air

Above: A pre-war photograph of Graf Spee *herself. German 'pocket battleships' were long-ranged heavy cruisers with 11-in guns, designed to out-run anything they could not out-fight. The only sure way to protect a convoy was to add an old battleship to the escort group.*

Left: Ramillies *escorted several Atlantic convoys, facing off the German battleships* Scharnhorst *and* Gneisenau *on their first raiding sortie.*

superiority and the potential of the Italian fleet. Convoys were either east- or west-bound. The former entered by Gibraltar Strait and were the responsibility of Admiral Somerville's Force H, sometimes reinforced by Home Fleet detached units. West-bound movements entered the Mediterranean via the Suez Canal and were covered by Admiral Cunningham's Alexandria-based fleet. A problem for each was that the confined geography of the central Mediterranean, where Malta lay,

required that the heavy cover turn back short of the island. This left the convoy's final leg covered only by light units and somewhat exposed.

The Royal Navy established an early moral ascendancy over the Italian fleet, so that the latter routinely used their superior speed to decline gun action. The occasional availability of a British carrier only enhanced this pattern. It could be argued that a carrier's presence was, in that respect, counter-productive in being able to field sufficient aircraft to deter the enemy surface ships without being in sufficient strength to damage and slow them, to bring about a gun action. The Navy's primary duty was, however, the safe and timely arrival of the convoy; it is to their credit that the vast majority of the losses borne by the mercantile marine were caused, not by the Italian fleet, but by air attack.

When battleships were absent, the Italians could be bolder. In March 1942, for instance, Admiral Vian had to fight the brilliant, but desperate, action of Second Sirte, his light units pitted against a battleship. In the June, the 'Harpoon' convoy was badly mauled by Italian cruisers after Force H had turned back short of Cape Bon. Its complementary convoy

H.M.S. REVENGE.

Above Convoys to Russia demanded battleship protection after a powerful German squadron was established in Norway. This picture remained secret until the end of the war: King George V was badly damaged in a collision with the destroyer Punjabi off Iceland.

Left: Revenge and the other 'R' class were a tough proposition for a German raider: they were slow, but well armoured and carried eight 15-in guns. A well-aimed 15-in shell would doom any 'pocket battleship' operating alone in the Atlantic.

('Vigorous') with only light escort, was obliged to return to Alexandria when threatened by two enemy battleships.

Commenced in September 1941, convoys to North Russia were flanked for much of their passage by enemy-occupied Norway, whose deeply indented coastline gave perfect cover for German heavy units. Admiral Tovey, C in C Home Fleet, was responsible for the convoys' distant escort. He adopted a policy of passing an outward-bound (PQ) and a homeward-bound (QP) convoy in the

region of Bear Island. It was thus possible for the Home Fleet squadron to cover one movement outward and the other on its return. Again, however, the real danger could lay beyond the limit of heavy escort.

The *Tirpitz*, *Scheer*, *Hipper* and, for a time, *Lützow*, exerted a baleful influence on this route. In March 1942 the *Tirpitz* made a sortie but both sides missed each other in the Arctic murk. In the July, after its Home Fleet cover had turned back, the Germans made a move. While they never came into

contact, the convoy PQ17 was scattered, losing 24 of its 37 ships to submarine and aircraft attack.

Badly wrong-footed by an British light escort on 31 December 1942, the German heavy ships were put under sentence by Hitler. It fell to the *Scharnhorst* to try to earn redemption but, on endeavouring to attack a convoy on Boxing Day 1943, she was deflected by a cruiser force onto the heavy cover of *Duke of York* and was defeated in a classic gun action.

Shore bombardment

During World War I the northern end of the Western Front was firmly anchored on the Flanders coast near the Franco-Belgian border. The enemy-held coastline was looked upon by Vice-Admiral Bacon at Dover as an excellent means of outflanking the opposition through offshore bombardment, for which no established procedures appeared to exist. Bacon, one of the Navy's intellectuals, set-to to develop them. His only heavy support at the outset was the twenty-year-old, but totally obsolete, battleship *Revenge*. She had survived thus far only through being used for gunnery trials. Her ancient 13.5-in guns had been sleeved down to 12-inch, but she had a lofty spotting top and a useful 6-inch secondary battery. These were all casemated, and the ship fitted with anti-torpedo bulges which, it was found, could be flooded to improve the guns' elevation and their meagre 16,000 yard range. With her 29-foot (8.84 m) draught, she was a poor choice for approaching a coast beset by sandbanks but, relieved occasionally by the newer *Venerable*, she pioneered methods later perfected by purpose-built monitors.

Aircraft spotting

Because of the ranges involved, spotting from the ship herself was usually difficult. Bacon quickly dismissed aircraft assistance ('like talking to stone-deaf people in the dark') and had tripods built, which could be unobtrusively 'planted' offshore preparatory to a shoot. Utilising two of these, each with a crew of observers and signalmen, all elements using specially gridded maps, corrections were rapid and precise through simple triangulation.

At the Dardanelles, meanwhile, seaplanes were being used. The results were patchy and not encouraging. Still very unreliable, and with primitive communications, the machines needed to have their flying hours conserved, but it proved very difficult to synchronise the readiness of both bombarding ship and spotting aircraft. In near-ideal conditions, the *Queen Elizabeth* carried out a brief indirect shoot across the width of the Gallipoli peninsula but, more often than not, the seaplanes could not operate, either because of adverse weather or conditions so calm that they could not 'unstick' from the water. Higher-

performance land-based aircraft were requested but their arrival was overtaken by events.

Between the wars, the fleet carried out shoots at the islet of Filfla, off Malta, but these were just gunnery practice rather than serious exercises in precision shore bombardment. During the early, defensive phase of the World War II Mediterranean campaign, battleships from both Force H and the Mediterranean Fleet bombarded specific enemy ports, e.g. Bardia, Genoa and Tripoli. Understandably, these were urgent affairs rather than calculated shoots and, despite the ships having spotting aircraft aloft, damage inflicted on port areas was little more than the collateral destruction wreaked on the adjoining towns.

Operation Torch

Passing to the offensive, the Allies launched a series of amphibious operations - North Africa (Operation 'Torch' in November 1942), Sicily ('Husky', July 1943), Messina Strait ('Baytown', September 1943), Salerno ('Avalanche', September 1943), Anzio ('Shingle', January 1944) and the South of France ('Dragon', August 1944).

Unlike practice in the Pacific War, assaults usually went in during the small hours and with minimum advance warning. Without the highly concentrated and heavily protected defensive systems built by the Japanese, the targets were usually such as troop or tank concentrations, or mobile batteries, which could be handled by cruiser and destroyer gunfire. Battleship support was, however, available when required: e.g. two King George Vs did a diversionary shoot in Sicily; both Nelsons, the *Warspite* and *Valiant*, softened up positions around Reggio Calabria prior to the Messina crossing while, in the desperate week following the Salerno landings, the two older ships were used to break up enemy armoured attacks. Here, it was possible to have Forward Observer Officers ashore to call down fire very precisely and quickly, as required. The *Warspite* was also pierced clean through by a German gliderbomb and had to retire to Malta for emergency repair.

'Dragon' was considered a 'soft' operation but approaches to Toulon and Marseilles were covered by Napoleonic-era fortifications with walls of up to four metres in thickness. An American cruiser, firing at

Ile de Port Cros, saw her 8-inch projectiles bouncing off 'like tennis balls', but a dozen rounds of 15-inch from the old *Ramillies* redressed the situation.

The enemy's 'Atlantic Wall' posed much the same problem at Normandy (June 1944). Enfilading the British 'Sword' beach were German batteries clad and roofed in two-metre-thick reinforced concrete. Two of these, Houlgate and Benerville, attracted a total of over 500 rounds of 15– and 16-inch fire. However, despite careful spotting and largely undisturbed shooting, only three of the batteries' four large guns were silenced and, of these, only one was totally destroyed. From earliest times it had been recognised that gun duels between fixed fortifications and moving, fragile ships was non-productive. Modern technology had done little to change things.

Above: Seen from the cruiser Frobisher, Rodney *fires a 16-in salvo at German troops in Normandy. At Anzio and Salerno, German counter-attacks on the Allied beachheads were broken up by naval gunnery. At Normandy, the presence of a powerful battleship squadron gave the Allies a concentration of artillery that was not surpassed even on the Russian front.*

Right: Rodney's *16-in shells weighed over a ton each, and were propelled by a 640-lb charge. If they were fired a target 35,000 yards away, the shells would reach an altitude of 5 miles at the top of their trajectory. The muzzle blast from these guns was tremendous, and engaging a target ahead invariably damaged the decks.*

Madagascar to Okinawa – the Eastern fleet 1942–5

To safeguard her widespread Far East interests, and to assuage the fears expressed by Australia and New Zealand about aggressive Japanese policies, the United Kingdom built the new fleet base at Singapore between the wars. Construction was a slow business, paralleled by severe cutbacks in the strength of the Royal Navy and the adoption of the infamous 'Ten Year Rule'. With insufficient strength to meet commitments even in Home and Mediterranean waters, the Admiralty adopted the 'Main Fleet to Singapore' policy. On the Japanese opening hostilities, a naval force large enough to deter direct aggression would be mobilised and despatched eastward. Depending upon the political situation of the moment, it was expected to arrive in anything between 42 and 70 days, and be fit for battle within 120 days. (In the event, 120 days was more than sufficient for the Japanese to overrun the Far East).

Japanese threat

As the 1930s saw the Japanese acquire territory ever closer to Hong Kong and Singapore, the rise of the dictatorships in Europe made it increasingly unlikely that any credible Royal Navy force could ever be spared for the Far East; the direct threat to the United Kingdom saw to that. With hostilities upon him, Churchill saw the Mediterranean as the 'first battlefield' and was able to assure the Government that they could 'take it as quite certain' that Japan would not be so rash as to move against Singapore. As we have seen, the undefended British and Imperial interests were met with the pitiful bluff of sending the *Repulse* and *Prince of Wales*.

With the disaster that overtook Force Z, and the death of Admiral Phillips, the capable commander of Force H, Admiral Somerville, was transferred to head a new 'Eastern Fleet'. Unfortunately, the *Barham* had just been sunk, and the *Valiant* and *Queen Elizabeth* 'Tarantoed' by the Italians. Somerville's command, therefore, was founded on the *Warspite* and the four surviving Rs. On paper a considerable force, the Rs were in reality of little use; unmodernised and too short-legged for the theatre, they had been taken from convoy escort. *Warspite* was newly repaired from

damage sustained off Crete the previous May. There were, however, the modern carriers *Formidable* and *Indomitable*, together with the elderly *Hermes*.

The squadron was based normally on Colombo and Trincomalee in Ceylon (now Sri Lanka), although Somerville also had use of the secret fleet anchorage of Addu

Atoll ('an abomination of heat and desolation'), some 500 miles to the southwest. The Rs, barely capable of 19 knots, were grouped with the *Hermes* in a 'slow division', while *Warspite* and the new carriers formed a 23-knot 'fast division'. Still too weak to counter a major Japanese thrust, Somerville remained out of sight

Above: The Pacific War had been dominated by airpower, and the Royal Navy's Far Eastern Fleet was based around whichever aircraft carriers were available. By 1945 modern carriers like the Victorious *helped to create a respectable squadron, but it was dwarfed by the US Navy.*

Left: The battlecruiser Renown *concluded her career in the waters where her sistership was lost in 1941. Unlike the more powerful 'R' class or the Rodneys, she was at least able to keep up with fast aircraft carriers.*

even during the enemy's heavy carrier strikes against Ceylon in April 1942.

No more than a liability, the Rs were now based back on Kilindini near Mombasa, from where they could at least cover convoys in the Red Sea approaches. Unknown to the British, the Japanese had no further designs on the Indian Ocean, but

Churchill, stung by the Navy's manifest inability to control the waters, promised substantial reinforcements. All that was offered, however, was the *Malaya*, likewise rejected on grounds of poor endurance.

Lack of enemy interest in the Indian Ocean did not go unnoticed for long and, little by little, the Eastern Fleet's strength was whittled away to meet real demands in European waters. In September 1943, coincident with the armistice with Italy, Somerville's vast command, which stretched from Durban to Tasmania, was re-drawn to reflect the new command structure for the massive build-up against Japan.

The availability of two fine Italian Littorios brought the suggestion that they might be used in the Pacific theatre, but it was soon realised that spares would be unobtainable. By January 1944, however, Colombo was again host to a credible squadron, the *Renown*, *Queen Elizabeth* and *Valiant* being joined by two modern carriers. At last, an offensive move could be made. Supported by the American carrier *Saratoga* and the French battleship *Richelieu*,

strikes were mounted against Sabang and Soerabaya. The raids accomplished little in material terms but were designed to deflect Japanese interest away from an impending thrust in New Guinea. Somerville did, however, note that the Americans were far and away more advanced in flight-deck operations, and that his own control of events suffered by virtue of wearing his flag in a battleship, rather than a carrier.

By the end of 1944, what was now the British Pacific Fleet possessed five modern carriers and two King George V-class battleships. Following a series of supporting operations in the Indian Ocean, they finally joined with the US Navy (as Task Force 57) for the assault on Okinawa. Even here, they were confined to the suppression of secondary targets, and their lack of support, in the shape of a proper Fleet Train, made them very dependent upon their ally.

With their by now greatly enhanced AA armament, the battleships were reduced largely to the close-in protection of the carriers, as were their American peers. During the last days of the war, however,

the flagship had the satisfaction of bombarding targets on Japanese soil. The most powerful and homogeneous force fielded by Britain during the war, TF57's addition to American strength was yet scarcely relevant. It was a guest artist on the American stage, a contestant in a war already won.

Top: Resolution *off Madagascar during the British operations against the French-held island. Fears that the Vichy authorities might allow Japanese forces to base there led to an amphibious invasion in 1942.*
Above: Warspite *in eastern waters during 1942 with the Dutch cruiser* Jacob van Heemskerk *in the background. The* Warspite *was recalled to the Mediterranean in 1943 to support the landings in Italy.*

Vanguard

On the very day that the nameship *King George V* was launched, an order for the first pair of a planned quartette of follow-on Lions was placed. As treaty restrictions had now been abandoned, the limitations of the KGVs could be addressed. A Nelson-scale, nine 16-inch battery was adopted on a modestly increased displacement of 40,000 tons. The extra length meant that 30 knots would be attainable with only 4 per cent more power.

From the outset of war it appeared unlikely that they could be finished in time to be of use. Not the least cause of this would be the design and construction of new triple 16-inch mountings. There were still in existence, however, four twin 15-inch turrets, removed from the two Glorious class carriers at their conversions. Incorporated into a lengthened *Lion*, there

was every chance of a considerably-reduced timescale.

Construction of the Lions was suspended in October 1939, but the one-off *Vanguard*, as she was to be named, was not laid down until October 1941. With war priorities firmly set on mercantile and escort ship construction, she was not completed until April 1946. She carried the KGV secondary battery of sixteen dual-purpose 5.25s, but with no space devoted to aircraft, mounted also a much-enhanced anti-aircraft armament.

A great improvement was the inclusion of a pronounced sheer and flare forward. This made for dryness in head seas, but the resulting tendency to drive her harder put enormous strain on the hull. A more efficient, squared-off transom stern was introduced. Her armour was slightly more extensive than that of the KGVs but, in

view of the greatly increased length, was on a lighter scale. She proved an excellent seaboat and her clean-cut profile, though different, retained the features of the British battleship's long pedigree. Even on completion, however, she was anachronistic and, at a time of severe financial stress, enjoyed a short life, being scrapped in 1960.

Vanguard data:

Displacement, standard	44,300 tons
Displacement, full load	51,400 tons
Length overall	814.3 feet (248.2 m)
Beam	108 feet (32.9 m)
Design draught	36 feet (11.0 m)
Complement	1600

Armament:

Eight 15-in guns (4×2)
Sixteen 5.25-in guns (8×2)
Twenty-two 40-mm guns (11×2)

Machinery:

Steam turbines 130,000 shp (97,000 kW)
Four shafts 30 knots

Armour:

Belt	up to 14 in
Bulkheads	up to 15 in
Decks	up to 6 in
Turrets	up to 13 in
Barbettes	up to 16 in

Above: Laid down in 1941 and intended to be completed in 1943 with the four 15-in turrets taken from Courageous *and* Glorious, *more realistic building priorities delayed* Vanguard's *completion until after World War II. She is seen here as guardship at Dover during a French presidential visit in the 1950s.*

Battleships in the Royal Navy: 1900–1960

Above: Britain began the 20th century with the most powerful navy in the World. Here, the predreadnought Renown *passes the Royal Yacht returning from a Royal tour of India.*

Britain built a fleet of dreadnoughts second to none. The blockade of Germany did much to bring about an Allied victory in World War I. Here, Bellerophon, Superb, St. Vincent *and* Collingwood *follow* Queen Elizabeth.

Below: World War II was to be dominated by airpower, and aircraft carriers became the new capital ships. Furious, *once Fisher's 'light battlecruiser' was one of several major units converted to aircraft carriers.*

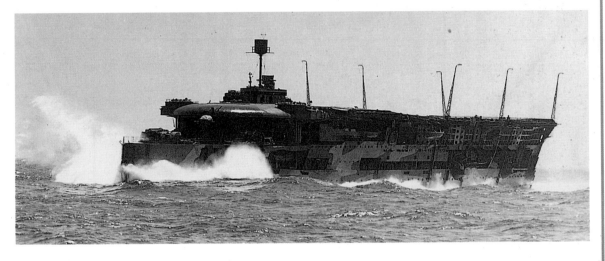

Certain of man's creations are so immense and so well embody his ambitions and emotions, that it seems inconceivable that they could ever disappear. Sentiment, however, is expensive and the battleship, like all else, had its day. Nonetheless, even now, the memory of the stripped *Vanguard*, en route to the knacker's yard, crabbing her way at the end of a rope through Portsmouth Harbour entrance that bright August day in 1960, can still awake that feeling of disbelief, the realisation that one was witnessing the end of a long and reassuring chapter in the nation's history.

To every force there is a counter force, to every threat an antidote. The United Kingdom's first true battleship, *Warrior*, preceded the locomotive torpedo by barely half a decade. Soon afterwards came the fast torpedo boat. For a while, the battleship was good business. Britain built the best and was happy to export them worldwide. Having tried, unsuccessfully, to stifle the development of the torpedo through the purchase of its patents, Britain proceeded to make a good living building the torpedo boats to carry them. These threatened the capital ships themselves, so antidotes were produced in the torpedo boat destroyer and the quick-firing gun. These were also good sellers, and the Royal Navy's battle line did not feel unduly threatened.

At the turn of the century, however, when our narrative begins, engineers (not seamen!) developed the first practical submersible, carrying an inboard, reloadable torpedo tube. A couple of years later, the Wright brothers went aloft in the pioneer powered, heavier-than-air machine. Few would have seen in these unreliable creations the genesis of the battleship's downfall.

For the whole of the First World War the vast panoplies of the Grand Fleet and High Seas Fleet achieved little except mutual stalemate. It was the older units, particularly the predreadnoughts, that saw the best action. The Dardanelles campaign saw the aircraft already advanced sufficiently to be useful in spotting and attack. It saw also the end of close blockade, that very British way of war, which lasted no longer than the arrival of the first U-boat.

Between 1914 and 1918 aviation at sea advanced from cross-channel packets carrying seaplanes to the first true aircraft carrier. Having created it, the Royal Navy saw it as a helpmate to the battleline - reconnoitring, spotting and, under favourable circumstances, slowing an enemy for the battle fleet to run down and despatch. It took other fleets to see the potential. Aviation was a weapon in itself; spread thickly, it could smother any defence.

During World War II, the battleships of both America and Japan were reduced largely to consorts of the aircraft carrier.

In the Royal Navy the battleship's decline was slower, the enemy fleets having little aviation content. Not until the British Pacific Fleet saw action in company with the Americans in 1945 did the truth emerge.

To quote Professor Arthur Marder: 'There was little doubt at the end of the war that the experience of serving alongside the American Fleet had educated the Royal Navy. In 1941 the relationship had been British master and American pupil; four years later these roles had been more nearly reversed.' In terms of range and ordnance-on-target, the carrier won hands down. The battleship was dead.

USA

The US Navy at the turn of the century

Following the exhausting Civil War, and having no foreign enemies, the United States allowed its armed forces to run down. An advisory committee was set up eventually in 1880 to address the potential vulnerability of the long coastline. Although it recommended naval expansion, the existing collection of rams and monitors could be increased only by three protected cruisers laid down by 1883, such was the undeveloped state of American metal shipbuilding. Given its insular outlook, it was surprising when the United States acquired in 1878 naval basing rights in Samoa. Nine years later this was followed by a sugar-dependent Hawaii granting similar concessions at Pearl Harbor.

In 1890, Alfred Thayer Mahan began to publish the influential works in which he so forcefully argued that a pre-requisite for national greatness was thriving world-wide trade, backed by a blue-water navy and, in turn, by a global network of bases. During the same year a naval policy board was established.

This recommended a 100-ship fleet, including twenty battleships and sixty cruisers, of which at least ten would be armoured. Congress remained unenthused by such grandiose plans, and a decade later the numbers were still only twelve and two respectively. They were, however, indicative of a new spirit abroad in the United states, evident particularly in a changed attitude to foreign affairs.

The 'nineties saw war with Spain. This was rooted in popular support for Cuban insurrection against Spanish rule. Except for the *Maine* incident, this would have gone no further, but this second-class battleship was despatched to Havana in January 1898 to protect American interests at a time of widespread civil unrest. Three weeks later she blew up with heavy loss of life. The cause was almost certainly a magazine being

'cooked-off' by a fire in an adjacent coal bunker, but press-inflamed public opinion blamed sabotage.

In the 'splendid little war' that followed, Spain's colonial naval forces were defeated by Dewey at Manila, then Sampson at Santiago de Cuba. Victory brought territory. The anti-imperialist nation that had produced the Monroe Doctrine was now responsible for the Philippines, Puerto Rico and Guam. Cuba, now nominally independent, remained under American occupation until 1902. Elsewhere, part of Samoa was acquired in 1899, following an annexation of Hawaii.

A new century saw more bold foreign policy. Despite Mahan's advice that such an undertaking would be disastrous militarily with an American fleet still so limited in size, an inter-ocean canal across the Central American isthmus was now indispensable with territorial interests in both the Caribbean and the Pacific. French attempts to build such a canal had recently foundered in mud and malaria. With the availability of an antidote to the disease, Congress acquired in 1903 a 99-year lease on what was to become the Panama Canal Zone. Army engineers commenced construction of a new canal in 1907, completing it in 1914.

American Atlantic and Pacific fleet units could now be swiftly interchanged but the dimensions of the locks soon became limiting factors on capital ships parameters. The canal now needed to be defended as a national asset, while Latin America's natural tendency to burst into revolution also needed to be

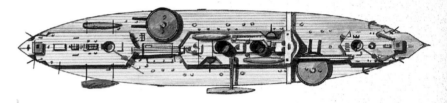

A major jolt towards a credible navy occurred in 1895, when President Cleveland used the Monroe Doctrine as a pretext to challenge Great Britain over a border dispute between Venezuela and British Guiana. The president found the British response humiliating and realised, like the Soviet Union in 1960s Cuba, that bluster was ineffective without a big stick.

By the turn of the century the 'big stick' had progressed as far as nine battleships commissioned, with eight more under construction. An extended series of armoured cruisers – longer and faster, but more lightly armed and protected – had been authorised. The Russo-Japanese war of 1904–5 opened President Theodore Roosevelt's eyes to the potential problems of safeguarding American interests in the Far East. As a show of strength and a test of mobility and endurance, he despatched a force headed by no less than sixteen battleships on a 'goodwill cruise'. Known popularly as the 'Great White Fleet', the force circumnavigated the world between December 1906 and February 1909, to impress upon friend or potential foe alike that the USA was now the world's third-largest naval power.

controlled. Aid and education programmes aimed to assist the path to democratic government but, when these failed, direct military intervention, as in Haiti, Mexico and Nicaragua, was resorted to. As national interests moved ever further afield and, with them, trade, a proper fleet became a sine qua non. Mahan had been proved correct.

Above: The arrangement of Maine's two 10-in turrets was a common one in the 1880s, although by the time she was commissioned in 1895, centre-line turrets were becoming the norm.

Top: Missouri was refitted with cage masts 1909-11: these were an American innovation intended to reduce topweight and resist shell damage better than conventional masts.

Below: The Maine as she appeared on her voyage to Cuba in 1898. US investigators reported she was sunk by an external explosion, but decomposing ammunition or a fire in her coal bunkers are considered more likely explanations for her loss.

Illinois (BB7) class

The three Illinois class units were authorised in 1896 before the war with Spain. Like the pair of Kearsarges that preceded them, they were categorised 'sea-going coastline battleships', a naval euphemism calculated to ease funding from a Congress still committed largely to home defence rather than to foreign expansion. This left the design with a low freeboard and shallow-draught, neither of which features enhanced their performance deep-sea.

They were modern in the sense that their armament was the first that was clearly divided between main and secondary batteries, with no intermediate calibre. Their two predecessors, built otherwise to the same main parameters, had interposed four 8-inch weapons, mounted in twin gunhouses perched atop the turrets of the main 13-inch guns and, thus, committed to sharing a common training angle and target. They also adopted the 5-inch gun for tertiary armament, this being the largest capable of using 'fixed' ammunition and, therefore, classed as quick-firing. The two storey major weapon arrangement made ammunition supply a real headache, the reason that it was abandoned in the Illinois class. These were able to site the forward mounting one deck higher. The reversion to a 6-inch secondary calibre made for improved logistics but the larger mountings required to be casemated over two levels rather than one.

Re-arranged boiler spaces saw the introduction of twin funnels abreast, an arrangement favoured earlier by the Royal Navy. With their generous beam-to-length ratio they were able to ship a fair measure of protection. The main belt was 16 inches thick amidships, tapering to 4 inches at either end. Main turrets and barbettes were reduced in thickness from the 17– and 15-inch of the *Kearsarge*, but were still generously covered when compared with later practice.

Illinois class data:

Displacement, standard	11,565 tons
Displacement, full load	n.k.
Length, overall	375.3 feet (114.4 m)
Beam	72.3 feet (22.0 m)
Design draught	23.5 feet (7.2 m)
Complement:	710

Class: *Illinois* (BB7), *Alabama* (BB8), *Wisconsin* (BB9)
Completed 1900-1901

Above: USS Alabama *and her two sisterships were the only American battleships to have their funnels side-by-side. Their secondary battery of 6-in guns was more effective than the mixed groupings of 8-in and smaller guns fitted to early US predreadnoughts.*

Armament:

Four 13-inch guns (2 × 2)
Fourteen 6-inch guns (14 × 1)
Four 18-inch torpedo tubes

Machinery:

Steam reciprocating machinery 10,000 ihp
Two shafts 16 knots

Armour:

Belt	up to 16 in
Decks	up to 4 in
Turrets	up to 14 in
Barbettes	up to 15 in

Below: Alabama *was distinguishable from her sisterships by having two boat cranes, as specified on the original design.* Illinois *and* Wisconsin *had a single crane amidships.*

Predreadnoughts and Armoured cruisers

The early years of the century saw the US Navy acquire armoured cruisers and battleships at much the same rate. Origins of this policy were various, but lessons of the Civil War, and the disproportionate amount of disruption and loss that could be wreaked on commerce by a few determined raiders, remained fresh. This concept had been developed further by the French '*Jeune Ecole*', which advocated war on trade as the best means of defeating a more powerful maritime power. In place of creating and maintaining a hugely-expensive battlefleet, which would probably never have been strong enough to defeat its enemy, it was better (it was argued) to build fast, affordable raiders which would inflict economic ruin on an adversary by destroying his trade.

Putting theory into practice, the French built the prototype *Dupuy de Lôme*, capable of 23 knots and the undertaking of extended forays. Suitably concerned, the British began constructing counters from 1899. These, in order to combine the requisite speed and firepower, evolved similar in concept to the French. To the Americans, engaged in rapid fleet expansion, the type looked attractive; in being threat and antidote combined, it offered flexibility in strategy. A measure of its importance was that it initially took the names of states, nomenclature reserved otherwise for battleships.

What, then, were these revolutionary warships? Most preceding cruisers, built to limited displacement, were of the 'protected' type. Owing much to the Italian designer Benedetto Brin, their vitals were sited below a continuous armoured deck, as much as possible of which was below water level. The deck was vaulted, in both fore-and-aft and athwartships directions. The level above was closely subdivided. Its sides were unprotected but backed by coal bunkers. Any shell exploding in this level would have its effects largely contained,

Left: The Russian Admiral Makarov was typical of the armoured cruisers built in the first decade of this century. Her fore and aft turrets carried a single 8-in gun, and she had a eight 6-in guns sited in low casemates. Such cruisers proved vulnerable underwater damage: her sistership Pallada sank with all hands after being torpedoed by a U-boat in the Baltic.

with only the largest fragments penetrating downward to the vitals.

New metallurgical processes, such as those of Harvey and Krupp, arrived in the 1890s. Earlier plate tended to shatter when hit squarely, but the new methods allowed a very hard surface to be formed onto a tough interior. For the same level of protection against penetration, armour could now be made much thinner. The weight thus saved allowed the protected cruiser to be given a belt over a limited length. This combination of 'protected' and 'belted' cruiser was known as an 'armoured' cruiser.

Thus the Pennsylvania class of armoured cruisers, at 13,680 tons, were directly complementary to the contemporary Virginia class battleships of 14,950 tons. Their major dimensions were 504 × 69.5 feet (153.6 × 21.2 metres) against 441.3 × 76.3 feet (134.5 × 23.3 metres), the bluffer battleship having only 19,000 ihp for 19 knots against 23,000 ihp for 22 knots. The cruiser was thus longer, finer and faster. Her armament was, of course, inferior (four 8-inch and fourteen 6-inch, against four 12-inch and eight 8-inch) and protection lighter (similar armoured deck but up to 6-inch belt against up to 11-inch). They were immediately eclipsed by the British Duke of Edinburgh class, which mounted a 9.2-inch main battery and which roofed-in the main belt with a second, lighter protected deck.

World War I proved the armoured cruiser to be terribly vulnerable to the battle cruiser and no more were built. The battle cruiser, in turn, gave way to the fast battleship.

Left: Scharnhorst and Gneisenau were the most powerful German warships outside European waters in 1914. They defeated a British cruiser squadron off Chile but were destroyed by British battlecruisers at the Falkland Islands.

Below: USS Milwaukee was one of the ten Omaha class cruisers built at the end of World War I. With a 3-in armour belt, and displacing 9,508 tons at full load, they were armed with twelve 6-in guns. Milwaukee was handed over to Russia in 1944.

147

South Carolina class (BB26)

Progression toward the single-calibre battleship was encouraged by the introduction of scientific fire control. Specialist optics permitted correction for fall of shot at greater ranges, but observers were confused when mixed calibres fired together. Between 1901 and 1905, several navies laid down battleships with only two major calibres. These were significant in comprising an intermediate stage between the predreadnought and the *Dreadnought* herself. Prime examples were the Italian Vittorio Emanueles, the British Lord Nelsons and the Japanese Satsumas. Of these, the last-named were most advanced in concept in as much as they were initially specified with an all-big-gun armament of twelve 12-inch guns, which intention was frustrated only through lack of funding.

The six American Connecticuts (BB18–22 and BB25) partially followed this trend. Their tertiary armament was casemated in the conventional manner but their secondary 8-inch weapons were disposed symmetrically in wing turrets. Much hull length in late predreadnoughts was devoted to boilers and machinery, with designers tending to spread superstructure over the same span. To keep hull length within bounds, a four-turret main battery would thus be disposed in a one forward, one aft and two wing mounting arrangement. This, even more so when increased to five-turret layouts such as that of the *Dreadnought* herself, was inefficient in restricting arcs of fire.

Authorised in the same year as the *Dreadnought*, the South Carolinas evolved naturally from the Connecticuts, owing nothing to the British concept. To mount eight 12-inch guns in a manner which maximised firing arcs meant siting

on the centreline. To avoid masking in axial fire, they had to be superimposed in pairs. The arrangement had been considered by the British but rejected owing to the supposed effects of blast on the lower turret. Following trials the Americans found the arrangement quite feasible, coupled with a shorter superstructure.

The pair were built in the same displacement and length as the preceding class, but were given extra beam to compensate for the higher situation of two turrets and their barbettes. Vertical protection was better than average, the long belt varying in thickness but, in way of magazines, exhibiting adherence to the American rule-of-thumb that the thickness should be equal to the main battery calibre, i.e. 12-inch in this case. It was slightly thinned over the machinery spaces and tapered toward either end. Horizontal armour and underwater protection were criticised as sub-standard but the all-up weight was still such as to require the hull to be reduced aft by one level.

The design's greatest weakness lay in its designer's unwillingness to join the *Dreadnought* in adopting the steam turbine.

As a result, the machinery's power-to-weight ratio was much inferior, limiting the ships to a shade under 19 knots.

Two 'military' masts (i.e. poles with fighting tops) were to have been fitted. Uniquely, they would have been staggered off-centreline to provide facilities for a boat crane on either side. In the event, the new 'lattice' masts were fitted. The helical design of these was intended to de-couple shock and vibration, due to the heavy guns, from the fire control platforms.In this they were not completely successful.

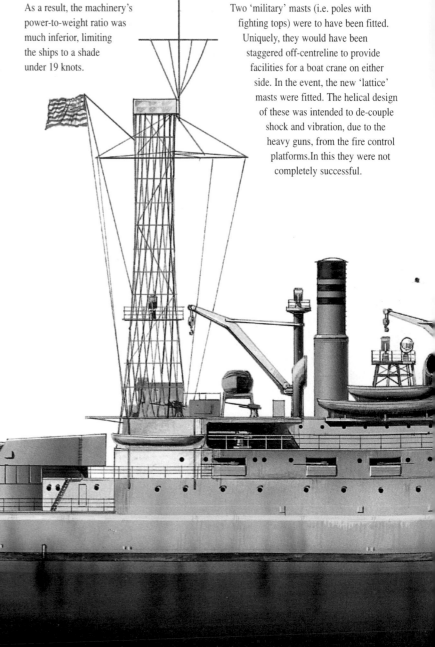

Left: USS Michigan *seen in 1910. The three black bands on her fore funnel indicate she belongs to the 3rd division of the battle fleet.*

South Caroline class data:

Displacement, standard	16,000 tons
Displacement, full load	17,900 tons
Length, overall	452.8 feet (138 m)
Beam	80.2 feet (24.5 m)
Design draught	24.6 feet (7.5 m)
Complement	870

Armour:

Belt	up to 12 in
Bulkheads	up to 11 in
Decks	up to 3 in
Turrets	up to 12 in
Barbettes	up to 10 in

Class: *South Carolina (BB26), Michigan (BB27). Both completed 1910.*

Armament:
Eight 12-in guns (4 × 2)
Twenty-two 3-in guns (22 × 1)
Two 21-in torpedo tubes

Machinery:
Two triple expansion steam reciprocating
  engines. 16,000 ihp (11,940kW)
Twin shafts 18.75 knots

Right and below: With its first dreadnought design, the US Navy introduced what would become the accepted standard turret layout. While many other navies experimented with echeloned turrets positioned to fire across the decks, the South Carolina's four turrets made the most efficient use of her eight 12-in guns. The 'basket' masts remained a standard US feature until World War II.

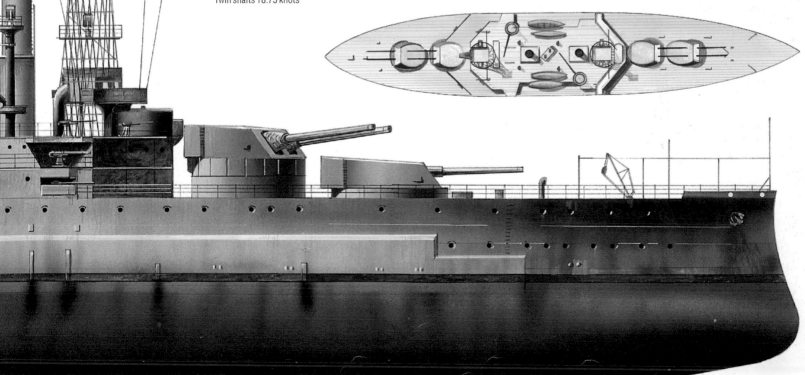

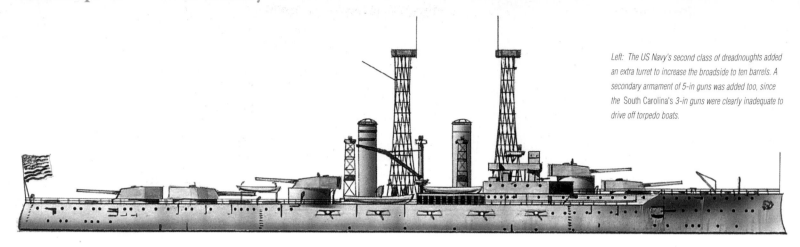

Delaware class (BB28)

Like the *Dreadnought*, the two South Carolinas had no secondary armament other than quick-firers for deterring torpedo attack by destroyers. Again, like the British, the Americans quickly realised that this could be a distinct drawback, the 13-pound (5.9kg) projectile of the 3-inch weapons carrying insufficient energy. The two Delawares, laid down in 1907, within a year of their predecessors were, therefore, given fourteen 5-inch guns in casemates. While the calibre was still smaller than that favoured by foreign navies, it threw a 60-pound (27.3kg) shell.

The critical improvement was the addition of a fifth turret, to make a ten-gun main battery equal to contemporary British practice. In the quest to maximise firing arcs this turret, too, needed to be placed on the centreline, adding twenty metres to the length. Its situation was unusual in being sited back-to-back with 'Y' mounting, an arrangement that placed a large concentrated mass at a position far aft. Both were superfired by 'X' turret but the considerable gap between them resulted from their trunks

and magazines flanking the engine room, fore and aft. The citadel-style amidships structure of the South Carolinas was abandoned for a British-style raised forecastle deck of restricted width and faceted at the sides. The longer hull required larger areas of protection but, with the extra available buoyancy, this could be maintained at the earlier standards (neither had torpedo bulkheads) though with a significant increase in displacement. The second ship, *North Dakota*, became the first American battleship propelled by steam turbines, although her Curtis machinery was later replaced by Parsons-designed geared units.

Delaware class data:

Displacement, standard	20,000 tons
	(*Delaware* 20,380 tons)
Displacement, full load	22,400 tons
Length, overall	518.8 feet (158.1 m)
Beam	85.3 feet (26.0 m)
Design draught	27.0 feet (8.2 m)
Complement	939

Class: *Delaware* (BB28), *North Dakota* (BB29). Completed 1910.

Armament:
Ten 12-in guns (5 × 2)
Fourteen 5-in guns (14 × 1)
Two 21-in torpedo tubes

Machinery:
Two triple expansion *(Delaware)* and two steam turbines *(N. Dakota)*
Twin shafts 21 knots Nominal output 25,000 ihp (18,650 kW)

Armour:
Belt	up to 11 in
Bulkheads	up to 9 in
Decks	up to 3 in
Turrets	up to 12 in
Barbettes	up to 10 in

Below: Nevada *and* Oklahoma *sailed to Europe in 1918. Operating from Bantry Bay, they patrolled the North Atlantic sea routes in case German battlecruisers tried to attack the convoys.*

US battleships join the Grand Fleet

In mid-1917 the Royal Navy's last five King Edward VII class predreadnoughts were paid off and, to maintain the Grand Fleet's margin of superiority over the High Seas Fleet, the Americans (who had declared war on Germany in April 1917) were invited to contribute four dreadnoughts to its strength. The Americans agreed readily, rotating four ships out of six that were committed. The *Delaware* was the oldest, the others being *Florida* (BB30), *Wyoming* (BB32), *Arkansas* (BB33), *New York* (BB34) (as flagship) and *Texas* (BB35). In command was Rear-Admiral Hugh Rodman, whose squadron joined Beatty's Grand Fleet at Scapa in November 1917.

In response to American wishes, the force was fully integrated into the British fighting organisation, becoming the Sixth Battle Squadron. Rodman and Beatty were immediately on excellent terms, the Americans quickly absorbing their ally's procedures and reacting well to the endless punishing round of exercises and sweeps conducted, for the most part, in long winter

darkness, cold and bitterly hostile conditions of the northern North Sea and, in particular, the Pentland Firth.

Until June 1918 Beatty had reservations regarding their battleworthiness, their gunnery being 'distinctly poor and disappointing', their signalling little better. What impressed him was their keenness and willingness to learn. Rodman's ships were attached whenever the Grand Fleet sailed and they took their turn with chores such as covering Scandinavian convoys and the laying of the Northern Mine Barrage. On the latter occasions, the American Admiral reversed normal status by commanding the accompanying British supporting forces.

The Sixth Battle Squadron was never granted the chance of proving itself in action. In April 1918 the British and German fleets missed a final major clash by less than 150 miles and, by chance, the Grand Fleet had deployed so that the Americans were in the van. Rodman's frustration with the missed interception was clear: 'I have often thought what a glorious day it would have been for the ships of our country to have led the Grand Fleet into action.' The successful co-operation boded well, however for the future and a war in which the relative fleet strengths would be reversed.

Admiral Rodman

Admiral Hugh Rodman, the 'Kentucky Admiral', was born in 1859, shortly before the Civil War erupted. Entering the navy through Annapolis, he was to be nearly forty years of age before seeing real action. He was gunnery officer on the cruiser *Raleigh* which was stationed in the Levant when ordered suddenly to join Admiral Dewey's Asiatic Squadron. She was present at Manila Bay, when the Spanish were defeated. Subsequent service in the Philippines brought him into contact with the British and Japanese navies, for both of which he developed admiration. This rapport was invaluable nearly two decades later when, as Rear Admiral, he was chosen to command the battle squadron that served with the Grand Fleet. His lack of pre-conceived ideas and his readiness to adapt to British routines greatly impressed Beatty, with whom he became firm friends. From 1919 to 1921 Rodman commanded the Pacific Fleet. He died in 1940.

Right: The US battleships very nearly clashed with the High Seas Fleet in 1918, as the Germans attempted to intercept convoys between the UK and Scandanavia. Delaware never had another chance of action: she was scrapped in 1924.

Left: USS Delaware opens fire with her 12-in guns on exercises in 1920. Serving with the British Grand Fleet, the American squadron learned the latest gunnery techniques developed in the wake of Jutland.

Below: The quarterdeck of USS Delaware in about 1913. Note the small spotting guns fitted on top of the 12-in main armament for gunnery training.

Left: Utah is fitted with heavy anti-aircraft guns at the Puget Sound Navy Yard, just months before her loss at Pearl Harbor. The old battleship had been used as a target ship until 1935 when she was fitted out as a training ship for anti-aircraft gunners.

Utah class (BB31)

The two Floridas, commenced in 1909, were essentially enlarged Delawares. Both were fitted initially with Parsons steam turbines and, if they had taken their planned main battery fit of eight 14-inch guns, would have marked a clear step into the post-Dreadnought era. Probably hastened by the pace of construction abroad, however, they also inherited the Delawares' ten 12-inch.

Originally they looked very similar to their predecessors, the main difference being that both funnels were sited between the masts. Adoption of turbine plant required an extra couple of metres' machinery space, evident in the slightly larger gap between the third and fourth turrets. An early feature was the provision of local range finders atop the second, third and fourth turrets.

They were the first American battleships to have quadruple shaft propulsion. As the power developed was much the same as the earlier turbine-driven

North Dakota there would appear to have been a problem with shaft speed. The Floridas' extra length allowed a degree of reduction gearing, while four smaller-diameter screws could be driven at higher design speeds.

The Floridas' protection marked an improvement on the Delawares' and compared well with that of the *Neptune*, their Royal Navy contemporary. Between 1926 and 1928 both ships were extensively modernised. The number of boilers were drastically reduced and turbines replaced by Curtis-type units, but their higher output was offset by the effects of the generous anti-torpedo bulges that had been added. Only one funnel was required, while the after lattice mast was replaced by a pole. *Florida* was stricken in 1931 but *Utah* went on to a second career as a fleet target ship.

Florida class data:

Displacement, standard	21,825 tons
Displacement, full load	23,400 tons
Length, overall	521.5 feet (158.9 m)
Beam	88.3 feet (26.9 m)
With bulges	106.0 feet (32.3 m)
Design draught	28.3 feet (8.6 m)
Complement	1000

Class: *Florida* (BB30), *Utah* (BB31). Completed 1911

Armament:
Ten 12-in guns (5 × 2)
Sixteen 5-in guns (16 × 1)
Eight 3-in guns (from refit)
Two 21-in torpedo tubes
Three aircraft

Machinery:
Steam turbines 28,000 shp (20.900kW)
Four shafts 21 knots

Armour:
Belt	up to 11 in
Bulkheads	up to 10 in
Decks	up to 6 in
Turrets	up to 12 in
Barbettes	up to 10 in

Both Floridas escaped the mass scrapping resulting from the 1921–2 Washington Treaties. As related above, both underwent a comparatively expensive updating during 1926–8, but they were to enjoy only a brief life extension from it. The 1930 London Navy Treaty required their disposal, along with that of one of the follow-on Wyomings. *Utah*, however, escaped again, by virtue of a clause in the original Washington agreement which permitted each signatory to demilitarise a battleship for the purpose of target and/or training. Like the British *Centurion* and Japanese *Settsu*, the *Utah* was fitted for remote radio control, in her case for Pacific Fleet gunnery and bombing practice. Re-graded AG16, i.e. 'Miscellaneous Auxiliary' she had removed all main and secondary armament, fire control equipment and searchlights. Turrets and casemates remained, but blanked-off. As a training ship, however, she could still mount eight 5-inch singles (of various marks) and automatic AA weapons.

When Pearl Harbor was assaulted on 7 December 1941, the Pacific Fleet carriers were absent. It was the misfortune of the *Utah* to have been temporarily allocated the *Saratoga's* usual billet, on the opposite side of Ford Island to 'Battleship Row'. From the attacker's viewpoint, it offered an unobstructed torpedo shot down the length of the shallow East Loch.

The sinking of the *Utah*

UTAH Used by the U.S. Navy as a radio-controlled target ship, the battleship capsized after being hit in the sneak raid. She was a 22,000 vessel.

Colours were in the act of being hoisted at 0800 when both the *Utah* and her next ahead, *Raleigh*, were instantaneously torpedoed. Seconds later, the 30-year-old battleship took a second hit. Both struck in the port side machinery space. Despite her bulges, these flooded rapidly, the ship taking an almost

immediate 15-degree list. The crew was ordered topside, donning life jackets while dodging strafing aircraft and a bomb that hit the superstructure, portside. Through supposedly-watertight bulkheads, the starboard spaces also began to flood. Steam pressure fell off, threatening turbo-generators and pumps.

Within five minutes of her being hit, she list to 40 degrees. She could not return fire as, due to her current role as bombing target, guns had been plated-in or struck below. For this role her decks had been given a cover of a double layer of 12 × 6-inch baulks of timber,

to defeat practice bombs. As *Utah's* crew abandoned, many of these broke loose with the precipitous heel, causing many casualties. At 0812 her mooring lines snapped as she rolled over, coming to rest with her superstructure on the muddy bottom and keel above the surface. One man was rescued through a hole burned in the double bottom, but 58 were dead.

In following months salvage teams removed ordnance, ammunition and fuel oil from the wreck. It was assessed that her poor condition would not allow her to be floated and moved on compressed air. As she was occupying a non-essential berth her salvage was not of high priority. Gradually, her tophamper was cut away and seventeen huge head frames welded to her hull.

Top left: Struck by two torpedoes, Utah capsized in a few minutes. She was never raised, and remains today as a memorial to those killed in the Japanese attack.

Top right: Utah seen during World War I with triangular baffles fitted to her masts. These, and the camouflage were a British idea supposed to confuse enemy spotters by breaking up her profile.

Winches ashore used these to parbuckle the hulk to within 38 degrees of upright. Officially not worth the expense of final salvage, the hull of the *Utah* remains still as a war grave. In company with the *Arizona*, on the other side of the island, she was the only ship never to be raised of the nineteen sunk.

Below: Utah served through World War I and into the 1920s, even visiting Germany in 1930 before decommissioning and becoming a target ship. Note how the 1918 camouflage scheme (also seen in the photograph top right) disrupts the line of the deck.

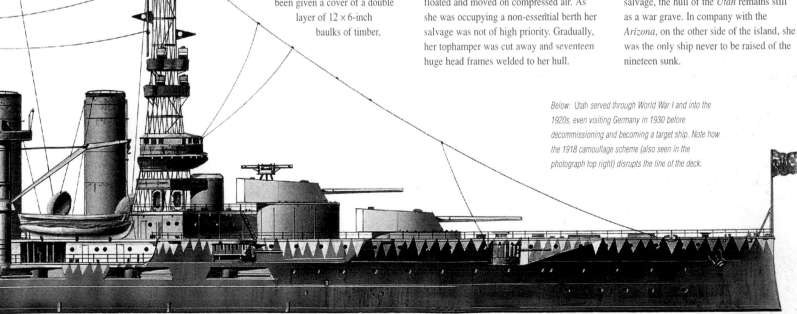

Wyoming class (BB32)

In the four Helgolands, laid down in 1908–9, the Germans increased their main armament calibre from 11 to 12-inch. Although twelve guns were carried, their poor disposition allowed only eight to fire in broadside. With the 'naval race' in full swing at the time, the British immediately introduced the 13.5-inch gun. Ten of these were designed into the four Orions of 1909–10 and, as all turrets were centreline mounted for the first time, a genuine ten-gun broadside was possible. The German ships' 6173 lb (2806kg) broadside was completely eclipsed by the Orions' 12500 lb (5682kg).

While not attempting to match this European rivalry directly, the Americans had no desire to be left behind. The initial advantage in firepower gained through their adoption of superimposition and all-centreline disposition had now been overtaken. A 14-inch gun was under development but was suffering delays, so the two Wyomings, scheduled for laying down in 1910, had again to make do with the well-proven 12-inch. Cuniberti, in the Italian *Dante Alighieri* and the Russian Ganguts, had shown that a triple 12-inch mounting was perfectly feasible. The Austro-Hungarians, in the *Viribus Unitis*, were about to go one stage better by superimposing them. All these classes could fire full twelve-gun broadsides of about 8772 lb (3987kg). Again, the Americans were designing a triple 12-inch but this, too, was not ready for production. The Wyomings therefore took no less than six centreline twin turrets of the type used previously. With the heavier American projectiles, their broadside was a respectable 10200 lb (4636kg) but resulted in an extraordinary turret layout, surpassed only by that of the seven-turret British

Agincourt, laid down in 1911.

American industry was also experiencing trouble with steam turbine and gearbox manufacture. It was proposed initially to fit a combined turbine/reciprocating engine arrangement, presumably with the turbines driving the wing shafts on an and/or basis. Finally, however, the necessary eight sets were produced.

The extra turret put eleven metres on the length and added very considerably to the displacement because of the extra area of protection required. Of the casemated secondary armament, those right forward and right aft proved to be unworkable in any sea and were removed.

During 1925–7 both were updated, undergoing a major change in appearance. Four oil-fired boilers replaced the original twelve coal/oil units, necessitating only one funnel. The after lattice mast was replaced by a tripod, stepped further aft, over the engine room. An aircraft catapult was fitted atop the amidships 'C' turret. Anti-torpedo bulges were added.

Wyoming herself ran foul of the London Treaty requirements, but escaped scrapping through conversion to a sea-going training ship. Only the two forward, and the aftermost, main battery turrets were retained. Vertical armour was removed and one boiler de-commissioned. She went on to

Above: The funnels and masts of the Wyoming class were grouped closely together to create space for the four turrets aft. This is Wyoming, seen in 1919 after the removal of her stern 5-in gun.

serve throughout World War II as a training ship for AA gunners, eventually losing her remaining heavy turrets and gaining a large number of 5-inch and automatic weapons, together with their associated directors.

Arkansas served through World War II as the oldest active American battleship. Heavy bombardment before and after amphibious landings proved to be

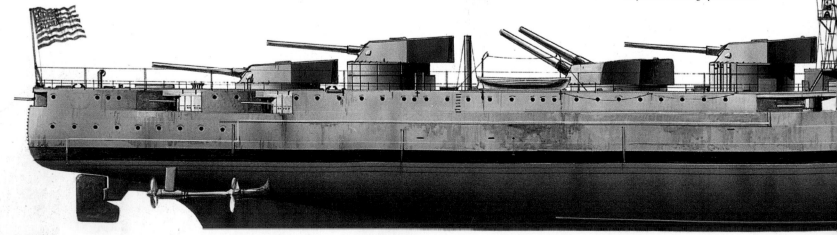

Left: The experience of the 'Great White Fleet' had already taught the US Navy that secondary armament had to be mounted higher. Here, Wyoming steams at high speed but most of her 5-in guns are clear of the water. The foremost 5-in casemate was plated over during World War I.

Below: Wyoming as completed in 1912. This was the last class of US balleships to carry 12-in guns until the Alaska class battlecruisers of World War II. Both Wyomings were fitted as llagships, the Arkansas was the flagship of the US Atlantic fleet in 1914.

indispensable and gave profitable occupation to older units. Again partly modernised, with a forward tripod, radar, reduced secondary battery and greatly enhanced AA armament, she saw action at Normandy, the South of France, Iwo Jima and Okinawa. Finally, she evaded the breakers again by being expended at Bikini, even then surviving the first nuclear explosion.

Above: With six 12-in gun turrets on the centreline, the Wyomings were only surpassed by the Agincourt. To protect the main armament, the main armour belt was 400-ft long from 'A' turret to 'Y' turret.

Wyoming class data:

Displacement, standard 26,000
(later 29,000) tons
Displacement, full load.........................27,700
(later 31,000) tons
Length, overall ....562 feet (171.3 m)
Beam ....93.3 feet (28.4 m)
Later 106 feet (32.3 m)
Design draught ....28.5 feet (8.7 m)
Complement 1060

Class: *Arkansas (BB33), Wyoming (BB32)*

Armament:
Twelve 12-in guns (6 × 2)
Sixteen 5-in guns (16 × 1)
Two 21-in torpedo tubes

Machinery:
Steam turbines 28,500 shp (20,900kW)
Four shafts 20.5 knots

Armour:
Belt ....up to 11 in
Bulkheads ....up to 11 in
Decks ....up to 3 in
Turrets ....up to 12 in
Barbettes ....up to 11 in

The 'Maximum Battleship'

The avowed American intention to create a navy 'second to none' resulted in a variety of responses. William A. Moffett (a commander in 1916, a rear-admiral by 1921, and destined to greatly influence the development of aviation in the US Navy) awoke Congressional interest in a study to determine the parameters of a capital ship that would render obsolete all existing battleships. Assuming no limitation on displacement or cost, what would be the ideal balance of protection, armament or speed?

An immediate limitation existed in dimensions. For rapid interchange between Atlantic and Pacific Fleets, all American warships had to be able to transit the newly-opened Panama Canal. Moffett assumed (possibly incorrectly) that any foreign competitor would be similarly constricted by the size of these locks. His maximum dimensions were thus fixed at 998 feet (c.304 m) overall length by 108 feet (32.9m) beam, with a draught of 34 feet (10.4 m).

The largest American battleships, the then-building 32,000-ton New Mexicos, had a length of 'only' 624 feet (190.2 m) but a 97.5 foot (29.7 m) beam that was already not a lot short of the limit. This length to breadth ratio of about 6.15 to one was typical of battleship forms: to maximise dimensions to those of the locks would give a ratio of about nine to one, more appropriate to a fast cruiser. It was obvious already that there would be several solutions, depending on which of speed, armament or protection was to be maximised.

A starting point was the already-designed 90,000 horsepower (67,100kW) machinery plant designed for the Lexington-class battle cruisers. To save time, this was adopted as a yardstick. A minimum of a 16-inch main armament calibre was envisaged, but 18-inch would be better, and 20-inch was considered. Full data was, of course, available on the extant 16-inch gun, enabling estimates to be made on the weights and dimensions of twin, triple, quadruple and, as an exploratory exercise, sextuple mountings. It is known also that the Americans proof-tested an 18-inch gun,

Left: Treaty limitations left ship designers with little flexibility. With their 14-in guns and modest displacement, the British King George V class followed the Washington Treaty restrictions. US and Japanese battleships built at the same time carried 16-in guns.

although it never entered service. Statistics for a 20-inch weapon would needs have been extrapolated 'guesstimates' from the Bureau of Ordnance.

With weight and size estimates available for machinery and a variety of armament fits, it was then possible to match them to hull dimensions to arrive at suitable protective schemes and displacements. This quickly demonstrated that the critical hull parameter was, in fact, the 34-foot limitation on draught. The Colorados, already under design, would draw 30.5 feet (10.3 m) on a displacement of 32,600 tons.

As the projected ships would displace anything between 60,000 and 80,000 tons, the designers were set the problem of at least doubling the Colorado's displacement without increasing the draught by more than 3.5 feet (1.1 m), nor the beam by more than 10.5 feet (3.2 m). Inevitably, this resulted in maintaining maximum beam over the greatest possible length, yielding portly proportions with block coefficients more appropriate to the lower-speed, pre-dreadnought era. For those variants that maximised protection and armament, the 90,000 horsepower plant proved over-powerful. By reducing its output by over one third, maximum speed was reduced by only 1.5 knots, yet 1250 tons could be saved.

The final designs are interesting, not least in showing that even an apparent carte blanche will soon attract limitations. Because the 'maximum speed' version needed to be slimmed, her displacement fell to 63,500 tons. This still permitted the full 90,000 hp machinery fit, for a speed approaching 30 knots. Four triple 16-inch turrets could also be carried, but there remained sufficient margin for only a 13-inch belt, making her inferior to contemporary practice.

Two 'maximum armament' variants were evolved, a 26.5 knot, 70,000-tonner and the other of 25 knots and 80,000 tons. These carried thirteen or fifteen 18-inch guns, the latter being preferred as an arrangement that concentrated the battery forward and aft, with no amidships mountings to cause problems with dividend machinery spaces and adjacent magazines. With a belt of 18-inches, tapering to 9-inches at either end, and a 5-inch protective deck, this version would have totally outclassed anything

afloat. No less than five parallel anti-torpedo bulkheads were worked-in along each side, giving an 18-foot (5.5 m) depth of protection.

These monsters were never built as, just three months after Jutland, Congress had authorised a massive fleet expansion, which included ten battleships and six battlecruisers. As there was a tight, three-year timescale, the programme was in full swing and could not be allowed to be deflected or made obsolete by developments. Following the war, even the naval race that developed between the former allies could not disguise the fact that the US Navy no longer faced any serious threat. This, and the knowledge that its rivals would be fully ready and able to match even 80,000-tonners with 18-inch guns, quickly led to the conference table at Washington.

The 14-inch battleship series

The late entry into service of the American 14-inch gun, and an adherence to twin turrets resulted, as we have seen, in the ungainly six-turret arrangement of the Wyomings. Laid down the year after (1911) were the *New York* (BB34) and *Texas* (BB35). With the new gun still not approved, they were originally slated to receive five triple 12-inch but were finally able to ship five twin 14-inch. With one centreline turret less than the Wyomings they could have been shorter, but extra protection was worked in. This, and the heavier main battery, resulted in increased displacement. Steam turbine manufacturing problems enforced a reversion to reciprocating engines, an advantage with which was superior endurance at cruising speed.

In 1912 the *Nevada* (BB36) and *Oklahoma* (BB37) were laid down. Triple 14-inch turrets were fitted in 'A' and 'Y' positions, each superfired by a twin. With a reduction from five turrets to four, the opportunity could again have been taken to reduce length but protection was further increased. Heavy-calibre trials had demonstrated the ineffectiveness of medium-thickness plate under real punishment. This resulted in the philosophy of 'all or nothing', covering the concentrated vital zones of a ship with the thickest-possible protection, leaving the ends and upperworks 'soft'. An interesting feature of the pair was the provision of steam turbines for the *Nevada*, and reciprocating machinery for the *Oklahoma*.

USS Texas *seen in 1943 with massively increased anti-aircraft armament.*

Prior to World War I, the rate of battleship construction slowed, the *Pennsylvania* (BB38) and *Arizona* (BB39) being commenced in 1913 and 1914 respectively. As their superfiring 'B' and 'X' turrets were upgraded from twins to triples, displacement again edged upward. Cruising turbines were included in the machinery outfit to maximise endurance. Between the wars, all six were updated along similar lines, gaining aircraft and bulges, landing secondary armament from those casemates unworkable in a sea, increasing the maximum elevation of the main armament and exchanging lattice masts for tripods.

During World War II *Nevada* and *Pennsylvania* were thoroughly modernised with modern secondary and AA armament, together with full radar direction. Both *Oklahoma* and *Arizona* ended their careers at Pearl Harbor.

New Mexico class (BB40)

With this trio the US battleship received a new 'trademark' in the form of a heavily-raked 'clipper' bow. Their waterline length of 600 feet (182.9 m) was the same as that for the preceding Pennsylvanias but the new feature extended overall length by 16 feet (4.9 m). The four triple 14-inch turret arrangement was retained but the gun was an uprated, 50-calibre model with an increased muzzle velocity. A similar secondary armament was fitted, with the difference that eight guns were casemated at upper deck level. The four sited one level lower, and flanking the forecastle proved, as usual, to be unusable in any sea and were removed. The *New Mexico* was fitted experimentally with turbo-electric propulsion, her sisters having geared turbines.

Between 1931 and 1934, all three were modernised. In the process of this, all received new machinery and boilers.

Externally, the distinctive lattice masts were removed, the bridge built up with a substantial tower structure and a pole mainmast fitted. A new crane was added right aft to server the quarterdeck catapult. Important, but invisible, was a thickening of their horizontal protection.

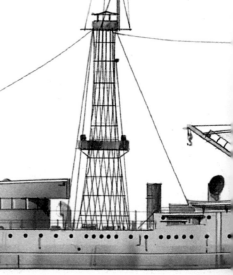

Already looking quite 'modern', the three were again uprated during World War II with radar, current fire control and a greatly-enhanced AA armament. *Idaho* had a new secondary battery comprising ten, destroyer-type, single 5-inch/38 gun-houses. Her

sisters 'made do' originally with open, old-style 5-inch/25s. All proved to be doughty performers in heavy gunfire support, being present at most of the major amphibious operations and surviving hits by both *Kamikaze* and air-dropped torpedo. *Mississippi* was also in Oldendorf's gunline, an assembly of veterans that crushed the Japanese in the Surigao Strait. She survived until 1956, having served for a decade post-war as a test-bed for guided missiles and prototype medium-calibre gun turrets.

New Mexico class data:

Displacement, standard ....32,600 tons
Displacement, full load ....33,500 tons
Length, overall ....624 feet (190.2 m)
Beam ....97.5 feet (29.7 m)
Design draught ....30 feet (9.1 m)
Complement 1085

Class: *Idaho (BB42), Mississippi (BB41), New Mexico (BB40)*
Completed 1917–19

Armament:
Twelve 14-in guns (4 × 3)
Twelve 5-in guns (12 × 1)
Two 3-in guns (2 × 1)
Two 21-in torpedo tubes
Three aircraft

Machinery:
Steam turbines (with turbo-electric drive in New Mexico only)
Four shafts 21 knots 32,000 shp (23,900 kW)

Armour:
Belt ....up to 14 in
Bulkheads ....up to 14 in
Decks ....up to 3.5 in
(later, 6 in)
Turrets ....up to 18 in
Barbettes ....up to 13.5 in

*Above left: New Mexico in Tokyo Bay after the Japanese surrender, with Mt. Fujiyama in the background.
Above right: Texas in December 1943. Note the AA guns on the roof of 'A' turret.*

Turbo-electric propulsion

Five classes of American capital ship, laid down between 1915 and 1921, incorporated electric drive, pioneered in the aircraft carrier *Langley*. In this system, the steam turbines are coupled directly to alternators. Current from these is fed aft to motors which, in turn, are coupled directly to the propellers. Advantages include the lack of long propeller shafts, resulting in much-improved sub-division. Power to propulsion motors may be cross-connected to give redundancy of supply in the case of action damage. No expensive gearboxes are necessary, speed being varied by switching in or out different numbers of motor poles. High astern power is almost instantly available by simply reversing the motor. Disadvantages include high voltages and efficiencies marginally lower than those of geared steam turbines. Its main drawback, however, was its 40 per cent lower power-to-weight ratio, critical to meeting treaty-imposed displacement.

Left: USS Pennsylvania introduced triple 14-in turrets for the main armament. Note the conventional dreadnought bow compared to the clipper bow of the New Mexicos. Pennsylvania was the flagship of the US Atlantic fleet 1916-18. Arizona was sunk at Pearl Harbor, where she remains as a war memorial.

Bigger, heavier and faster

Battleships, like national characteristics, tend to be classified in over-generalised terms. The accompanying diagrams, therefore, directly compare major parameters of American examples with those of their British and German peers. No battlecruisers are included; their extreme particulars would distort the picture and the United States did not build them in the period represented. This period reaches from the last predreadnought class to the planned American and British battleships abandoned post-Washington. To present a fair comparison, the British Lord Nelsons are plotted ahead of the *Dreadnought* although, in fact, they were commissioned later.

Figure 1 shows the variation in design displacement with time. Design displacement is that achieved at design draught. It is interesting in that, until 1916, there was little to choose between the designs of the fleets concerned. Britain and Germany commissioned no new classes after 1916 and, with this upward impetus

removed, the Americans (who were not yet involved in hostilities and were still building) retained virtually the same displacement. The plots are extended to a theoretical 1923 completion date for the monsters cancelled at Washington. Where the American South Dakotas would have represented a realistic 25 per cent increase in displacement, the unnamed British behemoths would have seen a 42 per cent hike, an extrapolation from an existing base that could have gone disastrously wrong.

Figure 2 shows that the proportions of British predreadnoughts were considerably more portly than those of the United States and Germany. Installation of steam turbines with the *Dreadnought*, however, demanded a finer hull form to realise the speed potential. British battleships thereafter remained finer, the results being apparent in the one-or-two-knot speed advantage seen in *Figure 3*. In the later diagram the Queen Elizabeths' claim to be the prototype 'fast battleships' is well illustrated by their 25-knot peak.

Figure 4 shows well the results of Fisher's 'speed is protection' dictum. In the slow predreadnought era, the Royal Navy's ships had the thickest belts, but speed meant shedding weight. The Americans closed with the solidly-protected Germans, leaving the British lightest. It is interesting that the

extra two knots of the planned South Dakotas would have shaved 2½ inches from their belts. It must be remembered that the stopping power of belt protection was reinforced somewhat by longitudinal anti-torpedo bulkheads, where fitted. The effect would be variable and is not included.

Figures 5 and 6 are interesting in showing that, where the Royal Navy generally maintained its policy of staying ahead in the calibre of its main batteries, American ships, by virtue of carrying more guns, generally had much the same weight of broadside. A further obvious point is that German ships were more modest in fire power and speed but considerably better protected.

Above: USS Pennsylvania off Port Townsend in August 1943. Although the British Queen Elizabeth class had 15-in guns, they only had eight to the ten 14-in guns shipped by the American Nevada class and the twelve carried by the Pennsylvanias.

Left: The magnificent sweep of the New Mexico's clipper bow revealed by a spell in dry dock at the New York Navy Yard in the summer of 1919. The New Mexico's protection included a 13.5-in belt and 3.5-in deck which was repeated on both the Colorados and the uncompleted South Dakota class 'super dreadnoughts'.

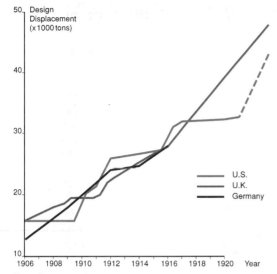

Figure 1

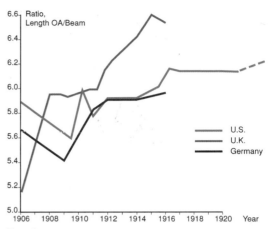

Figure 2

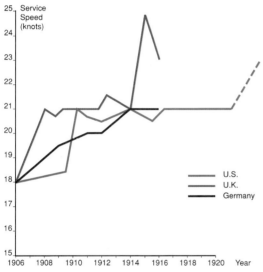

Figure 3

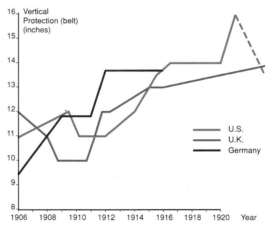

Figure 4

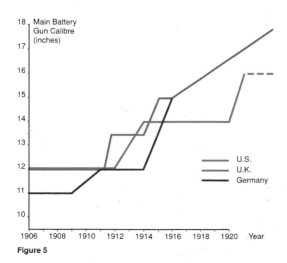

Figure 5

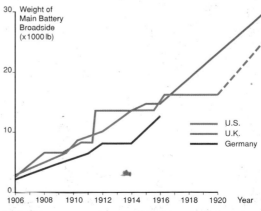

Figure 6

Colorado class (BB45)

As the New Mexicos had virtually repeated the hull of the preceding Pennsylvanias, so the *Tennessee* (BB43) and *California* (BB44) continued the series, with the significant differences of an improved machinery layout requiring a reversion to two funnels and, for the first time, a hull with no casemates, all secondary armament being located above the upper deck.

America was still not embroiled in the European war and was able to observe, and act upon, developments by the Japanese, of whom there was growing distrust. In the two Nagatos, to be laid down in 1917–18, the gun calibre was to be increased to 16-inch. The four Colorados, the first of which, *Maryland*, was due to be laid down in 1917, thus also took 16-inch guns, the development of which had been long in hand. As the previous classes possessed a tried and efficient hull form, it was again adopted, with little change except for a thickening of the belt. Four triple 14-inch turrets were simply exchanged for four twin 16-inch.

Standardisation in successive classes already assisted more rapid construction and, at this time, included the turbo-electric propulsion systems and bridges. None of the four could be completed during hostilities, the Washington (BB47) falling foul of her

eponymous treaty agreements and, about three-quarters complete, being expended as a target. The *West Virginia*, put on the bottom in shallow water at Pearl Harbor by six, possibly seven torpedoes, was virtually beyond repair. Becoming something of a symbol of recovery, she was salvaged, towed stateside and spent two years undergoing total rebuilding benefiting more than her sisters in the process. She recommissioned in July 1944, in good time to be with Oldendorf at the Surigao Strait, satisfactorily settling old scores in firing ninety-three 16-inch rounds.

Colorado class data:

Displacement, standard	32,600 tons
Displacement, full load	33,590 tons
Length, overall	624 feet (190.2 m)
Beam	97.5 feet (29.7 m)
Design draught	30.5 feet (9.3 m)
Complement	1090

Above: USS Maryland *seen during the early 1930s. Like the Tennessee class, the Colorados carried larger, heavier masts, with an enclosed top.*

Class: *Colorado (BB45), Maryland (BB46), Washington (BB47), West Virginia (BB48)*
Completed 1921/23

Armament:
Eight 16-in guns (4×2)
Twelve 5-in guns (12×1)
Eight 3-in guns (8×1)
Two 21-in torpedo tubes
Three aircraft

Machinery:
Turbo-electric drive 29,000 shp
 (21,600kw)
Four shafts 21 knots

Armour:
Belt	up to 16 in
Bulkheads	up to 13.5 in
Decks	up to 3.25 in
Turrets	up to 18 in
Barbettes	up to 13.5 in

In July 1921, months before the Washington Conference, a bombing trial was staged. While contentious, it exerted great influence on subsequent capital ship design. Brigadier General William ('Billy') Mitchell was devoted passionately to the interests of the-then Army Air Service. His belief in the power of the bomber was passionate and all-consuming. At a time of scarce defence dollars, he was determined to prove his force's value.

The navy was in possession of several ex-German war prizes, including the ten-year-old battleship *Ostfriesland*. Through intense political lobbying

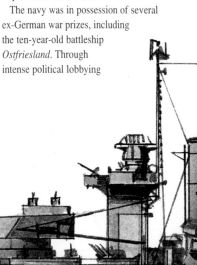

Death from above

Left: USS Alabama *(BB8) was also expended as an aerial bombing target in Chesapeake Bay during 1921. Although the bombing trials were heavily slanted to produce the results General Mitchell wished for, the sight of battleships sinking under air attack had a major impact.*

Right: The US Army Air Corps experimented with phosphorous bombs for their incendiary effect. There was even talk of using poison gas bombs against warships after the widespread use of chemical weapons in World War I.

of the President-to-be, Mitchell succeeded in sharing in the navy's intentions of evaluating the effect of aerial bombing on warships.

For the trial, the battleship was anchored, with all possible openings secured. Five Marine and three Navy aircraft opened the proceedings. Nine of the 33 bombs hit, but only two detonated. Comparatively small 230-pounders, they caused only superficial damage.

Six Army and three Navy aircraft then released eleven 600-pounders and eight 550-pounders respectively. Of these, only two of the former detonated at all. One hit, causing heavy damage, but all of it above the protective deck. The second, a near miss, caused leaking in the hull. Unstopped, this admitted water overnight. On the second day, six Army and five Navy bombers

arrived, each with two 1000-pound bombs. The trial orders prescribed that, following any heavy hit, there would be a pause to allow official observers to board the vessel to record and assess the damage. Mitchell's men, however, were marching to a different tune. Before they could be halted, the *Ostfriesland* had suffered three direct hits and three near misses. None affected her watertight integrity, but one uptake had been demolished (which would have slowed her considerably) and heavy fragmentation would have been lethal to guncrews.

Although it was now the Navy's turn, Mitchell's men again muscled in to prove their point. Six one-ton bombs were dropped. None hit, but two were very near misses. That forward caused no apparent damage but the other, port side aft in way of the after turret, presumably caused massive rupturing of the hull. Allowing no time for examination, the battleship rolled over, sinking in eleven minutes.

The trial was totally unrealistic in that the ship was stationary, not firing back and lacking damage control teams. Bombing was thus carried out in straight runs and from only 1400 feet. Nonetheless, the sinking was not entirely wasted. It proved that battleships, if not actually rendered obsolete by aircraft, could be sunk by them. Dedicated high-angle, anti-aircraft armaments began to make their appearance. Even an obsolescent horizontal protective scheme could obviously defeat quite heavy non-armour-piercing bombs. The major lesson, however, was the lethality of the mining effect of near misses, where the explosion shock wave passes through near-incompressible water, virtually without attenuation, to expend itself against the comparatively resilient shell plating of the ship. Many were to be sunk in this manner.

Left: USS Maryland *in 1944 with enlarged aft superstructure and additional anti-aircraft guns.* Maryland *received more AA weapons after being damaged by Kamikaze attack in 1945.*

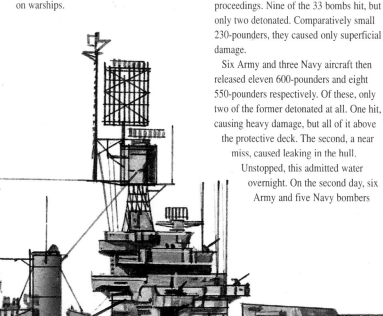

American coup: the Washington conference

The Anglo-Japanese Alliance of 1902, renewed in 1911 for ten years, included agreement that each would remain neutral in the event that the other was at war, except where one was attacked by more than one enemy. Great Britain was, therefore, not involved in Japan's trouncing of Russia in 1904–5. Newly confident, the Japanese participated in World War I and, for minimal involvement, profited well from post-war settlements.

Across the Pacific, the Americans viewed the emerging Japanese as a threat to their Far Eastern interests, a threat underpinned by the prospect of British military support. Despite British assurances that the Alliance would not operate against the United States the latter (still pursuing a fleet 'second to none' policy) became embroiled in the beginnings of a naval race with Japan. Great Britain, with vast interests in the Far East and Pacific, was also committed to a naval 'One-Power Standard'. Predictably, she, too, began to build.

All three powers became saddled with enormously expensive programmes. Each wished to be rid of them but none could do so unilaterally. The United States was able, secretly, to crack diplomatic codes at this time and realised that it was they who would need to take the initiative. They therefore set up a naval disarmament conference, to be opened in Washington at the end of 1921. While the major objective was clear, the Americans had a hidden agenda. The USA's first objective, to achieve parity with the Royal Navy, was an open secret. The second, to terminate the Anglo-Japanese Alliance, was suspected. The third, to bind the Japanese to controllable limits, was predictable.

With little preamble, the American senior delegate launched into a series of proposals that were breathtaking in their scope. Capital ships would be taken as the measure of naval power, with lesser types pro rata.

Regard being made to established strength, the United States, Great Britain and Japan would be permitted to maintain total capital ship tonnage in the ratio of 5:5:3. If this proposal could be made to stick, the Americans would instantly achieve two of their hidden aims.

As the proposal did not conflict with its One-Power Standard commitment, Great Britain raised little objection. The Japanese, however, felt penalised by being confined to lesser limits. Realistically, they knew that parity with the two greater powers was out of the question and pressed for a face-saving increase to 10:10:7.

Quietly, decoding their diplomatic interchanges, the Americans knew that Japanese public argument was not matched by behind-the-scenes resolve. The Americans thus pressed for the original ratio and, four weeks later, the Japanese fell into line. For good measure, the French and Italians also accepted parity, finally agreeing relative strengths of 5:5:3:1.67:1.67.

Ratios were one thing, tonnage ceilings were another, and savage scrapping schedules were required. Initially, the United States would retain 18 capital ships and scrap 30; Great Britain would keep 22, scrap 19 and abandon construction of four; Japan was allowed ten, with those planned or building being abandoned. By selective replacement programmes, the agreed ratios would be achieved by 1931. At this point, the United States and Great Britain would each have a maximum of 525,000 tons, the Japanese 315,000.

Capital ships would not be replaced within twenty years of their completion date. Replacement would not exceed 35,000 tons nor carry guns of greater than 16-inch calibre. Certain, once-only exceptions were made to assist initial alignment and each power was permitted to convert up to two capital ships, which would otherwise be scrapped, to aircraft carriers. The treaty would be binding for fifteen years.

In being required to scrap thirty existing ships, totalling nearly 850,000 tons, the Royal Navy considered itself to have received a raw deal, since the Americans were set to discard only nineteen of 580,000 tons, most of which were incomplete hulls from the recent naval expansion programme. As Australia and New Zealand

were as suspicious of long-term Japanese expansionist aims as the United States, the latter's objective in ending the Anglo-Japanese Alliance was also facilitated. Its military obligations in any case now fell foul of the principles of the new League of Nations. It was renewed in the form of a Four-Power Treaty, with the United States and France becoming signatories. Japan could thus not be offended by an outright abrogation, while the participation of the other two would technically remove rivalries in the Pacific. All agreed not to further fortify any Pacific island possessions.

Beyond minor cheating, the Washington agreements proved to be an effective regulator, but had the unforeseen side effects of promoting the development of naval air power, and starting a new naval race in heavy cruisers.

Right: Colorado, Maryland *and* West Virginia *seen from the* California *during US fleet exercises in the 1920s. These were the most modern American battleships and formed the core of a fleet now second to none.*

Below: The Japanese 16-in gun battleship Mutsu *seen in 1921. Japan was now capable of building battleships at least equal to the latest US and British designs. Treaties prevented a follow-on class of giant battleships.*

Lexington (CC1) class

The US Navy had less use for the battlecruiser concept than the British, and a half-hearted proposal to build them in 1913 was defeated by a greater requirement for more conventional battleships. British war experience at the Heligoland Bight and the Falklands, however, soon demonstrated their real value. Ironically, a class of six battlecruisers was authorised by the Americans just three months after the battle of Jutland which had so thoroughly discredited them.

A requirement for 35 knots demanded 24 boilers and a hull as large as that of the British *Hood*. Seven funnels were arranged, uniquely in alternate singles and pairs. Ten 14-inch guns were to be fitted, with twin

Left: USS Lexington *seen two months before Pearl Harbor. She is ferrying a number of Brewster F2A Buffalos, with SBDs and TBD Devastators on deck aft.*

super-firing triples at either end. A second draft up-graded the main battery to eight 16-inch and the secondary to 6-inch. Boilers were reduced to twenty (some above the horizontal protection) and funnels to five. Both versions displaced about 35,300 tons.

As wartime shipbuilding priority had been given to smaller warships, none of the class

had been laid down when the close of hostilities permitted further re-design, to incorporate all recent experience. A further 8,000 tons of protection was worked-in, reducing design speed by a couple of knots. Rapid advances in boiler technology permitted a further reduction to sixteen. All could now be situated below armour, while

only two large funnels were required. An interesting feature was the inclusion of ten, later eight, torpedo tubes.

Enormous for its day, the ship's power plant could put 45,000 horsepower onto each of the four shafts. Power was supplied by four turbo-generators, each shaft being coupled to two drive motors, working in

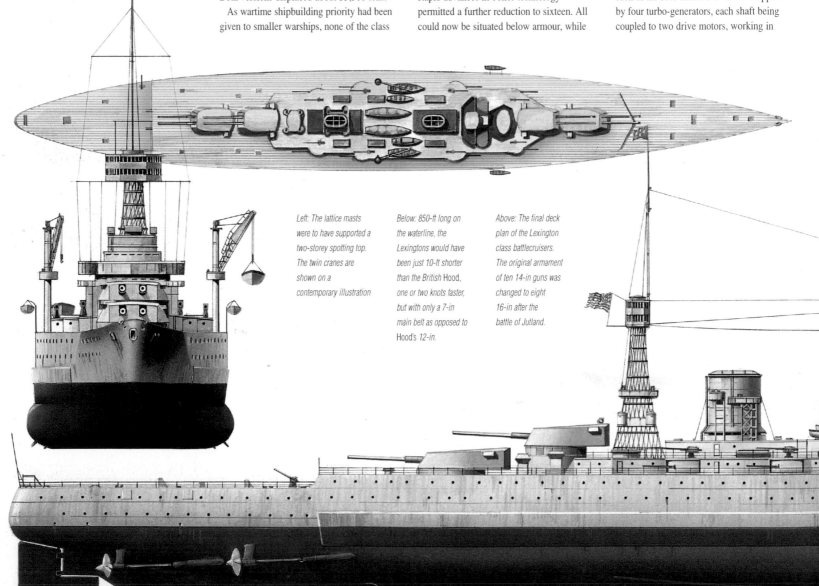

Left: The lattice masts were to have supported a two-storey spotting top. The twin cranes are shown on a contemporary illustration

Below: 850-ft long on the waterline, the Lexingtons would have been just 10-ft shorter than the British Hood, one or two knots faster, but with only a 7-in main belt as opposed to Hood's 12-in.

Above: The final deck plan of the Lexington class battlecruisers. The original armament of ten 14-in guns was changed to eight 16-in after the battle of Jutland.

Left: Lexington is
abandoned after
attempts to save her
finally failed. She was
lost in the first naval
battle during which
neither fleet's warships
were in visual contact.

tandem. Trials realised speeds of 34 knots.

Belt armour tapered from a thickness of
7 inches top to 5 inches at the bottom. It
conformed to current British practice in
being sloped at 11 degrees to increase
resistance to penetration. Two armoured
decks totalled 4 inches.

All six were commenced in 1920–21,
but following the Washington Conference,
work was suspended early in 1922. Under
its terms, the four least-advanced were

scrapped. The other pair, *Lexington* and
Saratoga, were allowed to be converted to
aircraft carriers, commissioning as such in
1927. At this stage, displacement was about
36,000 tons, of which some 3,000 had to be
'exempted' to comply with a treaty limit of
33,000. Much armour had been

retained but extensivebulging was necessary
to give the slim hulls the requisite stability.

Between the wars they contributed much
to the US Navy's expertise in aviation.
Lexington was an early war casualty, being

sunk in the course of the Coral Sea action of
May 1942. *Saratoga*, whose career saw two
torpedoings, three kamikaze and three bomb
hits, survived to be expended as a target
ship at the Bikini Atoll tests.

Below: Saratoga as she appeared in 1944 in a dramatic
'dazzle' scheme. By 1945 she was still the largest and
fastest aircraft carrier in the world.

Right: The original design for Lexington had to achieve a speed
of 35 knots and carry ten 14-in guns. It had seven funnels.

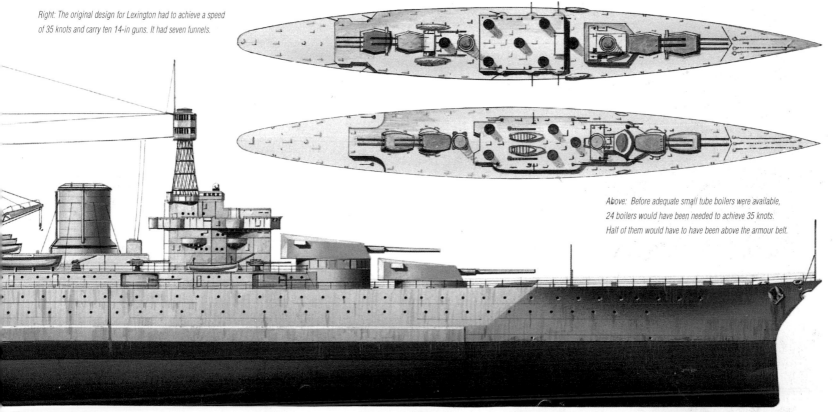

Above: Before adequate small tube boilers were available,
24 boilers would have been needed to achieve 35 knots.
Half of them would have to have been above the armour belt.

South Dakota (BB49) class

The two Japanese Tosas, laid down in 1920, stretched the still-completing Nagatos from eight to ten 16-inch guns. As the planned British equivalents would mount nine, the Americans capped it with twelve. At 43,200 tons, the six South Dakotas would represent a stage intermediate between the preceding Marylands and the 'ultimate' designs under preparation.

They would have been imposing and handsome ships, the clipper bow leading a long forecastle deck, with high freeboard for hard driving. Ten boiler spaces flanked the turbo-generator rooms. Exhausting then required four sets of uptakes, which were trunked into a single arched casing, which released stack gases well abaft the bridge structure. Lattice masts were still proposed but the US Navy was considering tripods, so they might very well have been completed with these. While the four triple 16-inch mountings required no greater length to accommodate them than the twins of the Marylands, their extra weight and increased protection demanded a larger hull. Beam was increased almost to Panama Canal limits. No bulges were included but two thirds of the length of the hull was flanked by up to five parallel bulkheads, whose enclosed void spaces were boxed

in at either end with 14-inch transverse bulkheads. Speed increase was modest, limiting the demands of machinery and length. The resulting after run was full, with virtually no cut-up, so that the four propellers were set unusually far aft. One, very large, rudder was fitted, but manoeuvrability might have been idiosyncratic.

At the point where their construction was halted under the terms of the Washington Treaty, three were about one-third complete and approaching launching stage.

South Dakota class data:

Displacement, standard	43,200 tons
Displacement, full load	47,000 tons
Length, overall	684 feet (208.5 m)
Beam	105.6 feet (32.2 m)
Design draught	32.8 feet (10 m)
Complement	1190

Class: *Indiana (BB50), Iowa (BB53), Massachusetts (BB54), Montana (BB51), North Carolina (BB52), South Dakota (BB49).* None completed.

Armament:
Twelve 16-in guns (4 × 3)
Sixteen 6-in guns (16 × 1)
Six 3-in guns (6 × 1)
Two 21-in torpedo tubes

Machinery:
Turbo-electric drive 60,000 shp (44,750kW)
Four shafts 23 knots

Armour:
Belt	up to 14 in
Bulkheads	up to 14 in
Decks	up to 3.5 in
Turrets	up to 18 in
Barbettes	up to 14 in

Above: USS New Mexico *leads a column of battleships headed by* Oklahoma *and* Nevada *during April 1919. Their 14-in guns were already surpassed by the 16-in guns of the Colorados and the Japanese Nagato class.*

Plan 'Orange'

For war-planning purposes, the United States was code-named 'Blue' and potential opponents were labelled by other colours. Japan was 'Orange'. War plan Orange grew from a series of sketch scenarios postulated about the turn of the century. Only with Japan's runaway defeat of the Russians in 1905, however, did it begin to be treated seriously. The American territories of Guam and the Philippines were seen as vulnerable to Japanese expansionist aims. As the latter were 7000 miles from the United states, any response to attack would rely totally on the navy's ability to transport an expeditionary force and be capable of defeating an enemy fleet at previously unheard-of distances from base support.

Questions posed by the planners were to have profound significance for the development of the navy. Were the territories worth defending? If so, should a deterrent-sized force be permanently based there? What was the relative importance of each island?

To meet and defeat a large and competent fleet such as the Japanese, capital ships would need both size and extended endurance. Distant operations demanded a fleet train – oilers, ammunition ships, fleet tenders. Forward bases would be necessary for routine maintenance and the recovery of action-damaged ships.

With the mandate of ex-German island groups to Japan came the spectre of a fleet having to endure continuous land-based air attack. The obvious requirement to take its own aviation made the US Navy very carrier-minded. The completion of the Panama Canal was hurried to allow a rapid transfer of the Atlantic Fleet. New bases were constructed on the West Coast and on Hawaii which, at 3500 miles from Japan, was considered to be at a safe range. Theory has it that the efficiency of a fleet decreases by ten per cent for every thousand miles that it has to operate from its main bases. The associated arithmetic underlay the tight construction ratios that the United States forced through at the Washington Conference.

Continuously honed and refined, Plan Orange visualised a three-phase war. Phase I saw the Philippines and Western Pacific possessions overrun. Phase II involved the despatch of an expeditionary force and its initial establishment at a forward base. Phase III dealt with the recovery campaign, including a decisive naval action. The difficult second phase involved a rolling, island-hopping advance, seizing previously-identified locations as required.

Above: US warplans during the 1930s envisaged a fleet action which would ultimately be settled by the battleships' big guns. The US fleet would have to operate over unprecedented distances if it came to war with Japan.

All suitable islands along the route from Hawaii, via the Marshalls, the Carolines and Palau, were surveyed as opportunity arose. Although it had to be assumed that Orange anticipated this line of attack, there was little scope for major departures from it.

Events in Europe forced Plan Orange to be superseded by Rainbow 'Five' in December 1940 but, when war came, the original plan proved remarkably prescient. While the sheer extent of Japanese gains had been under-estimated, as was their tenacious defence of them, the whole island-hopping strategy, the vital requirement for local air superiority and the final, decisive fleet action, were accurately forecast. Few plans have so well stood the test of war itself.

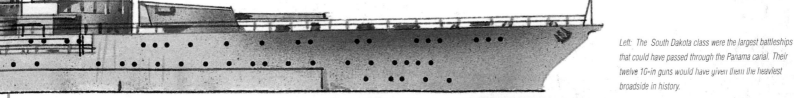

Left: The South Dakota class were the largest battleships that could have passed through the Panama canal. Their twelve 16-in guns would have given them the heaviest broadside in history.

Amphibious assault

The wisdom of retaining older battleships was realised during World War II, when the developing doctrines of amphibious warfare opened up new requirements in support. Effectively damned by the negative effect of the chaotically-managed British Dardanelles campaign of 1915, amphibious warfare was explored again from first principles during the 1930s, this time by the US Fleet Marine Force. During practice landings on Caribbean cays, gunfire support was rendered by the elderly Wyoming and Texas-class battleships, backing cruiser and destroyer shoots.

An early conclusion was that ammunition load-out would require careful thought. Bombarding ships would need armour piercing and semi-armour piercing rounds if they expected to be attacked by other heavy ships, but such projectiles were of limited value for shore targets. Here, high-capacity rounds with plenty of terminal energy and a large bursting charge were required, capable of breaking down hardened defences yet still being lethal against the defenders.

Radio communications had advanced considerably since the first hesitant flights of the *Ark Royal's* aircraft over Gallipoli and the Americans found that aerial spotting and forward observation parties could well support indirect fire, i.e. where the target was not visible from the firing ship.

Experience showed that the leader of the Shore Fire Control Party needed specialist training to fully appreciate both the capabilities of the bombarding ship and the requirements of the troops that he was accompanying. Thus was created the Gunfire Liaison Officer (GLO) who landed alongside the first waves, together with his spotter and radio crew. By the outbreak of the Pacific War both the Navy and Marine Corps had a good idea of the likely problems but could have had no conception of the ferocity that lay ahead.

Guadalcanal and North Africa saw the theories first tried out in earnest. During the first, the landing went in virtually unopposed, but the troops had the new experience of running in under a ceiling of friendly firing, arcing closely overhead. North Africa, too, saw little real opposition to the actual landings, but these were followed by an urgent need to neutralise mobile batteries and strongpoints. It was discovered that, despite theory, ships were able to engage forts successfully, while casualties from friendly fire were unlikely if close liaison was maintained with the GLOs.

Pacific landings typically had difficult offshore approaches and were usually undertaken at dawn. On large islands, the Japanese operated a defence-in-depth system, allowing the assault to go in before mounting a massive counter-attack. Where small islands were concerned, they integrated medium-calibre coastal defence guns with lighter mobile batteries, automatic weapons and a labyrinth

Above: US amphibious landings used techniques developed in pre-war exercises.

Top: US troops ashore at Kwajalein, February 1944. A chain of Japan's island fortresses had to stormed before the enemy homeland could be brought under effective air attack.

Below: Texas' old reciprocating engines could not make more than 19 knots by World War II, but her big guns supported US landings in North Africa and across the Pacific. Taken over by the State of Texas in 1948, she is preserved in San Jacinto National Park.

of interconnected strongpoints. Support ships had to go in closely, which made them vulnerable. The solution was a structured bombardment, a prolonged carrier-based air strike at first light, followed by a comparatively long range battleship and cruiser shoot. This overlapped the commencement of the assault phase. Before the small craft hit the beach, a further heavy air strike went in to keep the defender's heads down, and to cover the movement inshore of bombarding ships. The latter were then available to fire on demand.

It was found that the standard 5-inch 38 was valuable in that, due to its relatively low muzzle velocity, its projectiles had a high trajectory which could reach into hidden features such as re-entrants and valleys. Not the least problem was the choking clouds of coral dust that were raised, soon obscuring any target. The GLOs and phosphorous markers were essential. Though the Wyoming and Texas classes received only a minimum of up-dating, they performed valuable service, even in such hotspots as Normandy and Iwo Jima. The *Nevada*, completed in 1916, was the oldest to receive full modernisation. Undertaken in 1942/3, it recognised that bombardment ships,

constrained in speed and in room to manoeuvre, would be vulnerable to air attack. Cranes and boats were stripped out and other tophamper reduced to give clear arcs of fire in three dimensions. Radars and state-of-the-art fire control complemented eight of the standard twin 5-inch gunhouses, the older casemates weapons being landed. About forty each of 40 and 20-mm guns appeared in tubs. Aircraft and their support gear, retained for spotting purposes, but vulnerable and inflammable, were banished right aft.

Much the same modifications were made to the *Pennsylvania*, the three New Mexicos and all six Tennessees and Marylands. The worth of these old-timers is reflected in their battle honours. *Tennessee*, fairly typical, covered the Aleutians, Tarawa, Kwajalein, Eniwetok, Kavieng, Saipan, Guam, Tinian, Palau, Leyte and the battle in the Surigao Strait, Iwo Jima and Okinawa.

Above: As the landing craft headed for the beach, battleship gunfire helped suppress Japanese defensive fire and also served to break up counter-attacks as they developed.

Left: USS Texas served in the North Sea 1917-18 as part of the Grand Fleet. This is how she appeared in 1942. The lattice masts were replaced by tripod masts during the 1920s.

Tennessee (BB43) class

The two Tennessees, commenced in 1916–17, were close developments of the preceding New Mexicos. Externally, the most obvious difference was the reversion to twin funnels, indicating a more 'unitised', and survivable, compartmentation of their machinery. All secondary armament was raised above main deck level, so that the faceting of the forward hull, so much a feature of earlier ships, was at first omitted. As the superstructure block was of a length sufficient for only five casemates per side, four guns were sited in open mountings one deck higher. These were soon removed in favour of eight high-angle 3-inch guns, as anti-aircraft armament began to be taken more seriously. The late 'twenties saw these replaced in turn by new-style 5-inch. Two catapults were carried, one trainable unit on the quarterdeck, the other on the roof of 'C' turret (Turret III) which was trained by turning the turret itself. The aircraft, at that time fully exposed to the elements, were usually the float-equipped version of the Curtiss SOC (Seagull) series. Tough little aeroplanes, they also proved a bit problematical in service, being replaced by the SO3C Seamen.

Both ships were slated for modernisation in 1940 but plans were deferred owing to the likelihood of war. As it happened, the injuries that they sustained at Pearl Harbor necessitated repairs of a level that soon turned into a full rebuilding. The hulls were extensively bulged and little of the original ships was retained except the hull, machinery and main armament. Extra horizontal armour was added. Boiler room exhausts were trunked into a single massive funnel casing. Masts were removed in favour of the truncated conical towers that supported the directors and which also became characteristic of American heavy ships.

Tennessee class data:

Displacement, standard	32,300 tons
Displacement, full load	34,000 tons
Length, overall	624.7 feet (190.4 m)
Beam	97.4 feet (29.7 m)
Design draught	30.2 feet (9.2 m)
Complement	1090

Class: *California (BB44), Tennessee (BB43)*
Completed 1920/21

Armament:
Twelve 14-in guns (4 × 3)
Fourteen 5-in guns (14 × 1)
Four, later eight, 3-in guns (4 × 1)
Two 21-in torpedo tubes
Three aircraft

Machinery:
Turbo-electric drive 40,200 shp (30,000kW)
Four shafts

Armour:
Belt	up to 14 in
Bulkheads	up to 14 in
Decks	up to 3.5 (later 5) in
Turrets	up to 18 in
Barbettes	up to 14 in

Raising *California*

When Pearl Harbor was assaulted by the Japanese, the *California* was berthed alone, ahead of the 'Battleship Row'. With nothing outboard, her port side was wide open to a torpedo run from the direction of the Navy Yard opposite. She closed up quickly and damage control conditions 'Y' and 'Z' were ordered, closing off and securing most watertight doors and hatches. Little ready-use anti-aircraft ammunition was to hand, but before this could be rectified, a torpedo struck her on the port quarter, causing a loss

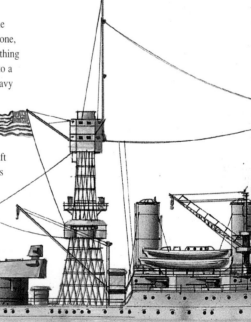

Right: California was scheduled for reconstruction by 1940, but nothing had been done by the time the Japanese sank her. Note the deflection markings on 'X' turret.

Below: California in 1944 after her extensive reconstruction. Her profile now resembled that of the South Dakotas. The secondary armament now consisted of 16 5-in dual purpose guns, 40 x 40-mm and 50 x 20-mm anti-aircraft guns.

of power and preventing the functioning of ammunition hoists. As ammunition was laboriously passed up by hand, the ship began counterflooding to control a developing list.

There was then a second torpedo hit, more serious, abreast 'B' turret (Turret II) and again to port. Two boiler rooms were flooded

on the starboard side to compensate. Several bombs then fell close aboard on the starboard side, causing heavy concussion. They were followed by a direct hit amidships, again to starboard, the bomb penetrating to the lower armoured deck before detonating. Althou... it caused no vital structural damage, it generated a serious fire

A new hazard was an advancing carpet of b... oil, coming down on the fresh ... the stricken *Oklahoma*. ... *California*, it obliged ...ent, but it caused only ...d on, the *California* ...proached ...om ...he was ...r, and as ...ely ...le

main damage. She fetched up on the bottom, with some of her maindeck above water.

In preparation for salvage, the *California* was lightened extensively through the removal of accessible main and secondary guns, armoured conning towers, mainmast, boats, catapults, cranes, anchors and cables. Timber cofferdams were installed, and hundreds of scuttles and openings secured. Heavy salvage pumps began to reduce the internal water level and work could begin on cleaning the interior of fuel oil, removing or preserving equipment and removing the fifty-or-so bodies still aboard. Finally, the heavy ammunition could be removed and all remaining fuel pumped out.

The ship refloated on 24 March 1942 and spent six weeks in dock for reinforcement of her patches. Yeoman work had succeeded in reconditioning one of her turbo-electric systems, so that she was able to sail under her own power for the United states. She spent over a year in Puget Sound Navy Yard being fully modernised. Recommissioned at the e... nuary 1944 she emerged with ...mpletely up-to-date secondary ...t batteries. The single funnel ...lmost identical with that of ...d her near-sister *West* ...d also been sunk at Pearl ...rved at the major Pacific ...the satisfaction of ...rs at the Battle of the

South Dakota (BB57) class

During 1937–8, the United States commenced the pair of North Carolinas (BB55–6). In accordance with treaty agreements (they had been approved in 1936) they were direct replacements for BB33–4, and also did not officially exceed the 35,000 ton limitation. They were sensibly equipped with the 16-inch of their Japanese peers rather than the 14-inch of the British King George Vs. First of the 'new generation' of American battleship, they achieved their displacement by a reversion to more orthodox geared steam turbine propulsion and an extensive use of welding.

The four South Dakotas (not to be confused with the earlier, discontinued BB49 class) were laid down in 1939/40, and were very much refinements of the North Carolinas. American practice followed German in putting emphasis on striking power and survivability rather than speed. By maintaining beam, increasing depth and shortening the hull (by about 15 metres), less area had to be protected. Armour could thus be disposed more efficiently and, even thickened slightly in places, without weight penalty.

With the interactive nature of ship design there had, of course, to be a drawback. This, the reduced length-on-breadth ratio, made for a hydro-dynamically less-efficient hull form. Lines were customarily optimised by experiment, but the class required an increase of some eight per cent in installed power, over their predecessors, yet remained about a knot slower.

Some of the earlier weight-saving was expended in the more powerful machinery, the spaces for which were arranged in a very compact form, which allowed for a truncated superstructure and a reversion to a single funnel. Tall, tower-like tophamper was topped-off with very light pole masts. A novel feature was the suspension of a 5–8-inch (16-mm) splinter barrier just three feet beneath the main (5-inch) armoured deck.

South Dakota class data:

Displacement, standard	42,000 tons
Displacement, full load	44,375 tons
Length, overall	680.8 feet (207.5 m)
Beam	107.9 feet (32.9 m)
Design draught	32.5 feet (9.9 m)
Complement	1795

Class:

Alabama (BB60), Indiana (BB58), Massachusetts (BB59), South Dakota (BB57)
All completed 1942.

Armament:
Nine 16-in guns (3×3)
Twenty 5-in guns (10×2)
32 to 68 40-mm guns
Three aircraft

Machinery:
Steam turbines 130,000 shp (97,000kW)
Four shafts 28 knots

Armour:
Belt	up to 12.25 in
Bulkheads	up to 11 in
Decks	up to 5 in
Turrets	up to 18 in
Barbettes	up to 17.25 in

Below: Indiana in the scheme she wore in September 1942. She arrived in the Solomons just in time to replace the damaged South Dakota. A Vought OS2U is seen on the catapult.

Night battles off Guadalcanal

Above: USS South Dakota's conning tower decorated to mark her victories during the Solomons campaign.

For six months, between August 1942 and February 1943, the Solomon island of Guadalcanal was bitterly disputed. It triggered many clashes between the American and Japanese fleets, with a disproportionately large number of ships sunk. American success hinged upon their occupation of the single airstrip at Henderson Field. Their enemy well understood this and it became a regular target for nocturnal bombardment.

During the night of 12–13 November, two Japanese battlecruisers, *Hiei* and *Kirishima*, headed a cruiser/destroyer squadron engaged on such a mission. They were intercepted by an American force which, lacking heavy units and saturated with torpedoes, lost four destroyers and two light cruisers in a confused melee. In the course of this, however, the two American heavy cruisers present, *Portland* and *San Francisco*, put about a hundred 8 in shells into the thin-skinned *Hiei*, leaving her so severely damaged that she was finished off by aircraft the following day.

Undeterred, the Japanese followed-up with a partially-successful cruiser bombardment during the next night. This resulted in the detachment of Rear Admiral Willis Lee's Task Force 64 from the covering *Enterprise* carrier group. Lee's flag was worn by the battleship *Washington*. She was accompanied by the *South Dakota* and four destroyers.

On the night of 14–15 November, the persistent Japanese returned with the *Kirishima*, four cruisers and nine destroyers. Lee intercepted them shortly before

midnight but the enemy, scattered widely in four groups, were able to again surprise his destroyers with overwhelming gunfire and torpedo salvoes. Three were quickly reduced to blazing wrecks. *South Dakota*, concentrating on the visible cruisers, suffered a major power failure when the shocks of her own 16-inch salvoes caused main breakers to trip out. For several blind minutes, she staggered around near-helplessly, brightly illuminated by burning ships and Japanese searchlights. She lost contact with Lee and suffered 27 hits in the space of a few minutes.

Her attention riveted on the *South Dakota*, the *Kirishima* failed to notice the *Washington* which, at virtually point-blank range, suddenly opened a devastating radar-directed fire. Only nine of the 75 heavy projectiles fired found their mark but, combined with

Above: Seen off the Norfolk Navy Yard in February 1943, with part of her AA armament still to be fitted, USS Alabama was completed in just over 30 months.

Right: Alabama seen during the feint operation mounted against Norway in June 1943, while Allied troops landed in Sicily. South Dakota and Alabama joined a British task force that included Duke of York, Anson and Malaya.

an estimated 40 5-inch hits, wrecked the Japanese battlecruiser, which sank a couple of hours later.

The action once again proved the vulnerability of the battlecruiser concept, but the experience of the eight-month-old *South Dakota* was valuable. Even at the short ranges involved, it is doubtful if the

Kirishima's 14-inch fire could have disabled her. Some 25 of her hits were from enemy cruisers, whose armour-piercing shells passed, for the most part, through her superstructure without exploding, but causing troublesome fires and killing vital fire control personnel. With their radars disabled, the crews in turn had to

improvise, showing an over-reliance on technology. While there was some minor flooding, the danger in her temporarily-disabled condition was not from gunfire but from the many enemy torpedoes in the area. Her return to the East Coast for repair also caused the unavailability of a valuable marker for some three months.

Preparing for war

The bold ratio of 5:5:3, agreed at Washington, referred of course only to total displacement in capital ships. It was tied to maxima agreed by the three main signatories but there was naturally no compulsion to build to these maxima. Most other warship types were not covered by such tonnage ceilings. Thus, both democracies, the United States and the United Kingdom which had major problems with the recession of the 'thirties, put only a minimum investment into defence. Japan's navy building to its agreed treaty limits, legitimately became proportionately stronger and comparatively more modern.

Partly as a measure to stimulate the economy, the 1934 Vinson-Trammell Act provided for a five-year naval replacement programme. The Japanese response was a reiteration of her demand for full parity with the other two main signatories, when the Washington terms lapsed at the end of 1936. As agreement was not forthcoming, Japan formally announced that she would abrogate the treaty from that date.

This was the high water mark for the three dictatorships, whose demands and excesses, and latent threats from mutual pacts, shook the United states from its predilection for isolationism. Its interests were now too internationally-based to allow it to ignore events. War was not only a distinct possibility, but war on several fronts, with various alliances and multiple foes. Previous war plans, aligned against specific powers, such as 'Orange', would need to be re-cast. Thus quickly emerged the appropriately-named Rainbow series. Of the original Rainbow One to Four and T̶ ̶ ̶re serious

a strength sufficient only to contain that of the Japanese, releasing powerful forces for the Atlantic, providing relief for the Royal Navy, which could then implement its 'Main Fleet to Singapore' strategy.

The barriers of strict American neutrality tumbled in sequence. Laws were not repeated, but interpreted imaginatively. For instance, loans and the sale of munitions to belligerents were forbidden, while goods purchased by belligerents had to be paid for in advance and transported in those states' own bottoms (the 'Cash and Carry' Act).

As Japan's campaign in China was not a declared war, American materiel could legitimately be supplied to the embattled Chinese. The British, as declared belligerents, could legally purchase materials from the United States, and were able to ship it out by virtue of sea control. The Germans, lacking sea control, could not. As the crisis deepened, however, the President obtained sanction to relax the embargo on munitions supply to the United Kingdom and France.

Establishment of the Neutrality Patrol, which soon extended from the Canadian border to South America, was useful to bring many ships out of reserve, and to call up reservists for sea training. The Patrol eventually became the nucleus of the re-formed Atlantic Fleet.

From June 1940, America envisaged Germany in effective control of the fleets of France and Italy, in addition to the Kriegsmarine. Britain faced imminent invasion and defeat. with a possibility of the

orted by the other two.
ifying the neutrality laws,
ansformed the 'Cash-and-
system to 'Lend-Lease', avoiding the need for Britain to drain her current

Above: Anglo-American alliance: USS Washington *joins* HMS *Duke of York escorting convoy PQ-15 to Russia in May 1942.*

account. Where the latter depended upon the effectiveness of the convoy system, but was desperately short of escorts, the President made a transfer of venerable destroyers and coastguard cutters, legalised by their exchange for basing rights. Making it clear to Germany that her behaviour towards neutrals had forfeited her right to correct consideration from neutrals, the President froze Axis holdings in the United States and seized Axis ships already interned.

Following the joint declaration of the Atlantic Charter, American destroyers undertook convoy escort in the Western Atlantic. Following predictable incidents with U-Boats, the Americans allowed their own-flag ships to become involved in the shipping of Lend-Lease materiel. Thus, by the time that the Japanese hit Pearl Harbor, the United States already had a fleet on virtually a war footing and, thanks to the Presidential policy of buying time, with major building programmes well on stream.

Right: The sheer size of the Maryland *is revealed in dry dock at Hunter's Point, California as she is readied for President-elect Hoover's 1928 trip to South America.*

North Carolina (BB55) class

Completed in 1941, the pair of North Carolinas were the last truly pre-war design. They were the first American battleships to enter service since the *West Virginia*, back in 1923, reflecting the effectiveness of the Washington Treaty. Because of the leisurely pace of replacements imposed by the treaties, there was ample time to develop a whole series of battleship designs, based on the limit of 35,000 tons and dimensions dictated by the Panama Canal. All the proposals fell short of what the Navy Board considered adequate, in particular showing that any requirement for 30 knots would be unlikely to be met within the treaty limits.

To allow a reasonable speed of 28 knots, the main armament initially reverted to the 14-inch calibre last used in the Tennessees. Twelve new-pattern 14-inch 50 calibre weapons would probably have been mounted in three quadruple turrets. Japan's non-renewal of her treaty obligations, when they expired at the end of 1936, together with the excessive secrecy regarding her intentions, caused the navy to take the unusual step of up-grading the armament to three triple 16-inch guns after construction had commenced. It was a good example of anticipation that the new quadruple 14-inch had been designed to virtually the same weight and barbette diameter as a triple 16-inch, reducing the problems of substitution.

An interesting feature was the late adoption of external bulges, which actually formed the outermost of five void or tank spaces, running parallel along the centre section of the ship. Only the centre one of the five bulkheads involved was armoured. The main armour belt was inclined and was seated on the inboard side of the bulge structure. The upper edge of the belt supported the outer edges of the main armoured deck. Inboard of the torpedo bulkheads a triple bottom was fitted. A pair of close spaced, but well-proportioned, funnels and an unfussy superstructure was combined with a long graceful sheerline to give a pleasing profile.

Armament:
Nine 16-in guns (3 × 3)
Twenty 5-in guns (10 × 2)
52 to 96 40-mm guns
Three aircraft

Machinery:
Steam turbines 121,000 shp (90,250kW)
Four shafts 28.5 knots

Armour:
Belt ....up to 12 in
Bulkheads ....up to 11 in
Decks ....up to 4.6 in
Turrets ....up to 16 in
Barbettes ....up to 16 in

Below: North Carolina as she appeared in June 1942. She had her baptism of fire in the...

Last of the pre-war battleships

Despite the 'ultimate battleship' studies that had been conducted, it became obvious during 1935 that any new battleship construction would still be subject to limitations. A second London Naval Conference was due to be held in 1936 to debate measures to succeed the expiry of the Washington agreements, which had a 15-year validity. Japan had already indicated her intention not to renew her obligations, but the British were known to be planning to table a proposal for 'affordable' capital ships with individual standard displacement not exceeding 25,000 tons and a maximum main battery calibre of 14 inches.

The Americans thus studied a series of designs ranging from the above lower limit to those which could ship nine 16-inch guns and/or sustain a sea speed of 30 knots. Bottom end design proposals were

Above: US transports under attack off Guadalcanal. Washington's intervention on the night of 14-15 November proved decisive.

dismissed quickly as being able neither to out-gun nor out-run the great majority of foreign contemporaries and, therefore, not worthy of further consideration. At the top end it was also apparent that the twin ideals of a nine 16-inch main battery and a 30-knot speed were not possible on the existing 35,000 ton limit. The resulting 40,500 ton proposal would, admittedly, have had a massive 17-inch (432-mm) main belt and a 6.25-inch (159-mm) main protective deck to

meet the initial navy requirement for a scheme to defeat the largest contemporary foreign projectiles. This onerous demand was later relaxed to call for 'adequate' protection against a 14-inch shell.

As was usual, speed was subordinated to firepower and protection. Extra beam conferred stability and depth of protection, but needed to be balanced by increased length in order to achieve a reasonable speed. Even without rumoured Japanese intentions, it is doubtful if the navy would ever have accepted a reversion to 14-inch, while 15-inch was not a calibre that was familiar. The accepted penalty was a completely 'soft' forward end as a weight-saving measure.

Although the official figures for post-Washington battleships displacements can all be expected to err generously on the side of optimism, much effort was made to maximise weight-saving. Such efforts, internationally, had a considerable impact on design and construction methods. Welding offered enormous weight reduction as not only could plates be joined by edge-to-edge butts but also the considerable weight of rivets could be obviated. Welding was, however, still an emerging technology. A shortage of skilled welders was exacerbated by the sheer scale of battleship construction. Construction procedures had to be modified but, quite often, abandoned in order to revert to riveting.

As mentioned elsewhere, the midships section comprised a triple bottom bounded by a five-deep void/tank space and roofed by the main protective deck. The arrangement was severely tested when the *North Carolina* was torpedoed off the Solomons in September 1942. It was fortunate that the weapon involved was the standard submarine 21-inch rather than the heavy

24-inch carried by Japanese destroyers, for it struck well forward, abeam of 'A' turret (Turret I) and close to the hard point where the longitudinal bulkheads met the thick transverse bulkhead. The low flexibility in this region resulted in a considerable transmitted shock wave, sufficient to crack several of the comparatively brittle 12-inch thick plates of the main belt, and to cause welding failures as high as the main radar pedestals. While the multi-bulkhead arrangement contained the explosion, it was still started sufficiently to admit about one thousand tons of flood water.

Left: Convoy PQ-15 forms up for the voyage to Russia, with Washington *joining the British Home Fleet for the mission. There was a serious danger that the German heavy units based in Norway would intercept the convoys, and the Royal Navy's margin of superiority in northern waters was reduced by its commitments in the Mediterranean and the Far East.*

Below: The previous generation of 14-in gun battleships like the Tennessee *could not match the latest Japanese super dreadnoughts.*

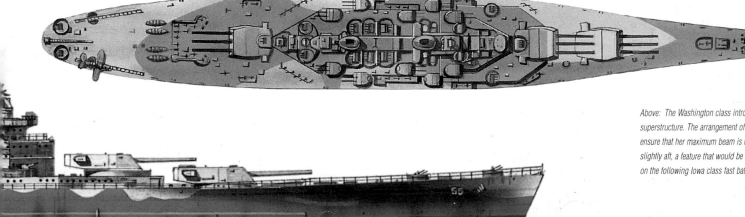

Above: The Washington class introduced a very compact superstructure. The arrangement of the powerplant helped ensure that her maximum beam is not amidships, but slightly aft, a feature that would be more strongly marked on the following Iowa class fast battleships.

Defending the carriers

Launched from a range of about 275 miles, the Japanese attack on Pearl Harbor in December 1941 ushered in a new era of naval warfare. Never itself at risk from heavy guns or of being out-manoeuvred, the attacking force inflicted more damage than could reasonably have been expected from even the most successful conventional engagement. War is not about chivalry and morals so much as profit and loss, and the Japanese loss of 29 aircraft bought a huge (material) dividend.

The big gun still enjoyed immense prestige but had reached that stage of development where vast inputs of research and experiment yielded ever-smaller improvements. At this point in any technology, a step change is required. The advent of reliable radar would have provided such an impetus, but its introduction was greatly overshadowed by the arrival of the carrier air strike, which could put ordnance on target at ten times the range of the largest gun.

Nagumo's carriers, which rightly took credit for the Japanese success at Pearl, were accompanied by a support and logistics group, built around a brace of battlecruisers. Their function was purely to safeguard the carriers. In that their role was subsidiary, and that they themselves were no longer the spearhead, the form of the major encounters of the Pacific naval war was already decided.

The US Navy's riposte was Doolittle's famous Thirty Seconds over Tokyo. For the battleship it made depressing news as it showed that carrier-launched medium bombers, on a one-way mission, could strike target from 650 miles' range, well beyond any means of counter-attack.

May 1942 saw the Coral Sea action where carrier attacked carrier without the opposing forces ever coming into visual contact. Neither side had fully worked up mature

as standard procedure, by now manoeuvred each of its carriers and dedicated escort independently, yet Nagumo was caught not only with his four carriers together but also far from the support of either the Main Body or the Strike Force. Nagumo had two battleships in close support but, at this stage of the war, their inadequate anti-aircraft batteries had no hope of defeating the well-co-ordinated American strikes, that employed large numbers of aircraft.

By the opening of the Guadalcanal campaign in August 1942, the Americans had seven pre-war battleships available in the theatre, yet none was suitably armed at that time for changing roles. The new *North Carolina*, however, showed at the Eastern Solomons action of 24 August that, by keeping station about 2500 yards astern of her assigned carrier, she could effectively disrupt attacking aircraft while, in acting as a less-vulnerable 'Aunt Sally', attracting some attacks from her charge. That the tactic was effective was shown by the *North Carolina's* services being passed on to two other carriers in turn.

At Santa Cruz the gap was closed to just 1,000 yards, with both the carrier and the *South Dakota* fielding the new quadruple 40-millimetre mountings for the first time. Although the carrier, *Enterprise*, took two bomb hits, her 'minder' was credited officially with destroying 26 of her attackers. In contrast, the carrier *Hornet*, without such cover, was bombed and torpedoed to extinction. If carrier warfare was now the key to supremacy in Pacific waters, the steady platform of a battleship, with search radars and a bristling armament firing the new proximity-fused ammunition, underwrote its feasibility.

In contrast with the long succession of vicious nocturnal cruiser/destroyer encounters to establish ascendancy in the Solomons, the carrier battles were fought on a large scale. During 1943, *Essex* and

Above: Alabama *joined the carriers, her 5-in and 40-mm guns proving more valuable than her main armament.*

amphibious assault, at which stage the old-timers came into their own with pre- and post-assault close fire support.

In June 1944 the Japanese Navy was reduced to effective impotence through the destruction of 90 per cent of its aircraft and aircrew at the Battle of the Philippine Sea, the so-called 'Marianas Turkey Shoot'. Of the four massive air strikes mounted here by the Japanese, the second and most costly lost 97 of its 128 aircraft attacking a six-battleship gun line with combat air cover.

Battleships began the Pacific war with, typically, a dozen 1.1 inch anti-aircraft guns, and finished with up to eighty 40-mm and fifty 20-mm weapons, which posed the twin problems of housing scores of extra gunners and tons of ammunition. From October 1944 even this became inadequate as the advent of the Kamikaze brought the urgent need to ship a weapon – the 3-inch 50 calibre – large enough to actually disintegrate a suicidally-inclined aircraft.

Right: A Japanese kamikaze bomber is shot down ahead of an Essex class carrier.

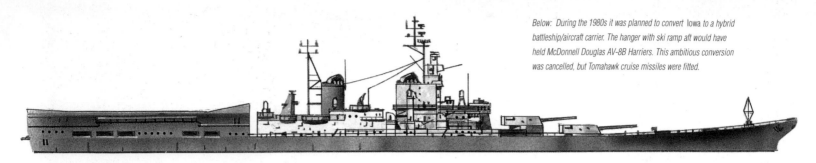

Below: During the 1980s it was planned to convert Iowa to a hybrid battleship/aircraft carrier. The hanger with ski ramp aft would have held McDonnell Douglas AV-8B Harriers. This ambitious conversion was cancelled, but Tomahawk cruise missiles were fitted.

Iowa (BB61) class

Design studies of the 1930s showed conclusively that a combination of three triple 16-inch turrets and a 30-knot speed would demand a displacement of well over 40,000 tons. The London Naval Conference and Japan's defection from all treaty agreements in 1936 gave the Americans the green light to build such ships. Earlier concentration on striking power and protection had produced battleships with speeds of up to about 27 knots. This was now viewed as unnecessarily inhibiting for fleet operations. A 45,000 tonner of only 27 knots could mount twelve 16-inch but a reduction to nine barrels was accepted for a promised 32–33 knots. Such a speed required a very considerable increase in length. On the same beam of the preceding South Dakotas, the overall length leapt by 193.9 feet (59.1 metres). Most of this dimensional increase was absorbed in the immensely long and fine-sectioned bow section, which was unarmoured. The forefoot terminated in a bulb, optimised for minimum resistance at high speed.

The Iowas took new 50-calibre versions of the well-tried 16-inch but hull protection was limited to defeating a smaller 45-calibre projectile. Even at this late stage of battleship design there was no consensus on the best manner of vertical protection. Where the preceding South Dakotas had a fairly narrow belt, set inboard about five metres, with four parallel void spaces outboard of it and overhung by both protective decks, the Iowas' belt was conformal with the hull, tapering from 310mm at the main belt level to about 40mm at a point just above the turn of bilge.

Two, widely-spaced funnels showed that the powerful machinery and boiler spaces were dispersed over the largest possible area to improve survivability.

The shape of the Iowa hull was unique. In plan it achieved its greatest beam about three-quarters aft. The after run featured a long cut-up, the inboard propellers being set in long skegs. This, with twin rudders, allowed for exceptional manoeuvrability.

Iowa class data:

Displacement, standard	52,000 tons
Displacement, full load	57,450 tons
Length, overall	887.8 feet (270.6 m)
Beam	108.3 feet (33.0 m)
Design draught	32.5 feet (9.9 m)
Complement	1920

Class: *Iowa* (BB61), *Missouri* (BB63), *New Jersey* (B62), *Wisconsin* (BB64); *Illinois* (BB65), and *Kentucky* (BB66) broken up incomplete. Completed 1943–4

Armament:
Nine 16-inch guns (3 × 3)
Twenty 5-in guns (10 × 2)
Sixty/eighty 40-mm guns
Four aircraft

Machinery:
Steam turbines 212,000 shp
  (158,000kW)
Four shafts 33 knots

Armour:

Belt	up to 12.1 in
Bulkheads	up to 14.5 in
Decks	up to 6 in
Turrets	up to 17 in
Barbettes	up to 17 in

Admiral Halsey

Hailing from New Jersey, William Halsey entered the Naval Academy in 1900. He commanded destroyers out of Queenstown, Ireland during World War I, followed by spells in Intelligence and as Naval Attache in Berlin. Qualifying as a flyer, he took command of the carrier *Saratoga* in 1935. At the outbreak of World War II he was Vice Admiral commanding Pacific Fleet Carriers. His pugnacious reputation led to his being responsible for the whole South Pacific Area in 1942. While no intellectual, he was a fine leader. After Santa Cruz he was promoted full Admiral, commanding the Third Fleet. His fine reputation was badly dented through his being neatly decoyed by the Japanese prior to the desperate battle off Samar, and by being blamed by Courts of Inquiry for the Third Fleet being overtaken by two damaging typhoons. He nonetheless gained five-star status in 1945. Retiring in 1947, he died in 1959.

Below: USS Missouri as she appeared in July 1944. The hull form helped achieve the exceptional speed of 33 knots, which made them the fastest battleships in the world.

Admiral Nimitz

Chester Nimitz was a bilingual German-American, born in Texas in 1885. He exceptionally gained command of a destroyer at age 22 but then widened his experience in submarines, carriers and cruisers. A rear-admiral in 1938, he commanded a battleship division. Following the disaster of Pearl Harbor, he relieved the C-in-C Pacific Fleet in four-star rank. It was he who improved morale by giving Halsey his command and it was he who masterminded the island-hopping Central Pacific campaign that complemented MacArthur's progress through New Guinea and the Philippines.

Courteous and punctilious, Nimitz delegated to the maximum, choosing his commanders with a sure touch and directing them to a series of victorious campaigns and actions. Made a five-star Fleet Admiral in 1944 he had the satisfaction of accepting the Japanese surrender. He served as Chief of Naval Operations from 1945 until his retirement in 1947. He died in 1966.

The 'fast-battleship' concept

Naval planners all tended to like the concept of the fast battleship, working on the fringes of the fleet to bring a reluctant enemy to action, or to head off his escape. Fisher took the concept of speed to dangerous extremes with his battlecruisers. Their German peers had speed and survivability, but only at the expense of lighter armament. Only with the Queen Elizabeths did the designers get the equation right with a considerable improvement in speed, adequate protection and an increase in gun calibre. This was possible, however, because there was no limitation on displacement. Similarly, it was only after 1936, and the expiry of the tight Washington agreed limits, that American designers could work-up a proposal that was adequate in each major parameter. The Iowa's

Above: Missouri *was the only Iowa class to be retained after World War II until the Korean war led to the re-activation of her three sisterships.*

Right: After the Korean war, USS Wisconsin *remained on the active list until 1958.*

six-knot speed improvement, from 27 to 33 knots, necessitated an increase in power of some 75 per cent. This, in turn, dictated the size of the centre section, the region of greatest beam.

Fast air-and-surface action groups became a reality. It was something of an anti-climax, therefore, that Halsey's headlong pursuit of Ozawa's carriers during the Leyte Gulf battles, which should have been a triumphant justification, instead proved to be what the enemy had intended.

Right: USS Iowa *was declared operational in August 1943. Her first mission was to take President Roosevelt across the Atlantic for the Tehran conference with Stalin and Churchill.*

Alaska class battle cruisers

Officially, the Alaskas were 'large cruisers' but possessed capabilities that put them far beyond even the later 17,000-ton giants of the Des Moines class. Their 12-inch armament and their length (only the Iowas were longer) naturally put them in the battle-cruiser bracket and, despite official discouragement, that is how they were usually categorised. This was reinforced by their 'CB' designators and their nomenclature. The latter was neither the 'State' names allotted to battleships, nor the 'Cities' associated with cruisers, all planned six took the names of American overseas possessions (Alaska and Hawaii were to become the 49th and 50th states post-war).

The Alaska design was pre-war and, while it was worked-up against a perceived threat, did not suffer from the restrictions carried over from the now-relaxed treaty agreements. The United States never built battlecruisers per se but these attracted the same criticism in being superior to any known cruiser but deficient in respect to

12-inch 50 was a very powerful weapon and, where the usual yardstick was to provide a realistic 'immunity zone' or protection against an equivalent foreign gun, this was not possible without a significantly increased displacement. Secondly, speed. Although capable of their designed speed of 33 knots, this gave no margin over the Iowas, which were already entering service, and which could be expected to provide an indication of the likely performance of new foreign battleship designs. In the event, the rumoured Japanese construction never materialised; with now no specific role within the fleet, only two of the Alaskas were completed.

Alaska class data:

Displacement, standard	32,100 tons
Displacement, full load	34,250 tons
Length, overall	808.5 feet (246.4 m)
Beam	90.75 feet (27.7 m)
Design draught	31.75 feet (9.7 m)
Complement	1370

Above: USS Alaska: a throwback to the battlecruiser concept designed partly at President Roosevelt's request.

Class: *Alaska (CB1), Guam (CB2)*
Completed 1944
Hawaii (CB3), Philippines (CB4), Puerto Rico (CB5), Samoa (CB6) cancelled.

Armament:
Nine 12-in guns (3×3)
Twelve 5-in guns (6×2)
Fifty-six 40-mm guns
Four aircraft

Machinery:
Steam turbines 150,000 shp
(112,000kW)
Four shafts 33 knots

Armour:
Belt	up to 9 in
Bulkheads	up to 10.5 in
Decks	up to 2.75 in
Turrets	up to 13 in
Barbettes	up to 13 in

Prior to the commencement of the expansion programme initiated pre-war, the General Board of the US Navy required a far-ranging study to be undertaken, covering the full range of each type of ship being considered. That for cruisers was typically thorough, encompassing main batteries of from 5-inch to 12-inch. As it happened, there was a requirement for both.

The threat of immediate war came from Europe, but the gaze of the United States was still directed primarily across the Pacific. Japan's building programme post-1936 was shrouded in mystery, fogged further by the effective leaking of 'disinformation'. It was through this latter conduit that the United States learned of Japan's interest in operating ocean commerce raiders which appeared not unreasonable in view of the enthusiasm shown for this type of warfare by her Axis partner, Germany.

Reasoning probably that the Japanese would use their excellent 'Treaty Cruisers' in the role, the well-protected, 32-knot, eight 8-inch cruiser was seen as the likely aggressor. A requirement was thus made for a 'cruiser killer', with a 10-inch armament, to be developed. This calibre would have required a totally new programme and, as the 12-inch was still in service, the recommendation was made, and accepted, to up-grade this gun. This meant a considerable hike in ship

Last gasp of the battle cruiser

size but, as treaty forbad a cruiser to mount any gun larger than an 8-inch, the new vessel would needs be termed a capital ship, in which case there was every justification in making it as survivable as possible. Paradoxically, the Japanese were victims of their own success for, having successfully bluffed the Americans into diverting resources to counter a non-existent threat they, themselves, had to set about designing a counter, armed with 14-inch weapons, although it was never built.

As usual, several draft designs preceded the final version, which was still being modified in detail shortly before commencement of the first-of-class in December 1941. Nine 12-inch in triple turrets were accepted as the minimum effective battery. A 33-knot speed was mandatory as was protection on a scale to defeat older marks of 12-inch

projectile. With no earlier experience upon which to draw, the final result recalled both the German *Scharnhorst* and a stretched version of the forthcoming American *Baltimore*. The German was shorter and beamier, very survivable but requiring higher power for a knot less speed. Her main battery was also 11-inch on a greater displacement.

The Alaskas shared with the Baltimores the standard 'large cruiser layout' of triple main battery turrets grouped forward and aft in a set arrangement with three twin 5-inch 38s. To maximise an all-too-fragile protective system, the main battery and freeboard were lowered as far as was practicable. Aircraft could not be stowed beneath the quarterdeck as the after hull

was too shallow. This necessitated an unpopular reversion to amidships hangars and catapults, with their attendant fire risk.

Once the American appreciated that the Japanese 'threat' was a chimera, the Alaskas might have been abandoned. They were, however, championed by no-less than Admiral King, who viewed them as potential close escorts for fast carriers.

Operation 'Crossroads' – the Bikini A-bomb tests

Between 1939 and 1945 the aerial threat to warships developed by a factor that could never have been forecast. As the war progressed, anti-aircraft gun armament developed from the risible to virtual sky saturation. However, where the latter would deter any normal pilot, the threat itself was changing. Stand-off glider bombs heralded the introduction of the air-to-surface missile (ASM), while the *Kamikaze* was a slow ASM with the ultimate guidance system. Tactics and weapons were still being modified to meet this menace when hostilities were terminated abruptly by the atomic bombing of Japan.

The existence of such destructive weapons had to have implications on both ship design and the manner in which ships were used. Peace had created a wealth of expendable hulls, both American and ex-enemy prizes. A total of 93 were thus brought to Bikini Atoll in the Marshalls for exposure to three atomic explosions. The 'guinea pigs' ranged from attack transports, through landing craft, submarines, destroyers and cruisers to a handful of battleships and carriers. Included among the latter were four American battleships (*Arkansas*, BB33; *New York*, BB34; *Nevada*, BB36; and *Pennsylvania*, BB38) and the much-repaired veteran carrier *Saratoga*.

In order, the tests were planned to be 'Able' – an air burst, 'Baker' – a shallow underwater burst, and 'Charlie' – a deep underwater burst. Infested with coral heads, Bikini Lagoon is nowhere much more than 31 fathoms in depth. Ships were anchored at a variety of distances from Point Zero, the aiming point. This was marked by the Nevada for Test 'Able', the veteran being painted orange and white to provide an unambiguous reference.

Early on 1st July 1946 a 'Fat Man' was released by a B-29 from a height of 29,000 feet. Ballistically a poor design, the bomb

THE BULL'S-EYE: THE TWISTED AND BROKEN SUPERSTRUCTURE OF THE 29,000-TON BATTLESHIP *NEVADA*, FOCAL POINT FOR THE AIMING OF THE ATOM BOMB.

Left: Nevada *seen on 11 July 1946. Despite the newspaper headline,* Nevada *actually withstood a 19.1 kiloton airburst remarkably well. Although her upperworks were devastated, the citadel survived. Even the second atom bomb ('Baker') left her afloat and she survived to be the subject of conventional weapons tests.*

THE 29,000-TON U.S. BATTLESHIP "NEVADA" (1914), ANOTHER OF THE VETERAN SHIPS OF "ATOM-BOMB TASK FORCE NO. 1."

Left: Nevada *survived bombardment by heavy guns and a massive underwater explosion, before finally succumbing to air-launched torpedoes.*

transmitted directly to underwater hulls, its effect probably concentrated by the ducting qualities of the shallow water. Within one second a column, containing an estimated half-million tons of water and two million cubic yards of spoil from the bed of the lagoon, towered 2500 feet above the anchored fleet. From its base radiated waves of unimaginable height, measured at 94 feet from trough to crest at a point 1000 feet from Point Zero. While they quickly diminished with range, closer vessels were affected catastrophically. A bare 250 yards from the centre, the *Arkansas* disappeared within seconds, while still obscured by the water column. She was found subsequently to have been 'crushed as if by a tremendous hammer blow from below',

surviving ships by hosing them down, but
radiation levels remained so high that Test
'Charlie' had to be abandoned.

The remaining three American battleships
survived 'Baker' in sufficiently good shape
to be towed to Kwajalein for longer-term
monitoring and research. All were finally
scuttled or expended as targets during 1948.

As no more battleships were built, the
experience of 'Crossroads' was to be
applied elsewhere. Superstructures, for a
period at least, became noticeably more
compact. Extensive pre-washing systems
were installed to prevent fall-out adhering
to topside surfaces. Personnel were sited
under cover, in 'citadels' capable of
excluding also biological and chemical
agents. Steaming dispositions for task
groups were changed to minimise effects
from one or more warheads. The concept
of beach assault from 'over-the-horizon'
was actively pursued to avoid vulnerable
concentrations of amphibious shipping.
Nuclear attack remains more probable on
ships than on shore targets owing to the
much lower political risks.

Above: Pennsylvania
fires her 14-in guns at
the Japanese garrison
on Guam during 1944.
She survived both atom
bombs at Bikini atoll but
her hull was left
radioactive. She was
towed to Kwajalein and
beached there for target
practice.

Left: Veteran of so
many Pacific battles, the
carrier Saratoga (nearest
the camera) was used as
an atom bomb target at
Bikini atoll. She is seen
here at Nas Alameda,
California in November
1945 with Enterprise,
Hornet and San Jacinto.

Montana (B67) class

Although ordered in September 1940, the five Montanas were never built. In appearance, their relationship to the Iowas was apparent, but their design brief emphasised hitting power and protection rather than speed. The Iowas would thus have been unique in their 33-knot capability.

Requirements for the Montana design included a very extensive immunity zone of 18–32,000 yards (16500–29300 metres) against a 50-calibre, 16-inch shell. This demanded a far deeper side protective system than that built into the Iowas. Although an 18-inch main battery was considered, 16-inch was selected, probably because it would be quicker to produce. In an effort to maximise the number of barrels, quadruple turrets were studied but their weight and large-diameter barbette cut-outs were incompatible with strength toward the extremities of a fine hull. Four triples were, therefore, specified.

Engineering limitations of the time put a maximum of about 50,000 horse power onto each shaft. As the beam was already (for the first time) to exceed the dimensions of the Panama canal, the prospect of adding a fifth or sixth shaft was unattractive. An increase in length would have permitted a refinement of the hull and a small speed improvement, but the launchways of existing yards were not able to accept the necessary increase and a 28-knot maximum was, therefore, agreed.

An innovation was a virtual double protective belt. The outer shell bore the main protection, 16-inch tapering to 10-inch at its lower edge. Inboard of this was a triple void space, whose inboard bulkhead tapered from about 7 inches at the top to about one inch at its junction with the double bottom. This arrangement covered both magazines and machinery spaces.

Montana class data:

Displacement, standard	65,000 tons
Displacement, full load	70,500 tons
Length, overall	921.5 feet (280.9 m)
Beam	121.0 feet (36.9 m)
Design draught	36.1 feet (11.0 m)
Complement	2150

Class: *Louisiana (BB71), Maine (BB69), Montana (BB67), New Hampshire (BB70), Ohio (BB68).* None commenced.

Armament:
Twelve 16-in guns (4 × 3)
Twenty 5-in guns (10 × 2)
Thirty-two/forty 40-mm guns
Four aircraft

Machinery:
Steam turbines 172,000 shp
(128,000kW)
Four shafts 28 knots

Armour:

Belt	up to 16 in
Bulkheads	up to 18 in
Decks	up to 6 in
Turrets	up to 18 in
Barbettes	up to 18 in

Naval surface fire support (NSFS)

The main argument for the continued retention of the Iowas was the US Marines' requirement for the crushing effect of their big guns. Unfortunately, the support of obsolete equipment on ships over a half-century old is prohibitively expensive, facilities for the manufacture and repair of their big guns have all but ceased to exist, while the ships themselves absorb a minimum number of 1500 crew apiece. And, of course, the fabric of the ships themselves is deteriorating.

Above: The 15-in guns of HMS Queen Elizabeth were used to devastating effect during the Dardanelles operations in 1915.

Alternatives have been sought for a considerable time but none was proved superior as long as the 16-inch remained available. The relative cheapness and flexibility of the naval gun have not been surpassed by the guided missile. For indirect fire only the enormously-

Below: Montana as she would have looked on completion. Far more heavily protected than the Iowas, these would have been the ultimate US battleships.

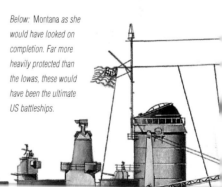

expensive Tomahawk cruise missile comes close, but this can be afforded in only limited numbers.

Extended range munitions and pinpoint accuracy will enable future guns to put more 'ordnance on target' because of far lower dispersions when compared with earlier guns. The ending of the Cold War and the re-definition of the Fleet's purpose in the context of the newly-defined era of littoral warfare has resulted in an immediate requirement for fire support to a range of 41 nautical miles (about 76km) and the ability to reach to 63 nautical miles (about 117km) for such roles as counter-battery fire.

In this context a 155-mm (6-inch) gun first appeared to be the best choice for calibre, but the increasing miniaturisation and robustness of micro-electronics has now made a guided 5-inch projectile an attractive proposition, particularly as over 150 examples of the 54-calibre Mark 45 gun are in service. In their conventional mode, these are credited with a horizontal range of 23,700 metres or about 13 nautical miles. A strengthened, 62-calibre barrel will fire rocket-assisted projectiles, using new propellants. The projectiles will be twice their current length.

By the year 2001 an accuracy of 10 metres at maximum range is being sought. Guidance techniques to achieve this may either be a self-contained Global Positioning System (GPS) or an Inertial Navigational System (INS), either of which would be fired from known co-ordinates against another set defining the target position. A

further possibility is laser or semi-active guidance, using either a remotely-piloted vehicle (RPV) or a Forward Observer to 'illuminate' the target, allowing the weapon to home. To compensate for its lack of energy and explosive content the munition, depending on the type of target, could be fitted with a shaped-charge warhead.

A Stand-off Land Attack Missile (SLAM) is under development for difficult 'area' targets such as armoured concentrations. Its capabilities are echoed somewhat by Tomahawk, Smart Anti-Tank (T-SAT), which scatters submunitions. Ground troops or 'soft' transport, would be attacked with explosive/fragmentation bomblets.

Above: With large stocks of ammunition left over from World War II, New Jersey's 16-in guns were called upon again during the Korean war, and she returned to provide fire support off Vietnam and the Lebanon in the early 1980s.

Top: 5-in guns carried by many modern US warships like the Spruance class destroyer Caron seen here, are to receive new ammunition for shore bombardment, extending their range to over 13 nautical miles.

Battleships against Baghdad

Last of the active Iowas, and more than 48 years after her maiden operational sortie, the *Missouri* (BB63) was decommissioned on 31st March 1992. Reflecting the cost of their operation, the class had enjoyed a curiously 'stop-go' career following the end of World War II. After five years in reserve, all were re-activated in 1950–1 for the Korean War. For this there was some up-dating of electronics, and the removal of aircraft and catapults. Useless against modern jet-propelled aircraft, all smaller automatic weapons were landed, although the plan to replace the sixteen quadruple 40-mm mountings with ten twin 3-inch 50s was never carried out.

This early in the Cold war, tactical nuclear interchanges were a real possibility. A 16-inch nuclear shell was developed and all the class, except *Missouri*, received a dedicated magazine and handling arrangements. In the 1950s, following the cease-fire, all four went back into reserve.

Strategic and anti-aircraft guided missiles were entering the operational inventory at this time and there was a strong proposal to finish the two-thirds-complete *Kentucky* (BB66) as a new-style guided-missile battleship. Firing nuclear shells, she would require only two, twin 16-inch turrets. The space otherwise occupied by the third mounting would be allocated to eight, 1000-mile range Regulus IIs. The secondary battery, of either 3-inch 50s or new 5-inch 54s, would be integrated with Terrier and Talos medium- and long-range SAMs. The scheme was not adopted, but the introduction of the Polaris ICBM soon afterward brought a rash of new proposals. It proved cheaper, however, to put SAMs into converted cruiser hulls and Polaris, more appropriately, into hard-to-detect submarines (SSBN), retaining the uniqueness of large-calibre guns to satisfy the Marine Corps' requirement for heavy fire support.

The Marines then went further by proposing that the whole after end of the ships be converted into a helicopter deck over storage/garage/accommodation facilities sufficient to support a reinforced battalion. Again, these aims were achieved economically by more-conventional means.

In 1968 the *New Jersey*, alone, was withdrawn from reserve and given a rapid and very basic, facelift to provide a year's fire support along the Vietnamese coast. A mid-1970s' proposal to install Aegis as the controlling element of what would have been a forerunner of the missile 'arsenal ship' also came to nothing.

It was the President's plans for the 600-ship 'Reaganavy' of the early eighties that saw the four veterans receive their most thorough modernisation. Quadruple launchers were installed for thirty-two Tomahawk cruise missiles and sixteen Harpoon anti-ship missiles. Four of the dated 5-inch mountings were landed to provide vertical access for services, a reduction in firepower redressed by the installation of four Vulcan-Phalanx close-in weapon systems (CIWS). A new electronics suite required a completely revised mast arrangement but the comparative sensitivity of electronics and modern weaponry dictated restrictions on the firing arcs of the main battery in order to reduce blast effects.

Wisconsin and *Missouri* saw the class's last active service when both were sent to the Persian Gulf for Operation 'Desert Storm', the 1991 re-conquest of Kuwait. Between them, they fired more than fifty Tomahawks, at ranges of up to 800 miles.

Top left: The F-117 Stealth bomber was able to overfly Baghdad in the teeth of Iraqi air defences, but naval fire support could hit the same targets without risking US lives.

Above: Carrier airstrikes can be prohibitively expensive against targets defended by modern SAM systems. The days when Grumman A-6s could deliver iron bombs with relative impunity are long over.

Above. The Iowas' upgrading included Harpoon anti-ship missiles, capable of over-the-horizon engagement and, ultimately, Tomahawk cruise missiles which converted the battleships into strategic weapons platforms.

Left: Missouri launches a cruise missile against Iraqi forces during the 1991 Gulf War. This was probably the last time these veteran battleships will ever see active service. All are currently mothballed as their maintenance costs are too high to justify keeping them operational.

Photograph credits

Imperial War Museum: 12, 13, 14, 15, 16, 18, 23, 25, 26, 27, 28, 29, 30, 32, 33,34, 37, 38, 40, 41, 43, 44, 49, 50, 52, 53, 54, 57, 61, 62, 63, 64, 66, 67, 68, 69, 71, 73, 75, 79, 81, 88, 89, 90, 91, 92, 98, 99, 100, 101, 104, 105–7, 109, 111, 116, 117, 120–126, 128, 131–9, 156, 157, 164

Jane's Information Group: 85, 88, 89, 96, 97, 113, 127, 135, 136, 137, 138, 140, 141, 153, 170, 189, 191

Marius Bar: 15, 22

Norwegian Defence Command: 94

Randy Jolly: 190

Woodes-Rogers collection: 14, 27, 30, 35, 36, 37, 39, 41, 45, 47, 48, 49, 53, 55, 56, 61, 63, 112, 113, 116, 117, 135

US National Archives: 147, 150, 151, 165, 170, 171

Naval Historical Center, Washington Navy Yard: 144–6, 148, 149, 151–5, 157–9, 162, 163, 165, 167–9